GW00858996

BIG BANDS & GREAT BALLROOMS

AMERICA IS DANCING . . . AGAIN

By John "Jack" Behrens

Author of the popular book, Big Band Days: A Memoir and Source Book
(1stBooks/2003)

AuthorHouse/2006

AuthorHouse™
1663 Liberty Drive, Suite 200
Bloomington, IN 47403
www.authorhouse.com
Phone: 1-800-839-8640

AuthorHouse™ UK Ltd.
500 Avebury Boulevard
Central Milton Keynes, MK9 2BE
www.authorhouse.co.uk
Phone: 08001974150

©2006 Jack Behrens. All rights reserved.

No part of this book may be reproduced, stored in a retrieval system, or transmitted
by any means without the written permission of the author.

First published by AuthorHouse 10/25/2006

ISBN: 1-4259-6977-1 (sc)

Library of Congress Control Number: 2006909260

Printed in the United States of America
Bloomington, Indiana

This book is printed on acid-free paper.

For information visit: www.writerjackweb.com

Graphics and production were prepared by Lisi Design, Holland Patent, NY
Front cover photo courtesy of the Airmen of Note, Washington, DC; Greater
Buckeye Lake Museum, OH and Chris Walden of Los Angeles

Table of Contents

INTRODUCTION

What is it that makes ballrooms the place to dance?

Ballrooms have an ambiance that other contemporary structures fail to achieve. A ballroom was designed to hold large crowds. There is just something about a large crowd sharing an exciting experience. As a ballroom operator these magical moments can give you a chill. I operated Matter's Ballroom in Decorah, IA from 1970 to 1999 before selling it. I grew up in the family business and began working at the ballroom in 1958. . . In the ballroom, I found, you are a participant, not a spectator.

. . . . John Matter, director,

National Ballroom & Entertainers Assn.

by John "Jack" Behrens

PROLOGUE

Where did big bands and swing music go?

They didn't leave… but the irony is many Americans actually believe they disappeared along with ballrooms and jukeboxes, bobby sox and zoot suits decades ago.

Band leader Brooks Tegler, who has recreated the great music of World War II with his Army Air Corps Review Big Band, offers a good response: "In order for something to come back, it needs to have gone away. Big bands have wrongly been put in that category. They never went away. Big bands live on in every way and like the recordings, concerts and dances that made them such a huge panel in America's cultural 'quilt' for the last sixty or seventy years, recording on paper the 'how we got there' story is of immense value."

In a sense that's the essence of the pages in front of you. My two years of research offer solid evidence that ghost bands, territorial bands and exciting music education programs on campuses everywhere flourish among younger generations of dancers and musicians who also enjoy the swing and dance music of the "big band days." Like our economy, the music business has spurts and depressions but it has never gone away.

The struggle to survive hasn't been without losses and a need for life support. It did when Glenn Miller, Benny Goodman, Harry James and Duke Ellington were in their heyday. For example, while the music and loyal followers remain, ballrooms have virtually vanished and jukeboxes have become museum pieces.

Too often, "jazz" is used to describe all parts of popular music including big bands when actually the concepts and music are quite different. Big bands feature music charts, arrangements, section work and musicians playing together as a unit. Jazz has always been improvisational music providing soloist's great latitude. Ken Burns' blockbuster television mini-series and book extravaganza probably created the confusion among those who were new to the musical experience. As Bill Crow wrote in his book, "Jazz Anecdotes" (Oxford University Press, 1990), it's difficult to define "jazz." Some historical etymologists think the word has its origin in the slang term for "gism." Jazzing was considered fornication in those early days of redlight houses and hot music in New Orleans at the turn of the 20th century.

We do know that in Chicago when the term was brand new, the underworld's use of the word "jass" was actually as an obscenity.

We also know that the Chicago mobs owned or influenced a number of clubs, speakeasies and dinner dancing spots and paid good money to musicians to play. Certainly Guy Lombardo benefited among the hundreds of unknowns who became national names in Chicago. Mobsters were willing to let good music and booze flow when family or independent ballroom owners couldn't . . . or wouldn't.

Inevitably, music and dancing evolved, matured and changed. The reasons are numerous and linked to our heritage. Like marching bands on a 4th of July, imagine a country club new year's eve without live dance music and a big band. Think about the many community engagements and high school and college proms that still insist on having live bands to play the foxtrots and swing numbers people enjoy. And don't forget the President of the United State – including '60s music fan Bill Clinton – needs big bands every four years for the traditional inaugural balls held throughout Washington. On a smaller scale but no less important big band music is traditional in places like a small village near where I live – Westmoreland, NY – where every year the high school holds a Senior Citizen Prom for those 55 and over. Like priceless art, the rediscovery process is in full swing . . . for swing!

Pete Jacobs who leads his Wartime Radio Revue band on the West Coast offers a great assessment. "Big bands are alive and well and while I grew up listening to Hendrix, The Beatles and Dylan once I played my first big band chart. . . I was hooked! Today my band plays over 50 dates a year keeping the music of the "Greatest Generation" alive in the hearts of a new generation. And kids today are bringing back the old dances – you know, the ones where people actually touch – and they show up for our gigs en masses. Welcome to the Second Era of Swing."

Consequently, this book is dedicated to something as much a part of Americana as national holidays and mom's pies; big band music, those who play it and those who appreciate it.

It's also dedicated to the many excellent, usually unheralded territorial musicians who play for events in your town or city. The pay is usually poor but in most cases, the music is similar if not better than the touring bands you paid far more to see and hear.

Today such music comes with more originality than my day when we played mostly stock arrangements and came together for the gig to dream about leaving where we were and going where we hadn't been invited. Most of us, unfortunately, never got an invitation or seized the moment. The consequences of being homeless in any distant city were too ominous.

Finally, it's dedicated to business people who for years created the venues for the touring and local bands and community dancers; the ballroom owners. Big bands wouldn't have survived if it wasn't for the ballrooms. Their demise left a sizable hole in the financial planning necessary for any bandleader yesterday and today.

Big band music and its players should be celebrated every season as uniquely American in a world that has difficulty defining what American culture means.

Jack Behrens
Clinton, NY
www.writerjackweb.com

TERRITORIAL BANDS
Where It All Began

Before Glenn Miller, Count Basie, Harry James and even the King of Swing, Benny Goodman, became household names in the late 1930s and during the 1940s, they played in territory bands. It was the place where everyone started. It was the place a great number stayed. And, thank goodness, territorial bands continue today.

Why? Countless reasons but think about the thousands of non-profit social affairs that benefit millions thanks to dance music, the numerous high school, college and civic social events that still enjoy sounds from the past and present, the corporate functions that use dance bands to embellish their entertainment and the country clubs and private organizations that yearly offer holiday activities where they traditionally have dance music. And that's just the outer edge of the need for such special music; the sounds of the big band.

Territorial bands are the backbone of the industry and, while there are very few touring bands anymore, there still are a good number of regional bands with excellent area musicians playing at the community center near you more than likely. They not only need your support . . . they deserve it.

They're the workers in the local grocery market or mall who you see on the stand on Friday or Saturday night at the Legion Hall or the Country Club gala. They are frequently the musical directors at local high schools. Yet, they can also be the surgeon at the local hospital, the insurance agent or real estate sales person. . . even the utility line person or plumber who handles your emergency and races home on Friday to change to get to the bandstand for your charity ball.

Gunther Schuller offers his definition of "territory bands" in his massive work, "The Swing Era: The Development of Jazz 1930-1945" (Oxford Press, 1989):

"Territory bands by definition were black. There were, of course, many white bands in the 'territories' . . . but they tended to have the more lucrative and permanent jobs and therefore were not required to travel as much as the black bands."

I find his definition rather narrow. During my playing days in the 1940s and '50s on several white territorial bands we didn't have "lucrative and permanent jobs" unless you count day labor in a dairy bar or clerking at a military surplus store. Worse, there were times we didn't get paid at all and we had little recourse given the cost of legal advice. Basically, the term used to have a negative connotation it didn't deserve. Territory bands were considered the "minor leagues" for national touring bands yet, at the same time, they were confined to specific regions or states. . . even parts of a state. They frequently were popular sweet bands that played a variety of community dances and events. They continue to perform the same purpose today.

> *"A man came over. . . and asked us if we wanted to play for a dance. We said sure and played from 10:30 until 12. The governor of Arizona was there. They gave us $2.25 a piece and we sure felt rich."*

A story in the "Naples Illustrated" described the dedication of these part-time players." I consider myself young at heart but my body is not as young," says 55-year-old Michael Mesnik, a percussionist in the band called "Phoenix" which plays the clubs in Naples and Marco Island, FL. He spends his playing nights working three sets of congas, claves, tambourine and other hand held instruments. "I'm a weekend warrior" he adds pointing out that he's self-taught and plays by ear.

The "Wednesday Night Band" at the Lyndon Elks Club in Louisville, KY, for example, offers the loyalty of the players and fans and speaks to the strength of the music and its history today. According to columnist Bob Hill in the Louisville Courier-Journal, band members of all ages who played with any number of bands including the city's territorial bands like "Sweet Street Big Band," the "Don Krekel Orchestra" and the "Ovation Orchestra Big Band," assemble every week to rehearse, have fun but take their playing and their music seriously.

While you won't necessarily find a band in the Yellow Pages of your telephone directory, go online with Google and you'll find 1,295 jazz bands and artists and 357 under the category of swing bands. Select the bands and artists listing and you'll be able to pull up nearly 51,000 names! A swing band in Boston could cost you between $100 to $500 a musician per hour while in Columbus you might pay a minimum of $499 for your musical evening.

What was it like in the Roaring Twenties to be a collegian like Glenn Miller and decide that your talent was good enough and your friends were footloose enough to go on the road playing your music?

My friend Jim Booker, a tenor saxophonist who played in a number of big bands in the 1950s, tells an interesting story of his father's early days on the road:

"In the summer of 1923 Homer (Booker) and four of his TEKE fraternity brothers . . . took a 4,000 mile trip to California and back in a Maxwell touring car. They left Ohio on June 22, 1923, and arrived back in Ohio on August 17, '23 . . . 56 days later. At least two of the five were musicians (Homer and Guz) and possibly all five were. Homer took his sax and banjo and, at times, they would play for a dance at the camps where they stopped for the night. Homer notes that at a camp in Arizona a man came over. . . and asked us if we wanted to play for a dance. We said sure and played from 10:30 until 12. The governor of Arizona was there. They gave us $2.25 a piece and we sure felt rich.'"

While I belonged to American Federation of Musicians for six years, I certainly played many gigs for less than scale. You took what the leader got for the engagement. End of story. Like many others, there were nights when we weren't paid although we had been promised a fee. On some occasions, club or ballroom owners matched receipts for the night against the band's cost and refused to pay us. They could. . . because, like Homer Booker, we played without contracts in those informal days of more fun than business sense. Today some say we lacked the commitment to be professional playing our music . . . others recognize that the times and the economy are totally different. But don't forget that Duke Ellington once worked as a sign painter to pay the rent and eat, singer Tony Bennett started as a singing waiter at 17 and bandleader Ray Conniff, who decided he wasn't going to write bop arrangements for Harry James, ended up digging ditches before he got back into the business and went on to success.

Yet even drawing large crowds and cutting records didn't always guarantee larger incomes for leaders or sidemen during the days when swing was most

JIMMY BARNETT
and his Orchestra

"The Midwest's
Greatest Doubling Band"

Management
Vic Schroeder Agency, Omaha

Jimmy Barnett and his Orchestra, a midwest "doubling" band based in Omaha in the 1930s. Doubling referred to the band members' ability to play different instruments. Photo courtesy of James Ronan Collection, Iowa

popular. Said NPR in an article about royalties in 2005: "In the early 1940s, jazz was recorded mostly on small independent labels for producers and label owners who heard both an artistic and commercial in the music. Unscrupulous ones would pay the band leaders an advance only to maintain later that their records never sold enough to cover the advance, much less provide royalties." Sidemen were frequently paid a flat fee for each recording . . . but were offered no royalties. A common royalty at the time was about 1 to 4 percent of retail.

Most musicians know that the success of the major touring bands like Miller, Goodman, Artie Shaw, James and others came because of marketing, booking agencies and, equally important, legally binding contracts that lawyers would have no hesitation to take to court. Yes, there was one more thing: talent. Lesser known bands didn't have the name or legal clout to threaten venue owners especially in their hometowns.

It had become a competitive business after the strong demand for music to fill ballrooms, country clubs and dance pavilions began to wane just after the war. In my hometown of Lancaster, OH, Dick Trimble, a music store owner and bandleader, had to buy broadcast time on local radio station WHOK to give listeners a chance to hear "Tempos with the Trimble Treatment." Like a bandleader he admired, Glenn Miller,

Dick squeezed as much music as he could in a half-hour Sunday afternoon show. His purpose, especially at particular seasons of the year like the fall and spring, was to let those who made decisions on dance programs, special events and club managers hear the band and the variety of tunes it offered. Said one of America's top bandleaders, Stan Kenton, about the music business to a West Coast radio audience in the late 1940s one of his principal tasks wasn't selecting music or hiring musicians it was "getting bookings for my band. We worked regularly and getting that work was difficult. George Shearing said the same thing."

And there were dangers that made the work more hazardous than simply whether you got paid or not. Walter Barnes took his Detroit touring band to Natchez, MS to play a place called the Rhythm Club in the spring, 1940. A fire broke out engulfing the whole building and the only exit was the front door. The leader and eight of his musicians as well as vocalist Juanita Avery perished in the fire. Barnes tried to calm the crowd stampeding toward the door by continuing to play. Said witnesses, trumpeter Paul Slott who had joined the band just a few days earlier, the only trumpet on the band, was heard still playing as the fire consumed the interior. Just the year before, Charley Barnet and his band lost charts, instruments and uniforms when the Palomar Ballroom caught fire.

But Barnet's loss also proved how supportive and tight the fraternity could be. Duke Ellington and Benny Carter, black bandleaders with similar styles, sent Charley their best scores. And Charley, who was never at loss for words, made sure that people understood the impact. The first number at his next gig?

"We're All Burnt Up!"

Territorial band leaders today give us more definition to what they do and why.

Joe Enroughty who leads his Virginia-based Royal Virginians is typical of bands that recognize their roles and, at the same time, are satisfied with their purpose.

Joe named his band, he says, because of his respect and love for Guy Lombardo, who certainly led one of the major "sweet" big bands of the early age of music. The primary focus is on Lombardo, Joe says, but "I don't just play Lombardo styled arrangements either. I have some Don Glasser, Chuck Foster, Jan Garber, Sammy Kaye and others. We mix it all up.

"I couldn't use 'Royal Canadians' because that is registered and owned by The Lombardo Estate. So I did the next best thing: since I live in Virginia, the name 'Royal Virginians' was an obvious choice. And, I think, just like when Guy Lombardo was alive and traveling, that having 'royal' in the name of our band is real classy. I don't necessarily agree with the term 'big band' because it seems to conjure names like Woody Herman and Benny Goodman, even though bands like Guy Lombardo and Jan Garber were considered big bands," he says.

Joe wanted to make sure of the authentic Lombardo sound so he spent the time to transcribe from 78 and LP albums the sound of the "Royal Canadians." "I want to make clear that we are not the official orchestra. . . My goal is to recreate a sound in American popular music that outlasted every other form of big band. Swing music had its heyday for about 10 years. While it's true that the swing band leaders came back from time to time and reformed bands for recording dates and special appearances, it was the sweet bands that never folded and continued to play with the same personnel night after night," he continues. The reason? Says Joe: "It's the music the people wanted the most."

Andrew Thielen, a drummer and bandleader from North Myrtle Beach, SC, tours through eight states playing gigs for corporations, dances and other audiences, says staying active takes plenty of vitality. "I can honestly say I know of no other band other than the currently traveling Dorsey and Miller Orchestras who are booked as regularly as we are. And they are ghost bands. We have actually created a strong interest in big band music throughout the Carolinas especially the coastal areas here and parts of Georgia and Virginia. But it has been a Herculean task. I have the double duty because I have had to educate musicians as well as audiences to get it all going. When I started in the early '90s I did research and found big bands didn't play much of what people seemed to be interested in. They were either way too jazzy and played charts way over their heads or they were too traditional and hokey. It was either 'Night in Tunisia' for the jazzy big bands or the old 'String of Pearls' all night long."

So he created a different band, he says. "Why not let today's audiences hear their favorite types of music and songs played by an exciting band? If you meet them on their own turf for three out of four tunes they are a lot more amenable to songs we in band know to be great."

The work was ground up, too. "That leads me to musicians. It was hard getting jazz musicians to look at a chart that says 'Old Time Rock'n'Roll.' I also had arrangers do many other popular songs for me from '50s to the '90s. Today we have charts from the hits of Norah Jones, Celine Dion, Michael Bolton, Wilson Pickett and others. Oh, yes, we had the moaners and groaners in the band but we moved on," he said.

Across the country in Pasadena, CA, a group of swing musicians who work at NASA's Jet Propulsion Lab found their interests were similar; they all wanted to continue playing. Says the spokesman for "Big Band Theory," Richard Machuzak, "The band started back in January, 1999, when Brenda Burkhart and Patrick Olguin (both trumpet players and still with the band) realized that there were enough musicians walking around JPL to form a big band. The band was originally called Jazz Propulsion Big Band. Putting together a lunch-time band was a challenging job, but not too bad. After all, it's not like it's rocket science. Seems that an interest in math and science go hand in hand with an interest in music. After all, music is a series of mathematical relationships. Those who are good with math and science also seem to be good with music and there are quite a few excellent musicians here. Most of our performances are to support JPL functions. We do some charity work off lab and have been hired from time to time for more professional gigs. We're now trying to 'break out.' We've been in a recording studio working our first CD. Having a CD to pass around will hopefully bring more invitations and exposure."

The NASA band, says Richard, finds that audiences aren't simply gray heads.

Hal Leonard and his Orchestra from Winona, MN.   Photo courtesy of James Ronan Collection, Iowa

"Most of the people in our charity audiences for example are the younger set whereas paying gigs seem to feature the older generation. There does seem to be quite an interest in swing dancing especially among the college crowd we play for," he explains. "We specialize in the music of Miller, Basie, Ellington, Dorsey, etc. So we do a lot from the '30s and '40s. But we also have a good number of Sinatra and other vocals and instrumentals from the '50s and even the '60s. We're trying to include more modern jazz charts as many of us also play in other bands which feature that kind of music."

On down the east coast, a re-creation band as they are called, has gained popularity across the country and abroad because of its approach to music of the past. Forbes magazine has called Doc Scantlin's Orchestra the "world's best band."

Doc and his 15 musicians give you a panoramic of America's Flapper Era with 1920 numbers like "Puttin' On the Ritz" and the "Charleston" and they take you through the musical 1930s and '40s with Cole Porter, Irving Berlin and, of course, the songs of Goodman and Miller. Doc calls his group "The Imperial Palms Orchestra." And the name fits the band uniforms. He is decked out in white tails, spats and slicked down hair. And there are gyrating dancing girls, too. He plays for balls, weddings, concerts, private parties and dances in the US and Europe.

Doc told me that "I have very strong opinions about the way things should be for

A Christmas card from Red Sievers and his Band looking forward to a busy season in the 1930s.

Photo courtesy of James Ronan Collection, Iowa

the band because it's not just music – it's a show, a stage production really. It's got a feminine part and a masculine part, an innocent part and a sexy part. It's every thing from Guy Lombardo to Louis Armstrong. And I love it all."

In Washington, DC, Brooks Tegler offers what he calls a band that not only recreates the sound of World War II big band music but a recreation of the WWII Army Air Force scene. Born in 1954, he has been a professional musician/bandleader/historian for 30 years. "I'm not a 'veteran' musician from that era but I've made it my professional area of expertise to focus on the music of the '30s and '40s with an emphasis on World War II. Devotion to the music and the people who played it would have to be my driving force as well as a re-enactor's attention to historical accuracy. " And it has been successful. "No band playing the music of my youth comes close to Brooks' group. They capture all the energy, drive and musicianship that we all remember so fondly from the war years. And they really look the part as well. . . . They put me right back in that cold hangar in England . . . swingin' to my favorite stuff," 8th Air Force veteran Johnny Sinclair said.

Brooks believes attention to detail and authenticity are essential. "I feel we're pretty unusual in that the band is made up of professionals who aren't just doing the 'obligatory' stuff and getting through it. We actually lost a gig after three years simply due to the fact that we were 'too accurate' and not (my words) 'campy enough.' There are many bands out there who wear the clothes but they're all pretty weak I think. Most recently, we have done five Miller AAF Band Tribute concerts where I use an exact replica of (Ray) McKinley's Radio King drum set. I built it entirely from spare parts." The band, which travels abroad, is a part of the WWII Allied Air Force Federation historical society.

A professional musician, bandleader and historian, Brooks takes pride as a re-enactor, too. His band not only plays the music of the '30s and '40s. . . it does recreations of V-Disc shows during the 1940s. "Devotion to the music and the people who played is my passion and 'driving force' and I offer a re-enactor's attention to historical accuracy in every respect," he adds.

In nearby Maryland, an accident site on old Route 32 near the town of Annapolis Junction more than 25 years ago created the name for another territorial band. The "Annapolis Junction Big Band" is a 17 piece aggregation that plays for the joy of playing dance music. "At the King of France Tavern, we are a bunch of easy going people who cheer for each other, admit our mistakes, insult the leader and play with manic energy," the band says at its web site. "We are a sandlot team that doesn't want to play in pinstripes. We play for the fun of it. In the ballroom or at a wedding reception we are well-behaved professionals; happy to stand in the background or get things going; it's all up to the boss, the person who hires us. And you will recognize nearly every tune. Our numbers are not dated despite their age. They are cool, not corny; powerful, not passé; beautiful not boring."

Down in the deep south, Vocalist Dorsey Tippett echoes Doc's love for swing and big band. Dorsey is a member of the "Auburn Knights," possibly the oldest band associated with a college in the country. The group traces its history back to 1930 at Auburn University in Alabama. Its musical history touches famous people and organizations. Gerald Yelverton was a clarinetist who graduated from the Knights in 1938 onto the Glenn Miller band. Music Corporation of America, one of America's premier bookers, signed the "Auburn Knights" for a summer tour.

It gained more notoriety in 1940 when John Philip Sousa II, the grandson of the march king, once fronted the band. The "Auburn Knights" played at Virginia Beach, Myrtle Beach and other well known resorts. Seven decades later how has it stayed together for so long?

Says Dorsey: "The love of swing music and the dedication to keep it alive. We are a separate entity of the university. We are in no way affiliated with it. We are a profit band. We play at any event people have. We normally play wedding receptions and private parties. This is just a little money for us to have on the side."

The band plays music from mainly the '30s, '40s and '50s and it stays alive by remaining in touch with its audience and Alabama campuses. "We hold tryouts each time a member leaves. We advertise by posting flyers up all over the area. We get the word out to students at Auburn and Columbus State. We don't worry about competing with other bands. . . we are the only 'big' band in our area and we try to play the swing music that people recognize as easy to dance to. Our audiences are usually made up of younger people but there are times when older ones come and listen. There is a swing dance association in Auburn and they enjoy dancing to our music and they're very supportive." At reunions each year packed houses of all ages show up, Dorsey adds. The band's history is packed with America's big band past. Tommy Dorsey and Buddy Rich joined the Knights for impromptu sets. So did Frank Sinatra, trumpeter and singer Ziggy Elman, Joni James, June Christy and the Four Freshmen. Before she joined the Captain and created the famous singing duo, Toni Tennielle sang with the "Auburn Knights" in the 1960s. She was a natural big band singer, many said.

Other bands capitalize on a particular sound and trace their success to meeting the audience's perception of something heard in another day. That has helped build the image and reputation of "The Sentimental Journey Orchestra" of Atlanta, GA. It implies the classical age of swing as played by the great bands of the period like Les Brown and his "Band of Renown." In fact, that's the way the band got its start. "I was playing trombone in an all-volunteer community concert band in Decatur, GA and during an after-rehearsal conversation with one of my friends I found he had a collection of old stock big band arrangements from years ago. It didn't take long to get enough musician friends to 'read down' those old charts. We've been doing it ever since," says Henry Mason one of the veterans of the band.

Says Mason of the Sentimental Journey band: "The name has had its downside but overall, it tells in the shortest form what we do. We provide the sounds and styles of great bands of yesterday and today. I do tell potential clients that, while we might play something with a rock type beat, most likely they won't be pleased with us if they are looking for a beach band. We are well known enough that when the client gets to us, they pretty much know what they are looking for." It took work and talent to get there, he quickly adds. "We finally 'went professional' when enough work started coming in to make it pay at least expenses. We still don't expect to make any money beyond having a good hobby that more or less pays for itself. . . doing it is hard enough and doing it right is even harder!"

Dealing with a changing audience is crucial, he continues. "We have been at it for 30 years and when we started, the World War II generation was still pretty young and

Touring sedans of the early big band days weren't the SUVs of today but they had to carry passengers and equipment. Here is Frank Robinson and his Orchestra who traveled the midwest in this "stretch" sedan. Photo courtesy of James Ronan Collection Iowa

vigorous. They were established enough to afford a dance band for special events. Looking back, we could have promoted it a lot better than we did but we are learning most of our lessons the hard way, I guess."

Is it difficult finding young players who still enjoy playing the music that was created and played before their birth? "Many of our members started with us fairly young and have gotten 'old' with us," Henry told me. " We have found that the really good younger players have no problem adapting to the style of the band. A good player will catch on pretty quickly. Since we have the best band in the territory, recruits are not that hard to come by. We have, for example, a long list of 'subs' who will fill in when someone has to be out and when someone retires or moves."

The Sentimental Journey band finds mixing tempos and musical styles in a program are no easy task these days. "One thing is interesting about our audiences; the hardest to please are those of the '60s generation. They want beach music and little else. The older ones love us and the young ones (who really figured it out) love us, too. We have played college dances when the oldest member was 22 or so. The ones from 55 to 65 (early rock through Beatles) are the most difficult to make happy and tend to have the narrowest musical horizons," Henry said.

In southwestern Ohio, bandleader-trombonist-arranger Tom Daugherty Pfrogner does more than just provide dance music for regional events, he teaches music and sees himself as the "keeper of the flame." "I've been called that and I guess that's my job. I do it several ways by leading the band, performing 'big band' recreational shows and also by my music transcriptions. I provide transcriptions – the original recorded arrangements – for bands across the country and even in Europe." And his accuracy and efficiency have been noted by the US Air Force Bands, the Tommy Dorsey Orchestra, Gene Krupa Orchestra and Frank Sinatra shows among others which have employed his services.

He prides himself on making sure of the authenticity of the sound. It's a time-consuming task you have to thoroughly enjoy. But, he insists, "There have been so many bad transcriptions of arrangements that bands have been using since the '50s. . . it does bother me. How can you recreate and carry on the tradition if you don't have the right charts to begin with? I spend the majority of my free time correcting this situation; it's my legacy so to speak." His memories over the years? Vanishing venues. . "What ballrooms are you talking about? When I was in my 30s, we played a few local ones but they are gone now. I do many shows and a few dances. . . probably more shows than dances, however."

Tommy knows that in his big band history, Tommy Dorsey was the greatest "all around band of them all. Others may have sounded more creative and others may have swung harder and more consistently but of all the hundreds of well known bands, Tommy Dorsey's could do more things better than any other could. . .There's no doubt about it. . . Tommy knew what he wanted and he was able to transmit his musical knowledge to those who were willing to listen. . . and who were able to put up with his temper tantrums."

James Bazen of Washington, DC, finds he can meet audience needs by having not one but three different versions of his big band. "The first is called the 'James Bazen Big Band,' the second is 'The Music Unlimited Big Band' and the third is 'USA Canteen.' The big band is strictly about jazz exploration and we play such venues as Blues Alley in DC and various summer jazz festivals. Music Unlimited plays the traditional (stock) authentic big band music – Glenn Miller, Artie, TD, Basie, etc – and it's strictly a dance band. Canteen is a big money group that plays conventions and corporate events. We dress in '40s costumes and have a costumed vocal trio singing authentic transcriptions – which I do – like those of the Andrews Sisters' time."

James doesn't have to worry about planning the gigs once the type of band is chosen. "I don't agonize over that . . . I just play whatever the client asks for. If that involves a stock chart . . . fine. If it doesn't then that's fine as well. My experience is people get bored unless you mix it up a bit. My approach is to play a variety of music each set and keep the pauses between tunes to the absolute minimum. And it works."

Southern California clarinetist Pete Jacobs made a conscious decision to put together a re-creation band of a different kind. He calls it "Pete Jacobs and his Wartime Radio Revue."

How and why the World War II concept?

"As I saw the vast numbers of young people begin to embrace the 'Lindy Hop' as a dance and dressing in forties' attire, I knew that a band which played the music of that era

The sax section of the popular Detroit band, "One Beat Back" led by trumpeter Gary Greenfelder (bottom left) playing a benefit gig in Port Huron, MI. The band raised $4,000 for a Detroit soup kitchen and leader dog for the blind organization in 2006. *Photos submitted by Gary Greenfelder.*

could be very successful. Really dancing is what it's all about! My wife and I have spent a lot of time learning as much as we could about swing dancing. I have an appreciation for what dancers want because we go dancing ourselves several times a week. I put our sets together with dancers in mind. It doesn't matter how great the musicianship of the band is if you can't dance to it. My goal was to make it sound like it sounded in that day. To do this, I knew I had to do more than purchase watered-down 'stock' arrangements of big band tunes. I listened to lots of old recordings and transcribed the music the way I heard it. As of today, I have transcribed over 70 charts, many of which are not even available commercially. I try to do at least one new chart a month," Pete explained to me.

And he knew he needed a particular kind of musician too. "I got a group of

Brooks Pegler and his unique re-creation band "World War II Army Air Corps Review Big Band" of Leesburg, VA.

Photos submitted by Brooks Pegler.

younger musicians with boundless energy together. They can really swing. When you go and play this music where the kids know how to dance the way they did in the late thirties, there is an almost magical synergy that occurs between the bandstand and the dance floor. This music MUST be danced to. It was never meant to be just listened to in a concert situation."

But Pete doesn't just play old standards to be an old time big band. "We do have many standards in our book but we have quite a few songs that are well known from the era but seldom played. For example, it's a very rare gig that would find me playing "In the Mood," or "Sing, Sing, Sing." Most of the audience we get is tired of those. They like it when we pull out some Jimmy Lunceford tune that really swings. When it's fresh, both the musicians and the dancers love it. Also I have a smaller horn section than most modern swing bands. Three trumpets, two trombones and four woodwinds . . . this is much closer to the pre-1940s band really. Most of them had no baritone sax for example. This helps get an authentic swing era sound . . . and it also cuts down the price, too," he smiles.

"The swing era is a very big part of my life and I want to do anything I can to help preserve this classic music," he insists. "Dance instructors have been largely responsible for bringing back the 'Lindy Hop.' This is almost as important as the music. Remember. . . jazz used to be the popular music of the day. It wasn't until jazz turned its back on the dancers that it became relegated to a 5 to 10 percent share of the recording market. R&B and then rock'n'roll came from jazz but retained the dancers at the same time."

What kind of music does he believe audiences want to hear when they go out for an evening of dancing?

"We just don't have that many ballads in our book. . . we have enough to do about an hour-long 'dinner set' but I never have felt the need to do that many ballads. I find that the crowds, regardless of the age, love the up-tempo swing charts. Many elderly people come up to me and tell me that 'they haven't felt like that since there were teenagers' or something to that effect. I might do one ballad and one Latin number per set. I have a total of exactly two waltzes in my book," he says.

"I actually decided at 49 to learn how to do the 'Lindy Hop.' It really opened my eyes as a bandleader to experience life from the other side of the bandstand. Now where I'm playing I often find myself wishing I was down there dancing. . . and when I'm dancing, I always wish I was up there playing! But it's a great alternative certainly to going to the gym."

One type of smugness that territorial bands don't have to deal with today that used to be a form of musical elitism was being labeled a "sweet band " or a "mickey mouse" band. Gene Lees, author of a number of books about jazz including a biography of Woody Herman, said that such bands and their musicians were usually despised. Jazz critic George Simon offered similar comments. But very few big bands of the 1940s and '50s made the money that "sweet" bands made generally. Who were the sweet bands of the era? Blue Barron, Sammy Kaye, Art Mooney, Gray Gordon, Emil Coleman, Lester Lanin, Meyer Davis, Ben Selvin, Anson Weeks, Vincent Lopez, Hal Kemp, Eddie Duchin, Shep Fields, Freddy Martin, Horace Heidt, Tommy Tucker, Dick Stabile, Ozzie Nelson, Vaughn Monroe, Larry Clinton, Art Kassel, Wayne King, Dick Jurgens, Johnny Long, Lawrence Welk and Guy Lombardo were the popular ones and there were many others. A great number of so-called "mickey mouse" bands were and remained territorial bands. Magazines like Downbeat and Metronome kept readers amused each year during the era by including a poll question that asked subscribers to list the best bands and to identify the "corniest" band. Who was the corniest winner? Guy Lombardo many times. Noticeably, though, it was the "sweet" bands like, Lombardo and Welk's that continued long after the big band era ended . . . and it was the same sweet bands that frequently hired former jazz soloists and section players when touring bands left the road. Said one veteran of the big band days when asked about his transition to the softer and slower pace "I was so used to playing an uneven set of 8 notes instead of the straight eight notes in these arrangements. . . I had to go back to private practice before rehearsals."

The difference is detectable immediately. Says Enroughty: "When we've been auditioned by potential bookers who suddenly realize that we are not what they wanted . . . we both move on. When we play a country club we do a mix of old and new songs. Music from the '20s to the '90s and a little bit of everything in between. There's Latin, swing, waltz and so on. We offer a product which is clearly advertised on our site and in our brochure. You wouldn't go to MacDonald's and order a T-bone steak would you? So why would we offer a different sound at a venue from what we advertise? I make it clear what we do and I don't veer off the path. And, to date, I haven't had any complaints."

Joe is an under 30 bandleader who has sidemen and women who are younger in his vintage band. "Finding young talent can be hard. I don't care how old or how young you are. If you play good, if you're in tune and you show up on time for rehearsals and gigs, you're in. The mentality of many of today's young musicians is not that of those who were in the Lombardo '46 orchestra. It's the way they're taught. Everything is about jazz nowadays. I could hire a 20-something trombonist who played in his high school marching band and in the community jazz band and chances are he'll get a great sound out of his horn. But will he have all the necessary mutes to play my book? Probably not. He didn't need them in the other jobs. . ."

Yet Joe insists that doesn't mean the Royal Virginians can't swing. "We do. But our swing arrangements are written in a boundary. "In the Mood," "Stomping at the Savoy" and others are played in swing time but the melody is always present. No obnoxious solos as I call them . . . just dance music. I don't want to play for an unappreciative audience. So if you're into Herman, James, Ellington, Shaw and those guys from another era and you're looking for their authentic sound recreated, then we are not for you. It's as simple as that. If our gigs are limited by the fact that we don't play the great swing hits then so be it. I want to play for folks who like what we do and show it with appreciation. And I can tell you right now that by advertising the fact that we are a sweet band and that we play ballroom dance music . . . it does limit our gigs."

Like every performer Joe believes you've got to be good at what you do. "Every bandleader should be enthusiastic about what they play. And, yes, I see myself as a lifetime bandleader. A 'lifer.' Each gig is great because you have the opportunity to make a new face happy for a few hours and you also get to see the same faces who show up and follow the band from ballroom to ballroom."

More important, he insists, "you have to thoroughly enjoy what you do. With me, that's true but I also get the most pleasure out of making other people happy. When people come up to me and tell me what a wonderful time they had and how much they are looking forward to hearing us again, it really makes me feel good. I'm making them happy. For just a few short hours, I made these people forget about their cares and they enjoy themselves. I can truly say I know how Guy Lombardo felt all those years. You can see it in his eyes (on tape or in photos) as you watch him lead his band but you don't truly know how it feels until you've experienced it yourself. And requests, well, the look on someone's face when you play the song they've requested is priceless. If there ever was work that was consistently gratifying, it's leading a big band. No matter how much trouble it may be to set up and take down all your stands and equipment, in the end, it's the most fun job in the world. The traveling can get rough, too, but the end result is the best part and it's what makes me so happy."

Henry Mason says that "Sentimental Journey" views it similarly although perhaps more clinically. "We try to vary our sets based on the demographic of the audience," he explains. "For example, we try to find out more in advance if possible. Sometimes we simply have to guess. A generic gig will have few ballads, several medium tempo numbers, a Latin or two and we see what works. The audiences seem to like whatever we do. Some enjoy the novelty of a live big band, some are reliving their youth and, for some, it is just 'different.' We rehearse weekly and our rehearsal director (a veteran of the "Auburn Knights" and numerous road bands) doesn't let us get away with anything. At the risk of sounding egotistical – which I do not wish to do – our standard is that of the road bands. If we don't play something well enough to sound like the fulltime pros we don't do it. We listen to recordings and work on our sound. We have top veteran players in the band who keep us 'honest.'"

However, there are those leaders who view the business differently. "I am not really interested in bringing back the dance stuff, " says James Bazen whose big band is based in Washington, DC." Yes, we play it when some corporation can pay us . . . for their holiday party but my main thrust is music for music's sake, not music for dancing. First of all, you have to understand that my preferred approach to the big band is more in line with Stan Kenton and Oliver Nelson than Glenn Miller and Artie Shaw. As an artist I find playing the authentic arrangements makes me feel like a history professor or a museum curator. It's great stuff and obviously is popular but I believe music . . .especially jazz and big band music – should be a living, breathing, evolving art form. An appropriate analogy is an art student learning by painting reproduction of the old masters. It's amazing that they can do that but in the real world why do we need another copy of 'the Mona Lisa?' Can the copy really even approach the quality of the original? That said, we all know that the best way to keep a band together is to make sure it's working. We use the same players but present music in different ways."

Farther north of the Mason Dixon Line in Detroit, MI, Gary Greenfelder leads a territorial band called "One Beat Back." It started as a rehearsal band – kind of a garage or basement band in the old days – in 1992 and had its coming out at a dinner dance. "Within a short period of time, we started to develop a following as well as a reputation and we started to work on a regular basis. We work all kinds of gigs from park concerts, weddings to corporate events," he says, but he adds that while the band has semi-pro as well as active "hobbyists" the band "rehearses every Thursday as a matter of fun and to continuously improve and add new music to our book. We're still a rehearsal band that plays out and gigs are the icing on our cake." Over the years, musicians have ranged from an 82-year-old trombonist who is also the band historian to those either in college or just graduated. But, without a doubt, finding capable players is tough. " I use local musicians with varying level of performance ability. But there is no doubt that ability and the ability to 'swing' are two different animals. I ask all my musicians to do one thing. . . just listen to the music! I have found that many musicians enjoy playing big band but may not listen to it. That, most often, simply doesn't work. I know that I spent many years trying to 'swing' and didn't realize that it has to become a part of you and that doesn't happen unless you listen all the time. What amazes me is that those who have taken the time to do so, usually swing well. It's those that haven't that don't know what they're missing," Gary adds.

Big bands that are successful need arrangements, he continues "and I'm fortunate to have arranger/trumpeter George Millsap who has transcribed many songs not available. He has transcribed many of the Sinatra charts we have.

Old standards do not work except for a few like, for example, 'In the Mood.'"

Dances, he says, are few and sometimes far between. "There is a reason for this: I find dancers only have their agenda in mind and more often than not, it doesn't fit what we like to play. Although we play for weddings these aren't 'swing dance parties' by any means. They do mostly like upbeat stuff but I have found that there are usually different people who want different tempos and you just can't please them all. "

He knows what it's like to keep his aggregation together when personal matters are the focus daily. "The band was a great source of support during my tough times and I truly appreciate that. During the period, I lost the focus needed to keep the band working and we suffered. . . A few years ago we played about 25 to 30 gigs a year. This past few years it has only been a fraction of that. We continue to practice weekly and we're positive about our future. There is work in Detroit for big bands. The largest challenge is that there are a growing number of bands without the same growth in gigs . . . it has become a competitive market." Audience age has changed, too, Gary points out. "I can say that the older age audiences are becoming smaller and smaller. We have some events we used to do that don't occur anymore. At the same time, we've played many yacht club events in recent years so you adapt to a newer generation and newer venues too."

Bandleader Andrew Thielen and his big band who play gigs at Hilton Head, Greenbrier, Ritz Carlton among other places believes live big band music on major TV shows like "American Idol" and "Dancing With the Stars" has had an impact too. "Because it makes all music sound great. That is why both these shows sound and feel so 'alive and exciting,' " he says.

"I created a different big band for a reason, too. Why not let today's audiences hear their favorite type of music and songs played by an exciting big band? If you meet them on their own turf for three out of four tunes they are a lot more amenable to songs we in the band know to be great. So, in effect, we have musically raised their tastes because we came into their world first, then they met us in ours. We did not force them back into the 40's. We did not put them in a coma by playing swing tune followed by swing tune. We also don't really care to do all that nostalgic crap either. If someone wants to wear vintage dress and dance to the band. . . that's fine, but we are not trying to be retro. I really don't perpetuate the brief swing era movement with zoot suits in the 90's either. All that stuff is limiting. When you try to be all retro or nostalgic you can leave half your audience cold and they in turn leave the dance, gala or concert in the park. . . very, very early..

"You like light country? We got a great arrangement of "Brown Eyes Blue." Shania Twain stuff . . . like rock? Here is a great big band arrangement of "Heard It Through the Grapevine. Like patriotic stuff? Some do. Sure, we have it. . . and we play it complete with horns."

How important is the big band to their communities around the country?

Columnist Wally Haas of the Rockford (IL) "Register Star" wrote a column about the lack of big band music on the radio and the response certainly demonstrated his readers agreed. More than 100 readers took the time to write letters of support.

But a letter in the Utica (NY) Observer-Dispatch from Gabe Brasie, a musician in Central New York, offered the other side of today's territorial band business.

"Being in a local band in the Utica area is extremely hard to get noticed. There are not places to play around here. . . It's not fair for musicians. We need a place to get kids off the streets and into a venue to see a band play. . . Please help local bands and music lovers across the city." Gabe could have been talking about anyplace in any state, really.

Says Joe Enroughty: "The band business has always been tough. Even in its hey-day. Now . . . it's worse. But we keep plugging along and keep playing our songs. There is a lot of promotion involved. You can't sit at home and wait for the phone to ring or work to come to you. . . I send out tons of brochures and info about the band to various venues and ballrooms across the state and beyond. By the simple fact that I am so young and so dedicated to this music should tell you that big band business hasn't died. Yes, it's hard to get good paying gigs today. I try to maintain a level at which I will not go below. That way I know I can pay my good musicians what they require. Otherwise, I might settle for less . . . and the sound of my band would suffer. . . so would I . . . and so would our audiences."

And owning and managing a ballroom over the years hasn't been an easier either, says John Matter, former manager of the family owned Matter's Ballroom, Decorah, IA. Today, John continues working with the National Ballroom & Entertainers Association. "When it came to big band or oldtime dances, they were something I did with the hopes of at least breaking even, " he told me. "And it was great if you could actually make some money on these dances. But I did them because it was something I felt a moral obligation to do. The people that still come to these dances were the ones that made your business successful years ago. You feel like this is a way to repay them. However, the ownership of ballrooms today is changing to another generation. I don't believe they feel that link to the past and (they) will continue the music only if it is profitable. Financially, that is not unreasonable, just unfortunate."

Territorial Bands: Where It All Began Bibliography

Gunther Schuller
"The Swing Era: The Development of Jazz,
1930-1945" (Oxford Press, 1989) (Territory Bands)

Andrew Thielen Big Band
www.bigbandonline.com
email 4/23/05; 4.25/05

Annapolis Junction Big Band
http://annapolisjunctionbigband.com

Auburn Knights (Dorsey Tippett)
www.auburnknights.com
email 5/26/05

Alumni Big Band
www.alumniband.homestead.com/theALUMNI~ns4.html

James Bazen Big Band
www.musicunlimited.com/bbb.htm
email 4/27/05; 5/20/05

Brooks Tegler Big Band
www.ww2aaf.org/band/band.html
emails 4/19/2005; 4/20/05

Big Band Theory (Richard Machuzak)
www.bigbandtheory.com

Big Band Era Marches on at Elks Club
Louisville Courier-Journal Jim Booker, letter, 2/5/03

Bill Elliott Swing Orchestra
www.swingorchestra.com/band.html

Chicago Metropolitan Jazz Orchestra
http://cmjo.com Cleveland Jazz Orchestra

Dave Hanlon's Cookbook
www.davehanlonscookbook.com

Dick Campo Big Band
www.dickcampobigband.com

Doc Scantlin's Imperial Palms orchestra
www.docscantlin.com

Don Burns Orchestra
http://members/aol.com/bigband200
email 4/23/05

Tom Daugherty Band
www.tomdaughertyorchestra.com
email tonpfrogner@sprintmail.com

Fort Adkinson (WI) Big Band Revue
Madisoncatholicherald.org/2005-01-13/arts.html
email 4/24/05

Joe Enroughty & Royal Virginians
http:snow.prohosting.com/Lombard/joeband.html
email 5/6/2005; January 1 2006; January 21, 2006

John Matter
former ballroom owner, director, NBEA
email Aug.16, 2005

James L. Dean Big Band

www.jldeanorchestra.com

MJP Big Band
www.mjobigband.com
email 4/23/05

Moonlighters
www.bigband-ri.com

One Beat Back (Gary Greenfelder)
www.onebeatback.com
email August 9, 2005; Aug. 23, 2005; Aug. 24, 2005; June 2, 7, 2006

Pete Jacobs and his Wartime Radio Revue
www.ww2aaf.org/band/band.html
email 4/22/05; 4/25/05

Rhythm Society Swing Orchestra
www.rhythmsociety.net

Roseville Big Band
www.rosevillebigband.com

San Francisco Starlight Orchestra
www.johnhoward.com/sfso.html

Sentimental Journey orchestra (Henry Mason)
www.thesjo.com

Stage Door Canteen
www.stagedoorcanteen.net
email 4/23/05

Starlite Orchestra
www.starliteorchestra.com

Steel Pier Remembered Big Band
www.cyberjaz.com/steelpier

Swingtime
http://melbourne.tripod.com/mmbst.htm

Switch In Time
http://members.tripodcom/switchintime

The Atlanta Seventeen
www.mindspring.com/~gordon17/index.html

Tom Smith Big Band
www.tomsmithbigband.com

Windjammer Big Band
http:fp1.centurytel.net/vcma/WJBB.htm

Vermilion (OH) Community Big Band
http:.1fpl.centurytel.net/ucma/wjbb.htm
email 4/23/05

"Lack of Big Band Music On Radio," Wally Haas,
Rockford Register Star, Feb. 25, 2005

"Takin' Care of Business" by William Pappalardo,
Naples Illustrated, January 2003

All Time Favorites
www.alltimefavorites.com

BALLROOMS... THEN... NOW

Older Americans will tell you "you had to be there to feel the excitement." No different, I suppose, than today when events or special occasions create more than the usual emotional tug. It's hard to top "Carmen Ohio" by the Ohio State Marching Band at a Buckeye football game in the Horseshoe with over 100,000 screaming fans. The same feeling of euphoria grips Southern California fans when the Trojan band plays "Fight On" or the University of Michigan Band begins a rendition of "Hail the Victors" in the "Big House."

In the days of the big bands, however, it was a combination of feeling, the ambiance of the ballroom, the musical group and the special person you were with. It was magnetic and it usually sprang from the buzz of high school hallways, campus student unions or street corners prior to the special night. From the 1930s through the twilight of the ballroom days in the 1960s, the get-away-from-it-all feeling was spontaneous when a big band was coming to a favorite spot close by.

Close by? I traveled hundreds of miles to hear favorite bands during the 1950s and I'm sure many others did, too. A $2.50 admission charge and gas mileage took all I had for a week but it was worth it. Today rockers and the jet set traverse the globe to attend U-2 concerts or see the Stones. . . so really little has changed in the music world. . . except the admission price.

What was so special about the "feeling" surrounding a big band during the swing era? A sense of excitement to learn a new dance step (or simply make sure you didn't embarrass yourself with foxtrot moves you hadn't practiced), hear a different sound or number or new soloists and finally, most important, to appreciate the musical moment . . . with or without a partner.

Little did we know the moment – which was during the middle of a war that took such a toll and so many lives – could end so quickly. Big bands, some music historians believe, were in trouble by the end of World War II less than a dozen years after the swing era officially began. Sadly, bands disappeared from coast to coast tours by late 1946. But ballrooms continued for another decade or so, struggling to find ways to draw crowds without the bands. Ballroom owners, mostly family businesses in the Midwest, were creative in continuing to attract a clientele and a number continue to do so today. It's one of the untold success stories of the period.

...really little has changed in the music world . . . except the admission price.

President Franklin D. Roosevelt delivered a stirring State of the Union Address Jan. 6, 1942, in which he enunciated a view of a world that would have four fundamental freedoms once victory was achieved. They were: free speech and expression, freedom to worship, the freedom from want and finally, the freedom of fear. I would have added a fifth; the freedom to enjoy the exciting and creative American swing and dance music that was now popular worldwide as the United States went to war.

Bob Montesano of Utica, NY, echoes my sentiments. "My fondness for big band music really grew from listening to late night remotes from big hotels around the country. We did local remotes from an outside dance setting at Bennett's Field near Utica in rural Frankfort. The bands I recall most from my announcing days were Chuck Foster, Bob Chester and Bob Eberle who also had a band at the time. My favorite was Foster because he was friendly and did not appear to throw his 'importance' around like other celebrities I met in those days. "

His interest in big band music started early. The Fulton Chain of Lakes in northern New York was rustic, still remote but he and his family spent quality time vacationing there during summers. "We would arrive on First Lake and park at the Lakeview Lunch along the boardwalk at 1 a.m. We usually had a boat reserved to get on the lake at dawn. However, even though I couldn't wait to start fishing at daybreak before I fell asleep I heard the big band music coming from the Hollywood Hills Casino which was just a few hundred yards from our parking spot. I was mesmerized by the great music. Jump tunes, ballads, all kinds of music. I was tempted to get out of the truck and walk a few yards to take in the action. The casino was a beautiful log structure built over the lake and the place really jumped. . . A friend of mine who worked at times as a busboy said he recalls many of the name big bands of the '30s and '40s playing at Hollywood Hills. . . After World War II when we returned to the lake, the place was closed and I believe fire destroyed the casino in later years."

Central New York was as attracted to the big band days as the celebrated spots on the east and west coasts. A young musician/composer/arranger from one of Mohawk Valley's most musical families, Torrie Zito, collaborated with world renown violinist Florian Zabach to create a clever violin/bass number called "Pussyfootin' in 1953 and began a career in music that led to work with national artists like Frank Sinatra, Tony Bennett, Bobby Darin, James Moody, Herbie Mann and others. He was on staff with Quincy Jones at Mercury Records to back such artists as Billy Eckstine, Sarah Vaughn and Barbra Streisand. Torrie's father Fred Sr., played bass with Phil Spitalny and his brother Fred Jr. was a trombonist with Artie Shaw, Gene Krupa, Stan Kenton and later Tex Beneke. Another brother Ronnie, a drummer, played with Woody Herman.

Hundreds of miles south, Dave Dodrill of Hurricane, WVA, never even considered music as something he wanted to do but he loved to hear the big bands. "Being musically challenged and from a poor family in a poor place I didn't have a chance to see a big band while growing up. In fact, I saw my first one when Stan Kenton came to my homecoming dance while I was in graduate school at the University of Iowa. He was great! My exposure to big bands came through radio, of course. I listened to radio as a teenager . . . I always admired the announcers' diction. Later, I worked at a daylight station in my hometown of Richwood, WVA. I worked there during high school years as a DJ and general announcer. The station format was whatever the DJ wanted it to be. It was mostly pop music but we used lots of recorded programs furnished by the military and Social Security and some freebies from recording companies. I still remember the women who called and said: 'Don't you have anything better to play than Wayne King?' The truth? No we didn't."

Don Cantwell, who later went on to lead his own bands, write books, teach and even do some cartooning, can still recall those weekly radio music programs. "Each evening from 7 p.m. until midnight there was the Make Believe Ballroom whether it was Sammy Kaye, Benny or Artie we listened to the music and, as high school musicians, we could buy the arrangements as it was recorded and that was even more exciting. Whether we'd perform it or not we would go down to the local record store and play those great numbers over and over again."

The big bands had arrived overnight by 1940, it seems. They came with so many other things. Burma-Shave roadside signs, Hemingway's "For Whom The Bell Tolls," Fibber McGee and Molly's closet, Bugs Bunny cartoons, Walter Winchell's staccato broadcasts to "all the ships at sea," V-Mail (the onion-skin like letter on blue paper),

The Dick Jurgens band from California playing at the popular hotel Pennsylvania Café Rouge on April 4, 1948.

Photo courtesy of Dick Jurgens Jr.

a double feature movie for 25 cents, $850 to $900 for a new car while 12 cents would purchase a gallon of gas and you could expect an average salary of $1,299 a year.

We knew where our money was; safe at Fort Knox, KY, where America's gold was deposited. George H. Gallup, a 34-year-old social scientist, had launched the first of millions of polls at his American Institute of Public Opinion. The famous parlor game, Monopoly, was showing up as Christmas gifts to entertain the family in pre-television days. Life magazine was just four years old but it already was the nation's picture weekly and would continue to be until 1972. The country was whistling or singing "Pennies From Heaven" and fast dancing to "Stomping at the

Savoy" as the threat of war grew daily.

Where were you that fateful Sunday, Dec. 7, 1941? I was 8, midway in the 2nd grade in Lancaster, OH, a long way from Pearl Harbor but still very connected to the events at the military base where my late uncle, Walter Danison, was assigned to Battery C 15th Coast Artillery and later told his daughter Jeanne Worachek in her book of her father's "World War II Remembrances" (2003) how he had just stepped out of his tent at Fort Barrette on a beautiful morning when he saw a Japanese plane flying so low he could see the pilot looking down from the cockpit. My uncle had his rifle. . . but no ammunition!

The Honolulu Advertiser, Dec 4, 2001, told the story of Pat Thompson and Jack Evans of San Diego, CA who had met the night before at a jitterbug contest at Bloch Arena, Honolulu, where they won the contest and took their trophies home. . . never to see each other again until a piano player on the USS California, John Rutledge, publisher of a survivors' magazine, the "Scuttlebutt," found Jack, a sailor at the time, and put the two in touch with each other. Surprisingly, they both had settled in San Diego not far from one another.

Bandleader Billy MacDonald certainly remembered the date. His band had extended an engagement in Honolulu and finished a long Saturday night gig and wanted to sleep in like any group of musicians would do on a Sunday morning. Falling Japanese bombs jolted them into the streets where band members "pitched in to help clean up and care for the wounded," Dec. 7th. It was the beginning of a nightmare for the MacDonald band because it took them more than 60 days to get back to the mainland . . . and when they did, a number of the band had induction notices waiting for them.

The late Steve Ambrose, a celebrated 20th century historian, wrote an opinion piece for the Wall Street Journal on the anniversary of the 60th anniversary in which he pointed out that the United States was as divided about it's political and economic future in those fateful days as they were when the World Trade Center was attacked on Sept. 11, 2001.

Dec. 4, 1941, for example, was the day the Chicago Tribune broke the massive story about America's Victory Plan which offered the details on how the country would fight the Axis powers (known to be Germany, Japan and Italy) if war came. It created shock, dismay and a search for those who leaked the ultra secret information.

But people were humming numbers they heard bands play and trying to forget the ominous daily news they read. Glenn Miller's "Elmer's Tune," which he borrowed from Dick Jurgens and put words to, was popular as was "Serenade in Blue" which featured a marvelous introduction written by his trumpet player/arranger Billy May; Peggy Lee's "Why Don't You Do Right" and Duke Ellington's "Don't Get Around Much Anymore" were also hits. Every territorial and touring band also included such popular wartime charts as "Deep In The Heart of Texas," "When The Lights Go Out

All Over the World," "Don't Sit Under the Apple Tree," "At Last" (from Miller's successful movie "Orchestra Wives"), "As Time Goes By," "All or Nothing At All," "Pistol Packin' Momma," "That Old Black Magic," "American Patrol" (another Miller favorite), "Praise the Lord and Pass the Ammunition," "Coming In On a Wing And a Prayer," "Do Nothing 'Til You Hear From Me," another Ellington hit, and a Woody Herman ditty that made little sense then and now but was a soft ballad that tugged at the heart called "Happiness Is Just a Thing Called Joe." The Joe in the song incidentally, oldtimers know, was what every soldier was called during the war.

Four years earlier psychologists had raised concerns about voodoo music and African drums. Social scientists were undoubtedly reacting to the events as the year began when Drummer Chick Webb's band excited dancers to his Lindy-hopping music at the Savoy Ballroom in New York City, which would be called "The Track" because of grooves worn in the floor by the shuffling feet. Said Downbeat Magazine in February, 1938: "The much herald Battle of Swing between Chick Webb's and Count Basie's bands took place Saturday, Jan.18, at the Savoy Ballroom. The affair drew a record attendance and hundreds were turned away at the box office with the crowds tying up traffic for several blocks in that vicinity. Applause for both bands was tremendous and it was difficult to determine which band was the more popular. . ."

The ballot showed Chick's band the winner and Ella Fitzgerald the top singer.

Cautioned the conservative New York Times, Aug. 14, 1938, swing music can cause unbalanced behavior and sexual permissiveness. However, few newspapers or magazines really wrote or published articles about swing bands, the music and the dancers. The exceptions were Colliers, Look, Esquire and an occasional piece in Life magazine. Big bands, meanwhile, were covered by specialty periodicals like Downbeat, Billboard, Variety and Metronome. The public generally ignored the psychologists and continued having fun where they could find it. You read about the bands and the entertainment business from writers such as John Hammond, Dave Dexter, George Simon, John Wilson, Leonard Feather, Barry Ulanov and Ralph Gleason among others as I did.

Top 10 bands? Billboard ranked Benny Goodman tops in 1938, Artie Shaw first in '39 and Miller was at the top for his last three years leading his civilian band.

Numbers two and three were held by two bands for five years; Tommy Dorsey and Kay Kyser. While the black dancers were enjoying Chick Webb and Duke Ellington at the Savoy and the Cotton Club, the only black bands to break into the Billboard list of predominantly white bands was Jimmy Lunceford in 1941.

Cab Calloway's language had "infected" us, too. Young people talked about "jive" which was actually Harlemese for stuff, liquor or to kid along; "icky" which meant not "hip," and you frequently heard about how the "joint is jumping" which meant a place was really hot with good jazz or swing. You also could be called a "Daddy-

O" which meant a hipster, a "cat" (or a "cool cat") which was insider talk for someone who loved jazz or swing. To Lionel Hampton everybody was a "gate" and for good reason, said Hamilton College Jazz Archive Curator Monk Rowe, who interviewed him before his death. "Alligator" was a slang term for a musician and Lionel simplified salutations. "'Gate' allowed Lionel not to have to remember everybody's name. He just called everybody 'Gate,'" Monk told me in a radio interview. "Chops" referred to a musician's technical skill on an instrument but black musicians frequently used the term to talk about false teeth or lips too.

And every musician who was a player knew what "bread" meant. The universal language. . . money.

But it was the ballrooms that gave a growing number of bands the place to be heard and allowed crowds to participate with them. Millions responded in the early days. . . and some do so today. Listen to these soundbytes from people asked to submit their interests at a national web site:

A poster of Anna Mae Winburn and her "own 12 Cotton Club Boys" and her traveling "RV" on a midwest tour.

Photo courtesy James Ronan Collection, IA

"I love gospel and jazz," Rita from Chesapeake, VA; "I love all kinds of music," LC from Indianapolis; "I enjoy most styles of music," James from OH; "Music is my life!" Tracy from Seymour, IN; "I love to dance," Cheri from CT; "Music is my life . . . without it. . . it would be so drab," Heather from FL.

"The success of the big band was largely dependent on its acceptance by the dancing public. The revolution of the 'Swing Era' was led by black bands and black audiences before being broken into by the first white band leader, Benny Goodman. 1935 marked a break-out year for big bands as Benny . . . was given the chance to play on a coast to coast radio show. All of America could now hear the sound of the big bands that Harlem had given birth to. It was the only time in history that the popularity of jazz

One of Iowa's celebrated ballrooms, The Inwood, which was built in 1920 in Spillville, IA. National talent and touring groups played the Inwood including Louis Armstrong and Lawrence Welk among many. In 1965, the original Byrds played the ballroom.

Photo courtesy James Ronan Collection, IA

music eclipsed all other forms of music in the US," said a swing music web site.

In 1940, Billboard Magazine surveyed ballroom operators in various places in the country to see what bands brought business to dance floors.

At Canadarago Park, Richfield Springs, NY, Guy Lombardo, Gene Krupa, and Cab Calloway were in demand. At King's Ballroom in Lincoln, NE dancers liked Henry "Hot Lips" Busse, Vincent Lopez and Hal Leonard. Sandy Beach Park crowds at Russell's Point, OH, loved Artie Shaw, Blue Barron and Jan Garber. Out west, Phil Harris and Eddie Duchin were popular at Natatorium Park in Spokane, WA while Jimmy Walsh and Anson Weeks were familiar names to dancers at Saltair in Salt Lake City, UT. At the Fiesta Danceteria back in New York, people flocked to hear and dance to Ben Bernie, Krupa and Shorty Allen.

So if the bands are coming back . . . is dancing already mainstream again?

It certainly is. In a 2005 web site about dancing called "Find A Partner" I counted over 100 entries from throughout the US and Australia from age 16 to over 70 who express interest in all kinds of dancing including one who was married to a non-dancer for more than 30 years and finally left to get a new life. . . dancing!

Legendary dancer Frankie Manning who grew up as a regular at Harlem's Savoy Ballroom in the '30s, offered his thoughts on the difference between yesterday and today's dancing in the Washington Post a few years ago. "In comparison of the top dancers of today, not everyone is on the same level. . . I would have to go with the oldtimers."

Says James Ronan of Iowa, a collector of big band postcards and a fan of ballrooms in his state, the era simply came and went far too quickly. "The first ballroom concert I ever attended was in Spillville, IA at the Inwood Pavilion. The Byrds from California were in town with the number one song, "The Tambourine Man." From that day forward I was hooked on not only the music but the great ballrooms in the tri-state area. Growing up in eastern Iowa, we had over 200 ballrooms at one time. We had more ballrooms per capita than any other state in the union. Sad to say only 15 remain that are still functioning. By the mid-1970s, things had changed and the dancing at the local ballrooms fell on hard times. Concerts rather than dances were being held. In Decorah, Matters Ballroom was in business for nearly 90 years until it burned down a few years ago. I have fond memories of big band, rock and roll in other ballrooms. I've never missed a Buddy Holly tribute show which is held every year in February. Another great ballroom I remember is the Lakeside in Guttenberg, IA. Ballrooms were simply a great place for families to gather, enjoy the live music and dance. . . especially in the pre-rock and roll days," he says.

"I moved back to northeast Iowa in the late '70s and I have tried to support the ballrooms by not only attending shows but renting and booking bands at these venues. In the old days, I could dance all night long for no more than $2 and meet lots of young ladies in town who loved to dance also. I'm especially in mourning for the next generation who will never experience what I did. Many great theaters and ballrooms are gone and never will be replaced."

James is right . . . young people now have far fewer opportunities to dance as those who grew up when bands were plentiful, ballrooms were everywhere and dancing was the "social scene." As a number of territorial bandleaders note in this book, young people today really like swing music and energetic jitterbugging. They bring their own water bottles and get an informal physical therapy session on the floor! In earlier days, couples on regular weekends found dark corners to do slow dancing, sometimes called walking or simply "standing together" music. Bob Crosby said it was called "dippers' corner; big dippers, medium dippers and quick dippers."

When a nationally touring big band was in town . . . a good number hovered around the bandstand most of the evening but dancers were still everywhere enjoying the moment.

The first band to be heard nightly on radio? Some historians say Paul Specht and his band in broadcasts from WWM, Detroit in September, 1920. Five years later, there was the Carlton Coon and Joe Sanders group which used the title "Coon-Sanders Band" from Kansas City. The band's remotes began at midnight and played for an hour or so. Typical of the bands looking for image at the time, one musician in the Coon-Sanders band wisecracked one night that only "nighthawks" listened at that hour and shortly after the band was known as the Kansas City "Nighthawk

Band." That same year, an accordion playing, dancing bandleader from Yankton, SD, Lawrence Welk, began broadcasting with his studio band at WNAX. And it was merely twenty-four months afterward that the famous Cotton Club in New York City featured Duke Ellington.

The National Ballroom & Entertainers Association is the official register of America's ballrooms past and present and the list of current dance halls shows how dancing moved from the east coast to the west. In the 1930s, Pennsylvania, New York and New Jersey dominated the scene with ballrooms that generated radio listeners, thanks to remotes, as well as crowds of jitterbugging teens and young adults who danced in the aisles of theaters as well as the streets when they heard the music. They later became the bobby sox fans of Frank Sinatra.

The irony is that NBEA records show that New Jersey, New York and Pennsylvania had a combined total of 40 ballrooms (24 in Pennsylvania, 10 in New Jersey and 6 in New York) while Midwest states like Illinois, Iowa and Ohio had a grand total of 71 ballrooms (Illinois 28, Iowa 23 and 20 in Ohio). Ballrooms were more plentiful in the Midwest than anywhere in the early years it appears.

Big bands had a special appeal within the years after jazz sprang from New Orleans. Jazz had its distinctiveness; small groupings, individual stylists taking riffs and running with them for up to a half hour depending upon the crowd and the mood. There was that solid two beat and a meandering pace that became the benchmark for jazz groups. You could dance to it. . . but most people tended to listen and watch jazz musicians who frequented more clubs, bars and taverns. Ballrooms were another matter because dancing was the focus usually.

That's why there was always a sadness associated with a ballroom closing. The late 1940s triggered the beginning of an end no one wanted. Residents in Johnson City, NY, fondly remember the George F. Johnson Pavilion as the place you frequented to shut out the stress of a Depression and the worries of World War II plus Korea and Vietnam. The 78 year old facility built in 1926 by and named after one of the founders of the Endicott-Johnson Shoe Co., would overflow its 10,000 foot dance floor and an outside patio with more than 1,200 couples when big bands like Miller, Goodman, Dorsey and others played. The pavilion demonstrated the company's interest in its community.

Johnson not only built the dance hall he subsidized top entertainment so you paid 75 cents to a $1 when a major band was playing. By the '50s big bands weren't traveling and to keep the place active, it became a roller skating rink. Then it became a rock'n'roll spot before it shut down in the summer of 2004.

The world was vastly different by 1950. Studebaker was urging you to take a trial run in its new Champion deluxe 4-door sedan which averaged 26 miles to a gallon. RCA was promoting its "horn of plenty" sound system for music lovers and Dumont claimed to be the "first with the finest television" emphasizing all the more reason

The crowded dance floor of the famous Roseland Ballroom on 239 West 52nd Street, New York City where the Woody Herman band played its first gig in 1936.   Photo courtesy Roseland web site

to stay at home weekends. GE, meanwhile, had a new 16" tube with the sharper contrast that made blacks blacker and whites whiter. Not to be outdone, Admiral announced a Smart set which had a 16" tube, AM and FM radio and a three-way phonograph in a beautiful cabinet for $499.95 "all the more reason to stay home and enjoy" rather than fight the crowds or so the advertising claimed.

Just 10 years later, Emcee Ronnie Reagan told a nationwide audience on a show called "Swingin' Singing Years" what had transpired in the brief big band years. We saw and heard the Woody Herman Herd, dressed in bright plaid sport coats that looked checkered in black and white, swing with a rendition of a World War II number called "Your Fadder's Mustache." Woody introduced it as a "good old Brooklyn folk song." And we listened to a singer and pianist recreate the music that made Johnny Mercer and friends' Capitol Records one of the major studios in Hollywood. Ella Mae Morse sang and Freddy Slack and his band backed her on the number, "Cow Cow Boogie." How much impact did the 78 single have on Capitol?

According to Reagan, mail addressed to the "Cow Cow Record Company" was regularly delivered to the company.

The big band sound was different and it continues to be so today although people think of the music as all a part of a bygone era. Said the Swing Era, 1932-1944 web site: "Because of this the swing era is also often known as the big band era. Some big bands didn't include a lot of improvisation. Other big bands such as that of Count Basie placed great emphasis on improvisations."

Big band enthusiasts and ballroom owners can probably thank Fletcher

Henderson for the disciplined section arrangements, the blending of woodwinds, brass and rhythm that formed the music of the first bands that played the larger pavilions in America, And we are also indebted to employers, whether racist or not, who didn't hire young Fletcher (who they called "Smack") fresh from Columbia University with his master's in chemistry. Hard to believe today but he was without job prospects in the early 1920s in New York City and he turned to music simply to make a living.

Like Freddie Martin, an Ohio big bandleader a few years later, Fletcher worked as a song demonstrator at the W.C. Handy Music Publishing Co.. Later, he doubled as a music director and pianist at Black Swan Records, a company he co-owned with his friend Harry Pace. He brought popular singer Ethel Waters to the label and he led the band that backed her in her first recording, "St. Louis Blues."

Within months, he formed his own band which became the resident group at the Club Alabam and then jumped to the Brooklyn ballroom, the Roseland, where he became known as the best "colored" band in New York. His arrangements were popular to listen to . . . as well as for dancing. His theme "Christopher Columbus" became a familiar tune to those who went dancing in New York City. He was heavily influenced by the popular Paul Whiteman band of California, an all-white orchestra in demand as the jazz age began. Within a year, trumpeter Louie Armstrong joined his band and Henderson realized the potential for jazz orchestrations in a big band. At the same time, he was joined by another innovative saxophonist/ arranger, Don Redman, who was credited with developing "block passages," where one section plays the same phrases together. Fletcher was well recognized by white and black musicians as the man who could find the answer to blending sections and creating pleasing sounds and good danceable music.

A swing score, for example, had specific notes for every instrument to play in every measure. Fletcher, his brother Horace and Redman charted arrangements for trumpet, trombone, saxophone and rhythm. The arranger would likely decide which measures would be used for soloists, too. It was the beginning of a time when musicians played together and read what was written.

Although popular, Fletcher didn't demonstrate managerial ability. Unlike the man he helped achieve great success, Benny Goodman, he wasn't considered a disciplinarian or a businessman. After an auto accident in 1928, he arranged for others like Teddy Hill, Isham Jones and Goodman.

Goodman's dramatic use of Fletcher's arrangements at the Palomar at a pivotal point in the clarinetist's career in the mid '30s led to virtually instant success with young dancers and he returned to the east coast to be chosen a house band for the "Let's Dance" CBS radio nationwide program. Goodman needed charts every week and Benny's friend John Hammond suggested Fletcher should be recruited to produce the new arrangements.

In 1939 Fletcher disbanded his own group and joined Benny as a pianist and arranger. Later he was a fulltime arranger with Goodman and the hits demonstrated his success.

Dance, of course, was evolving at the same time. It was popularized by Vernon and Irene Castle in a dance called the "Castle Walk" in the early 1900s in nightclub performances and was later given more exposure by Harry Fox in the Ziegfield Follies, New York's popular stage show. While there are various interpretations of how the "Foxtrot" began. . . Harry definitely played his role. It was described as a jerky kind of dance with a tempo of about 160 beats a minute. Famous dance studios like Arthur Murray and Fred Astaire still teach the steps. It's what every couple thinks of when they step on the floor to dance.

According to Don Herbison-Evans in the online "The History of Modern Ballroom Dancing," the word "ballroom" explained the location of a dance. Before radio and television, balls were important social events. Consequently, if you look at the large number of ballrooms in the 1920s and '30s, they might be on the second floor of a building, maybe a large room in the back or some other less likely spot.

Where did owners get such exotic titles like the Rendezvous Ballroom or The Shalimar or simply names of the locale?

The National Ballroom & Entertainers Association says the buildings were called all kinds of things more than likely to help attract the clientele. "Ballrooms refer to all establishments, whether called pavilions, parks or just dance halls, where large crowds would gather to dance to the new music of the times. Although ballrooms have long been associated with the big bands, it was the jazz age where many of them got their start. The '30s and '40s were undoubtedly the

highpoint of the ballroom era, and ironically, it was the end of World War II that also saw the downswing in the number of ballrooms across the United States."

In Detroit, to illustrate, there was a rich history of big bands and grand ballrooms. The Detroit News published an in-depth account of the city's big band past entitled "When Detroit Danced to the Big Bands," by Patricia Zacharias which captured the mood and the dress of the era.

"Among the well-to-do in the 1920's, modernism became the thing in music, dance, fashion and behavior. Old rules crumbled. Jazz became the rage, along with lively dances. Hard-working newly independent women now chose a new way of dressing. Layers of long, smothering garments fell in favor of simple clothing. The most daring even wore trousers. Women challenged the demure ladylike manners once expected of them. Drinking and smoking in public became more common. More women wore make-up and went to restaurants and nightclubs without a chaperone. . . People worked hard having fun. They tried to erase memories and its austerity and ballrooms became the public drawing room where Boy Met Girl," she explained.

Ballrooms and big bands and even radio were intertwined from the beginning. Glenn Miller's meteoric rise to fame came from back to back ballroom bookings – Frank Dailey's Meadowbrook and the Glen Island Casino – in 1939-40. And radio remotes, which attracted distance audiences, added to the demand for bands and their recordings. Unlike other leaders who either didn't see much beyond individual gigs or feel the necessity to promote themselves at the time, Glenn seized the chance to realize his dream. In fact, Willie Schwartz, a member of Miller's early bands, described Glenn's motives. He said Glenn sought what others didn't always do; a market for his music. When Glenn signed with Chesterfield Cigarettes to do 15 minute programs Tuesdays, Wednesdays and Thursdays each week from Dec. 27, 1939 to Sept. 24, 1942, he risked interfering with touring to play one-nighters. Willie said that Glenn was determined to spend the air time getting in as many Miller numbers as possible but the difficulty in an era before tape delay was doing these programs live from everywhere . . . and nowhere. It meant finding a good engineer and, more important, locating a site to do the remote. According to Schwartz, the band actually did a show in a boxcar on a siding once because Glenn couldn't find a suitable building.

Glenn believed that music would generate demand for the band throughout the country. . . and he was certainly right. Where was the risk? Carving up a schedule of one-nighters where three nights a week the band had to leave the premises early and take long breaks to do the radio shows.

Legendary jazz critic and big band drummer George T. Simon, author of the authoritative book, "The Big Bands," described the dilemma in a liner note on the 1968 33 1/3 album entitled "The Chesterfield Broadcasts, Vol. 1 and 2."

"The show itself was not difficult to do – at least under ordinary circumstances,"

George wrote. "Generally, it required a run-through, mostly for timing and balancing requirements, there usually was a dress rehearsal, which was followed by the broadcast. This routine occurred twice a night, once for the eastern part of the country and then, three hours later, for the west coast. This meant that the band was often forced to leave an eastern engagement for an hour or so while it went into the studio for its commercial broadcasts."

Imagine how a ballroom owner who promoted the Miller band appearance explained to the crowd that the band would take an hour or longer break and be back later in the evening. . . While ticket prices weren't what they are today, unhappy fans weren't always pacified easily. Several on the east coast remembered having their special nights interrupted when the Miller band packed up to get to the studio. "Dancers wanted the music to continue, they weren't interested in drinking and waiting," said one.

> In 1941, one out of every three records
> played on jukeboxes was a
> Glenn Miller record.

But they usually waited. That's because the Miller Band was the band to hear when he was in town. Schwartz, the celebrated clarinetist who discovered himself providing the lead when Glenn found "his sound," said that, prior to American Federation of Musicians President James Petrillo's recording ban in 1942, the band stayed east and recorded everything they could think to press into vinyl. A total of 45 songs in 1940 alone. It was Glen's idea to get ahead of others, Willie said. He was certainly right again. In 1939, record sales totaled $50 million up from $10 million in 1932. By 1940, sales zoomed to $70 million and in 1941, just ahead of the ban, sales soared to $100 million. Meanwhile, jukeboxes, which became popular in drug stores and confectioneries when they were introduced in 1934, also became the rage. In 1941 there were nearly 400,000 jukeboxes in the United States and, according to Miller drummer and singer, Ray McKinley, "one out of every three records played on those jukeboxes was a Glenn Miller record." On top of that, Miller's popularity from his whirlwind one nighters introduced more than 500 Miller fan clubs – called "chooches" – in the United States and Canada.

Yet, ballrooms were the place to be during those years. Singer Mel Torme described what it was like to be at the opening night of the Hollywood Palladium when Tommy Dorsey packed the place on Halloween, 1940. "For $1 you got dinner, singer Connie Haines and my friend Buddy Rich along with Tommy and the band. I was in heaven!" he told a PBS Special audience in the 1990s. "Duke Ellington and Fletcher Henderson had already formed large swing bands that played in the Kansas City area. Swing bands started to play a large part of people's lives in the late '30s as people tried to shake off the depression by dancing," a swing web site said.

The country was alive with big bands playing about anywhere there was a dance floor. Dance fans in Central New York had choices everywhere. Ozzie Nelson opened Russells Danceland in Sylvan Beach on Oneida Lake in 1939. He followed Chick Webb's hot band with Ella Fitzgerald into the region when Chick had a gig at the prestigious Yahnundasis Golf Club, New Hartford, NY and along with nearly a hundred or more touring bands they played places like the Mohawk Armory, Steuben Park Armory, Calvary Armory, Canadarago Park Pavilion, Skate-A-Rama in Yorkville, Bennett's Field, outside of Utica, Hotel Utica and theaters such as the landmark in the area, the Stanley Theatre and the Uptown Theater.

The Webb band played for the New Hartford High School Prom at the Yahnundasis, a first since Chick had become the "house band" at the world's greatest ballroom, The Savoy in New York City from 1931 to 1935. A drummer who didn't read music, Chick had lost some talented people like Louis Jordan and Johnny Hodges but musicians like Louis Bacon and Taft Jordan on trumpets, Sandy Williams on trombone remained and he had hired a lively and talented teenaged singer who had won vocal contests at the Apollo Theater and just finished a stay with the Tiny Bradshaw band. Ella was basking in the fame of her hit tune "A-Tisket, A-Tasket" which sold more than a million copies and stayed on the pop charts 17 weeks when the band appeared in New Hartford possibly one of the first black bands to play the club. She started with the Webb band on a trial basis at $12.50 in 1935. Sadly, Chick died of tuberculosis of the spine (he was suffering from the symptoms while on tour) a few months after the Central New York gig. Ella, who also didn't read music, stepped in and became the leader of the band now called "Ella Fitzgerald and her Famous Orchestra" and continued the tour. The gifted jazz vocalist, considered one of the most influential singers of the 20th century, had a three octave range and was considered to have an exceptional purity of tone.

The following year, New Hartford High School brought trombonist Jack Teagarden and his band to the Yahnundasis.

As the big band era faded, musicians like Bob Sterling of Herkimer, NY, pursued the dream regardless of the loss of places to play. According to good friend Jonas Kover who wrote a Utica Observer-Dispatch feature on Sterling in later years, Bob had been a drummer since 16. He organized his own band under the name Van Sterling and worked as an arranger. Said Jonas of Van's music: "Sterling's tunes emit a fanciful feeling of permanent, lost or fleeting romance that puts you in the mood for a moonlit night or a turn around the dance floor under the jittery bright sprinkles of a mirrored globe."

But like many of us who wanted to play, the end was already past. "I came in on the tail end of the big band era. We all knew it. We did a lot of college work and policemen's balls all over the state," Van added. But looking back, I'd say such musicians were just as important to their communities as going to hear touring bands who were trying to make monotonous one nighters memorable evenings. A number of big bandleaders who toured during the 1940s and '50s complained about the time it took scouring the countryside to find replacement musicians who left their groups because of the draft, illness or lack of interest in staying on the road. And bands didn't get much rehearsal time for new music when they were traveling either. The frenetic pace took its toll on the best of the name bands, their sidemen and vocalists.

More than twenty-five years later some bands were struggling to find gigs but playing similar kinds of places when they could find them. Steve Early was a drummer with Duke Ellington 1966-67 and returned briefly in 1968. "I came in at the end of the big band era, really. Strange as it seems I got to play with some of the best big bands . . .but there was very little work and they had all these great sidemen available. Duke's band was different from any other one I played with. Probably different than any other in the business. The scope was vast, everyone in the band had their own sound, and you couldn't take people in and out as in most bands tried to do without completely changing the sound. These so-called re-creation bands of his music are ridiculous in my mind because the guys in the band including Duke in those days . . . they WERE the band."

Ellington was, without question, a musician/composer/leader that others emulated. Woody Herman played tributes to Ellington and Basie from time to time. Even Lawrence Welk would play Ellington medleys occasionally.

Yet, music had its elitist faction that simply couldn't cross ethnic and taste barriers in the 1960s. A three-man music jury had recommended to the Pulitzer Prize advisory board that a special citation for four decades of musical accomplishments be awarded to Duke in the mid-1960s. The advisory board rejected the recommendation but made no mention of it until it was forced months later to admit it had turned down the application. Duke's reaction was typical. "Fate's being kind to me. Fate doesn't want me to be too famous too young," he said with his gracious smile. He was 66. That year, he was awarded a bronze medal by New York City for his contributions to New York life.

Swing as a music of the day was debated as much as rock and hip-hop in recent years. According to "The President and Fellows of Harvard College" in 1994, it was thought to be music for teenagers and adults but also perceived as a way to articulate thoughts and gestures which punctuated American culture. In the 1940s, it was dominant in literature, media and lifestyles. Hollywood gave it more of a voice too. Just a decade or so earlier, reviewers weren't tolerant of such music. Said a review of Paul Whiteman, one of the top bandleaders of the era in 1924: "There's no such thing as swing. Swing music doesn't exist, but swing musicians do. It is a verb, not a noun."

I loved fast dancing and the very vigorous and self-expressive dancing of the late 1940s and early '50s when the traditional box step was more a matter of tightly holding a partner and taking short steps together across whatever part of the floor wasn't crowded. Look at a number of photos of glamorous ballrooms of the era filled beyond capacity and you'll realize that dancing could be simply trying to navigate a space for yourself in a spot that could only take a lounge chair not a sofa.

Dance historians think the waltz and polka, which both allowed closer contact among partners, probably created the movement. But both allowed more freedom of than the foxtrot on a crowded dance floor.

Swing dancing had different styles. There was jive, jitterbugging, the Lindy, push, Whip, and east and west coast swing. It diversified easily over the years. Shag dancers, for example, could dance to beach music, bobby-soxers liked rhythm and blues, push dancers liked the blues too and lindy dancers actually liked big band music. And who from the '50s could forget the Bunny Hop?

And dance has simply exploded in recent years after its beginnings in clubs, cabarets and speakeasies. In the beginning, there was the Quickstep and the Charleston, which emanated from the Cape Verde Islands and showed up on the docks of the Port of Charleston when black workers performed the dance. It was first made public in 1922 in a black revue by George White. Black Bottom probably originated in Detroit but it was New York and New Orleans where it became popular with George White's "Scandals of 1926."

The Shimmy was another dance step that came to America from African slaves. It was a Nigerian dance called the "Shika" and it was Ziegfeld's Follies that gave it popularity in the states.

For most people in the early to mid 20th century, dance titles weren't that familiar but dancing was an individual thing that like-minded young men and women discovered from parents and Life Magazine. Try to recall the era; we celebrated Lincoln's Birthday on the REAL day, Feb. 12. George Washington's birth was honored on the day of his birth, Feb. 22. We were on War Time Daylight Savings from Feb. 8, 1942 until September 30, 1945. You called a New Yorker a "Gothamite" without knowing why really.

I remember dance classes while I was in grade school every Saturday evening which my parents insisted I take. It was needed socialization with the opposite sex, I was told. Actually, it was forced internment . . . males on one side of a large bare room . . . females congregated on the other. The gender segregation, I vividly recall, continued for a whole year although my first date came as a result of the class.

But the experience was valuable. We discovered the importance of the box step, for example, that made me a novice for the rest of my life. It also demonstrated clearly why the male led at a time when women had no problem with such initiative. That could be an issue today, I suppose. Said the US News & World Report in August, 2005, explaining the renewed interest in dancing in America: "Another ballroom dance myth is that it's a great way for couples to spend time together. Sixty-five percent of the students at Arthur Murray studios are couples but that doesn't mean they're all having fun . . . During group lessons, students change partners every few minutes, which inevitably leads to unflattering comparisons. The key is to find a class that teaches you solid basic skills. "

Talk to fourth, fifth and sixth graders in PS 115, Washington Heights, New York City. A few years ago, the school system mandated ballroom dancing and the success of the program continues, says the New York Times.

Most musicians from that era will tell you that watching dancers from the bandstand was more amusing than a matter of envy to be dancing although every band seemed to have lecherous guys who made comments that brought snickers.

One night playing a gig I remember the leader broke out in laughter just as he ended a solo that nearly brought dancers to a halt. Several members of the band joined in and the crowd, not knowing the source of the humor, also started laughing without realizing how or why. The leader became embarrassed at what he had done and nothing was said until we took a break and went outside. "Did you see that couple trying to dance?" he exclaimed starting to laugh again. Several had and didn't need to be prompted to become hysterical. Since I hadn't, I spent the rest of the evening searching the dance floor for this comical twosome. And I got my wish while we played that beautiful slow number, "Stardust," which ended the night. And I wish I hadn't. It was an older Ichabod looking man with a short, round, very overly endowed woman. I had a difficult time keeping the beat and controlling my laughter too. Fortunately, it was a slow number and I could keep my head down.

The difficulty for many touring musicians, a number told me, was staying focused playing the same music night after night and not making mistakes or becoming distracted. You simply didn't make mistakes on the stand with leaders like Isham Jones, Glenn Miller, Benny Goodman or Buddy Rich. If you took the view it was a job. . . it wasn't fun. On the other hand, if you got caught up in too much fun. . . your exuberance could take away from dancers' fun, too. Two leaders who usually looked taciturn on the bandstand probably struck the most appropriate presence for playing a dance date. Goodman and Count Basie said that balance was crucial every working night. Leaders not only set the tempo, they had to be the enforcers when playing a gig.

Benny's notorious "ray," a glare that came and stayed awhile when he suddenly went silent, told anyone in his band . . . he was in trouble. Other leaders, certainly

Woody Herman was one, wanted everyone to have a great time. Woody's band was usually enthusiastic . . . the crowd picked up on it and he always appeared to enjoy himself too. In a far less exuberant manner, Guy Lombardo and the Royal Canadians gave audiences the same feeling whether New Year's Eve or any night of the year.

I found it ironic that many people thought musicians must be good dancers because music was part of their lives. The best bandleader who danced with the moves of an Arthur Murray in my mind was Lawrence Welk. And he demonstrated that every TV show he did. To me, it appeared he loved dancing as much as he loved playing and leading. Stan Kenton, by contrast, didn't like to dance and rarely ventured from the bandstand. It was rare for Glenn Miller, who played lots of the sentimental music of the day, to get on the floor either. But Glenn was a businessman at work when he played dances. I remember Ray Anthony, Louis Prima, Dick Jurgens and a few other leaders who loved to dance while leading their bands . . . but I don't recall seeing Harry James, Glen Gray, Charlie Spivak, Ralph Flanagan or Vaughn Monroe among dancers on the floor when I saw them perform.

The Woody Herman band was a different story. Tommy Dorsey once told a music critic that of all the bands on the road, Woody's band was the most energetic. "I don't know how they play but they sure are good dancers," he laughed. He was more than likely talking about trumpeter Shorty Rogers, trombonist Bill Harris, tenor saxophonist Flip Phillips and one of the most gyrating bassmen in the business, Chubby Jackson, who also did scat singing and yelling during the band's up tempo numbers. Ralph Burns, the Herman Herd pianist and arranger probably said it best. "He (Woody) let us go and from time to time we could get out of control but when he had to crack down, he could do it, too." Woody once said that "Chubby once won the Downbeat poll for yelling."

Herman could swing with the best and, at the same time, he never bad mouthed his fellow bandleaders. He was a good friend of Glenn Miller and he listened to Glenn's advice as well as tried to help out when he could. "For instance, once in Boston Glenn had a lead trumpet player who was bothering him. Consequently, he called me and said he needed a new trumpet player immediately. So I wound up with this young man and when he arrived I saw that he had a slight. . . drinking problem. Glenn knew how to get rid of them gracefully," he laughed. Woody's attitude, said a number of his sidemen, was tolerance and patience as long as you could play the date and sound your best.

Yet, he could be exasperated by audiences when he got requests that other leaders made famous. Trombonist Jon Fedchock told Phil Holdman of the Browsers' that once a drunk continued to pester Woody to play other bandleaders' hits until finally the amiable Herman asked the man what he paid to get in the place. When the man responded, Woody handed him a twenty dollar bill and said "see you later, pal."

His sense of humor and wit was at its best when he played the Metropole Cafe in New York City, a place well known for its odd "bandstand." The Herman band, said Phil Holdman of the Browsers', had to play standing up in a straight line.

Woody stood between the saxophones and the trumpets and trombones. "It was something, " Herman smiled. "I used to see completely sober guys walk in, and during the course of one set – about 40 minutes – leave . . . in a bird cage. They would hustle you down along the bar and you'd go for doubles with a beer chaser and you'd walk out, out of your mind, saying 'That's the greatest band I ever heard!'"

While music and ambiance are vital to the mood, most club and ballroom owners know that if there is a return to the exciting swing era, dancing will be the key to success.

USA Today reported five years into the 21st Century that the 19th and 20th centuries pastime of dancing has returned and the indicators continue to build.

Arthur Murray Dance Studios, for example, reported its franchises are up reaching a pace of 20 percent, something unheard of a decade earlier.

Dance competitions jumped from a mere 25 a year to more than 90 with up to 13,000 entries, according to the president of the National Dance Council of America.

The popular television show, "Dancing With the Stars," on ABC primetime was a popular launch several years ago and continues.

Equally important is a documentary produced by Paramount Classics about a group of New York City fifth graders who competed in ballroom dancing in a program called Madhat Ballroom that expanded to 155 theaters and drew a cool $1.8 million. If you need further proof, talk to younger and mid-life folks you know and discover how many are taking classes at the local high school, community college, university, civic center or the YM or YWCA.

Arthur Murray's marketing director Thomas Murdock says media actually helped create the return of dancing. The October, 2004 film "Shall We Dance" with Richard Gere and Jennifer Lopez about how dance revitalized a marriage reverberated among couples and singles planning to be couples.

"Since the film there has been a big increase in men wanting lessons," Murdock told USA Today. "Our students used to be 55 and older, with the majority women. Now many men or couples are in their '20s and '30s. Lopez and Gere increased interest in a younger audience."

Bruce McDonald, president of the Dance Council, thinks many young people see it as artistic and, at the same time, a competitive activity too. That's supported by the venerable Village Voice in New York which published Terry Monoghan's article about swing shift, a growing generation of mostly white couples doing the Lindy Hop a black dance craze that came from World War II days.

"The best swing dance classes are as hard to get into as Studio 54 once was and Gap khakis are only the latest product sold via Lindy on TV. Swing nights at Lincoln

Center's 'Midsummer Night Swing,' were packed to capacity. . ., " she wrote.

The White House which had a distinctly jazz tone during saxophone playing Bill Clinton's presidency entertained Lindy dancers at one time. The east and west coasts still dominate and bring cutting edge to dance movements but the interest grows as dancers and dancing groups find public service and humanitarian causes to tempt those who once enjoyed it and entice those who have never experienced it.

At the Oceanside Municipal Pier, CA, couples gyrate to the sounds of good dance music at the annual big band concert, an event that is nearing a decade of fun. Patti Lovvorn and Chuck Potter told reporter Erika Ayn Finch of the North Country Times that "we love to dance." As members of a swing dance club, they were enjoying an afternoon that supported a resource center that provides scholarships for foster kids. In 2003, the group raised more than $7,000.

Some members of earlier generations have passed on their love of dancing to their sons and daughters. It demonstrates more about young people today than earlier generations that left dancing to spending weekends at their jobs, making money, TV, mall walking and treadmills. They never turned back. Some wished they had.

Dancing is certainly alive and well in the nation's heartland, too. Said the Daily Nebraskan in 2005, 380 dancers signed up to dance 14 hours non-stop for a University of Nebraska Dance Marathon that benefited Omaha's Children's Hospital. Farther north, Muncie, IN sponsors "America's Hometown Dance Band" and hosts the "USO Hanger Dance." The band plays music of the '30s, '40s and '50s and the dance benefits worthy causes and features dance instructors. Dancing will probably take on many different styles wherever you are even though one web site – www.swing.com – believes there's some rivalry across the country.

"East Coast Swing is more of a purer, faster, real Savoy Ballroom style of swing while the West Coast Swing is a subtler, slow variation of the Savoy Lindy Hop. The East Coast swingers find West Coast overly sexual, while West Coast aficionados find New York's traditional lindy as too wild. There is some bad blood flowing between the two styles because each fears losing dancers to the other side."

But dancing is dancing. Listen to Kevin Hoffberg of California describe his fascination in his letter to his daughter Emily when she chose swing dancing as an activity in high school. "Other parents haul their kids off to play team sports like soccer, swimming, basketball, and T-ball. For whatever reason we didn't. Instead you selected diving, fencing and swing dancing. This last was a mixed one for your parents. On the one hand, watching you turning and flying and tearing up the floor to the tunes of the great big band classics is nothing short of sublime. You were and are breathtaking on the dance floor, what with your dazzling smile, terrific performance presence and snappy moves." His son Kevin plays sax and has played in big bands since the 7th grade in a music program in Lafayette, CA public schools that nurtured the big band sound. His memory brought back my own memories too. My daughter Cindy loved to dance too. . . and still does.

In an earlier day, music, the urge to dance and being with people you like made it all worthwhile.

Woody and Anne Brindle of Pennsylvania love the big band music of a group called Sophisticated Swing who played at the George Mullen Activity Center, North Port, FL, the Sarasota Herald Tribune reported. Every Tuesday the 16 member band of volunteers entertain a crowd at the center for free and, of course, donations. It's the kind of performance that takes place in communities all over the country. The Sophisticated Swing group has been playing together for more than a decade and director Ted Buengen puts his 41 years teaching high school music to good use in his retirement years. He was a trumpeter at MacDill Air Force Base during the 1940s. The crowd never gets tired of Count Basie, Harry James music and pop hits from the '40s and '50s, he says. Barbara Choinere of Lake Suzy, FL is a regular and echoes the Brindles' feelings about the evening entertainment. "We love the big band sound," she adds.

If you want to be popular at a party...
learn to dance.

Most retirees and a growing number of young folks still find dancing the reason to get to the floor on any night of the week. Ask Luca and Gina Esposito who have been teaching ballroom dancing virtually ever since their first date. They didn't go to a movie. . . . they went dancing. The Espositos told reporter Linda Murphy of the Utica (NY) Observer-Dispatch that they believe dancing is as universal as the music. "If you want to be popular at a party. . . learn to dance. Whether you're a teen going to the prom or a long-married couple preparing to dance at your child's wedding, social graces increase as social dancing skills are gained. Now, keep in mind that women love dancing with a man who knows how to lead – it makes her feel effortlessly graceful. Dancing is romantic, " Gina told Linda.

Only an elite, usually country club members or those who were frequently pictured in New York, Washington, Atlanta and Miami newspaper society pages, took lessons in the days when big bands toured and holiday revelers danced to one of Lester Lanin's society bands at plush hotels. Everyone else picked it up from a dance partner or others on the dance floor.

Today, the Carleton Rugcutters of Minnesota offer the information and accoutrements you need to get on the dance floor in a web site http://orgs.carleton.edu/rugcutters. What kind of shoes and clothes should you wear? Leather was an easy way to be flat on the floor most of the night in my day. Crepe soles, tennis shoes were comfortable but never, never heels with metal pieces that could damage the floor. If management didn't escort you out. . . your partner might have left you. It also would be wise to know the variations before you trip over yourself doing the wrong dance to the wrong music. There are Blues Dancing, Texas Tommy, the Big Apple . . . even Balboa dancing which was created on the California island of the same name and the former ballroom that hosted the big bands.

Yes, it takes practice unlike the days when many of these steps got their start.

An organization called Flying Feet (www.flyingfeet.org) says you need to spend time with a partner practicing before you do air steps, slides, dips and drops. "Emphasis is on technique and safety, as well as musicality and dancing into/out of any of these moves so that they seamlessly integrate into your dancing. Partners are required and participants should be at an intermediate level or higher to enroll."

Practice time in my day came at the ballroom or the dance spot and we usually didn't think safety although I still have a chilling recall of a woman who put her foot through a wall and was badly bruised doing some high steps at a home party I played.

The 1950s featured dances like the jitterbug and variations of so-called jive dancing which are still very popular today because you can work the steps into the music of popular big bands, rock'n'roll groups or music played by bands like Big Bad Voodoo Daddy, Royal Crown Revue, Brian Setzer and Bill Elliott's Big Band.

In the Midwest, meanwhile, dancing and big bands broke down racial and social barriers and traditions . . .if only for an evening. Central Ohioans told me how in still racially divided communities close to the state capital, Duke Ellington and his band played the Memorial Day opening at the Pier Ballroom, Buckeye Lake, 1940, and swing music was what excited a large crowd.

Fans, it seems, remembered every second of a big band performance in every section of the country. Here's how Bruce Park, a Bates College graduate of the '40s, remembers his night watching and listening to the Ellington band at Kimball's Ballroom in Lynnfield, MA. "Sonny Greer (the drummer) so thin he could have disappeared behind (Frank) Sinatra, came on first, tuned his snare, hit a few muted rim shots. The rest drifted in a few at a time, noodled on their instruments and The Man himself was at the piano."

Certainly musicians and singers are equally as vivid in their reminisces. Kay Weber, who sang with the first Dorsey band and recorded for the first time in March, 1934 with two novelty numbers "Nasty Man" and "My Dog Loves Your Dog" recalls the Dorseys issued the recording as performed by Bob Snyder and his orchestra. She also remembers being on the bandstand when Tommy walked off at a rehearsal, too.

It was Glenn Miller who she remembers most fondly. Miller heard her when he was a trombonist/arranger with the Smith-Ballew band and when he formed his band she was among the first hired along with people like trombonist Don Mattison and saxophone player "Skeets" Herfurt. Kay said she traveled to New York City with Glenn and his wife, Helen, in that famous blinding snowstorm to find a club that had closed down. Glenn looked out for her like a brother, she continued. So when he ended his band after a new year's eve, he contacted Tommy Dorsey and took her to Tommy's home on Long Island.

A Tennessee big band fan vividly recalls the night he and his wife loaded up his 1958 Volvo with no muffler and started out for Cape Girardeau, MO, in the cold, freezing rain for a trip across two states to hear Duke. On a web site, he described it this way: "We got there early and sat at a front table next to the dance floor. It was an hour before the band was to play and Duke Ellington came out and played solo piano for an hour. It was wonderful. Then, Paul Gonsolves, Johnny Hodges, Cat Anderson, Harry Carney and Russell Procope and the rest of the band came out. Duke asked everyone to dance as much as possible. . . it wasn't a concert, he said. At intermission, Duke came over to our table and sat down and asked us who we were, where we were from and what we wanted to hear. He stayed most of the intermission. When they returned he dedicated two Hodges' numbers to us. Ray Nance soloed the second half on trumpet and violin and came on the floor and tap-danced while playing violin. . . It was a remarkable evening some years ago."

For others – especially women – the memories are more about dancing and special feelings. Barbara Rhodes of Rome, NY recalls one such evening in a suburb of Tokyo while she was located there. "I have fond memories of dancing. I wish dancing was in my life again. . . I have an indelible imprint of a special evening in August in Japan after the war.

"It was a pleasant, warm evening with blue skies and the sun just about to set. . . as I remember the two of us, I am sure we thought we were the only two people in the world, and we looked and acted like we were indeed. The big band sound of the music just melted our hearts. After a few drinks and toasting the evening and us, he asked me to dance. Shyly, I told him 'I'll try.' You see we had talked about this day earlier. I confessed at that time I had never danced in my life!

He found that to be the most incredible thing he had ever heard. How could it be possible that we lived through our teens and the 20s and into our 30s without ever dancing? To him, dancing was like breathing; a second nature. I was raised by parents who did not believe in dancing so I was taught not to ever trust anyone who danced. Music was okay but dancing was not."

When they got on the dance floor the first number was a slow fox trot, she continued. "He was good; I looked like a pro because he knew what he was doing.

My high heeled feet were twirling around like the best of them. But the crowning joy of that moment was not that I found out I could learn to dance while dancing. . . but that dancing was the most fun I had ever had! What made it fun was watching the look on his face," she says today savoring the details of that night. "I can never forget it. He looked like he was in heaven . . . He looked proud that he had found this unearthed gem and we both knew that very night that we would have an adventurous and wonderful life together. But I still cherish that first dance, that moment of pure ecstasy even after all these years."

In the Midwest, dancing was also the popular activity of choice. Mildred Opitz said she would rather dance than eat and she remembered traveling throughout the countryside to dance to Woody Herman who played in Grand Island, NE. Big Bands, she recalled, performed at the huge airplane hangers at a local Air Force Base and " we'd get to hear and dance to Sammy Kaye, Guy Lombardo and all those other big bands."

Meanwhile in Muncie, IN, things haven't changed five to six decades later. Students at Ball State University spend time weekly polishing swing dance movements and find it takes concentration. But they enjoy the exercise and how they can bring non-western student friends to see and participate in the "American culture."

Togetherness on the dance floor was being reinforced during the 1940s by the movie industry which capitalized on the public's demand for light and dreamy musicals that featured dance bands and were certainly low budget. Glenn Miller trombonist Paul Tanner said that the Miller band made its first movie "Sun Valley Serenade" in 1941 on a Hollywood lot. "The band never got to Sun Valley," he laughed. "I heard it was a beautiful place. You should go there some time."

Approximately 50 major films were made between 1940 and 1945 featuring big bands that included Artie Shaw, Miller, Gene Krupa, Jack Teagarden, Benny Goodman, Jimmy Lunceford, the Dorsey Brothers (Tommy and Jimmy), Woody Herman, Ellington, Les Brown, Charley Barnet, Joe Venuti, Harry James, Sammy Kaye, Count Basie, Xavier Cugat, Kay Kyser, Guy Lombardo, Freddie Martin, Cab Calloway, Ted Lewis, Charley Spivak, Johnny Long, Paul Whiteman, Carmen Cavallaro and Stan Kenton. The movies, of course, influenced decisions to see the bands when the major touring groups like Miller, Herman, Ellington, James, Kaye and Long went on one-nighters within weeks of the release of the films. Good managers and leaders who could keep the nucleus of talent together for months could profit from popular hits seen and heard in the movies and available on 78, 45 and later 33 rpm vinyls at record stores. What better than seeing the same band in person playing your favorite hits on the record you had at home or the current movie at the Rialto Theater?

Leaders and musicians of the era that I spoke to said Hollywood kept bands working and payrolls steady at a time when selective service was taking whole sections from some major bands. Some leaders had to disband because of lack of experienced sidemen.

Some studio decisions in selecting bands for movies were curious in light of the band's later image and distinctive sound. For example, the progressive sound of Stan Kenton was adapted for the movie "Wilson," the story of the 28th President, Woodrow Wilson. But both the movie and music were applauded by the critics. The film featured a powerful cast that included Dana Andrews, Jeannie Crain, Thomas Mitchell, Red Buttons and Eddie Foy Jr. 20th Century Fox gave the picture strong support . . . even during wartime. It was nominated later for best film of 1944 but it was the year Bing Crosby was named best actor for his role in the academy's top movie "Going My Way." The music of the day came from song writers Jimmy McHugh, Sammy Cahn, Mack Gordon and Jimmy Van Heusen and Johnny Burke who wrote the "Going My Way" winner, "Swinging On A Star."

However, 20th Century sound department received first place for its recording of "Wilson." The cast later accompanied the band on a special tour of Ohio where they were driven to the premiere in limos with police escorts.

In his fascinating account of his years with Kenton entitled "Stan Kenton: The Early Years, 1941-1947," Ed Gabel remembers how 20th Century provided brand new uniforms – red jackets, dark blue slacks, white shirts and red and blue neckties – for the musicians including a white gown for singer June Christie. Ed said the band played the closing portion of the stage show behind a scrim (a semi-transparent curtain used for dramatic effect). The last number of each show was "Shenandoah" with its haunting melody, and as the movie opened, "The Battle Hymn of the Republic."

But bandleaders, promoters, booking agencies and ballroom owners didn't like the dwindling numbers they saw out front. Critics pounced on announcements in Downbeat, which said that eight major bandleaders – Herman, Goodman, James, Brown, Teagarden, Benny Carter, Ina Ray Hutton and Tommy Dorsey – were disbanding in 1947. The big band era was over, many said. Media, of course, didn't report later that all of the leaders returned to the bandstand and some formed new bands and resumed touring as wartime gas restrictions eased.

Ironically, just months earlier North Texas State University began the first jazz studies program to provide more skilled talent for the big bands.

There was no question that ballrooms and clubs reacted to the revenue shortfall as defense plants shutdown and America tried to absorb millions of returning service personnel. The shift to normalcy meant a shift away from frantic production demands and the stresses that caused both men and women to look for clubs and ballrooms to relax with more money than they ever made in the pre-World War II years.

Touring big bands, however, faced the reality of rising costs and musicians weary of touring. The public, meanwhile, was spending more time at home watching that new box in the corner of the living room. Hollywood also felt the pinch and the change. Between 1946 and 1950, for example, only 11 films featured celebrity dance bands as compared to the first five years of the decade.

Yet, one bandleader was basking in a social scene most Americans don't get invited to and his music, strictly medleys of old favorites and some contemporary special arrangements added for an evening, created his success and generated a number of dance bands playing under his name. Lester Lanin got his major gig playing for President Dwight Eisenhower's inaugural ball and he continued performing at such galas for more than 50 years. His music, as old and foxtrot as Lawrence Welk's, was very popular in Washington, DC and on the eastern seaboard especially at lavish debutante balls, weddings and fund-raising affairs.

According to Lanin historians, his bands played for 20,000 wedding receptions, 7,500 parties and 4,500 proms!

Bandleaders of the day didn't talk much about it and dancers took it for granted but Lester also knew the importance of setting the right beat when playing. He told the Christian Science Monitor in a story I clipped in 1980 that he studied dancers by watching their feet. If they were out of "meter I knew something was wrong," he said. It was one of the major reasons Lester and his band were in demand over the years.

Like Lawrence Welk's rules on the bandstand, Lester was an enforcer of a strict code of conduct because of the culture of the crowds he played. For example, Lanin would not tolerate drinking or drug use on the bandstand. He also banned smoking while on the stand, too. Some leaders ignored it if the music was good. Not Lester. And he had rules for himself, too. He would never leave the bandstand during a performance and he never became over friendly with clients. He always referred to them as Mr., Mrs. or Mr. President.

Lester, however, could be confused by music tastes at times. One party goer remembers when Lester was asked by a groom to play Dave Brubeck's complicated rhythm number "Take Five." Without hesitation (perhaps thinking he had it in his book) Lester called it out and courageously tried to conduct it in 5/4 time continuing to motion to his drummer to find the beat. After a few choruses, he realized neither he nor the drummer could make it work and he yelled over his disorganized band to play the number "Five Foot Two" and turned to audience and smiled as if nothing had happened.

Ballrooms, which had become a social center in thousands of American communities for millions from the 1920s on had to find a new mixture of entertainment to entice people and remain solvent.

The answer was a guy who was as comfortable playing country western as he was playing anything. He started in 1949-50 with a group called the Saddlemen.

It was Bill Haley and the Saddlemen. A name change came after several numbers didn't make it and a friend who noted the significance with Haley's Comet suggested the new title; Bill Haley and the Comets. The band scored with a number called "Crazy Man, Crazy" which was the first rock and roll number to be televised nationally when it was included on a soundtrack for a 1953 play that starred James Dean.

By 1954, Haley and the Comets recorded "Rock Around the Clock," which started slow but picked up momentum. It sold more than 25 million copies thanks probably to the film "Blackboard Jungle" which was released a year later. The Haley number was re-released with the film and it climbed the hit parade and stayed for eight weeks. It was the first rock and roll record to become popular and it gave ballrooms new activity with a different kind of music.

Although Haley's impact declined by 1957, rock and roll garage bands were flourishing and they continued through the 1960s and '70s.

Big bands became a distant past in a hurry.

Ballrooms Then. . . And Now Bibliography

Barbara Rhodes, Rome, NY
emails April, 13, 2005; April 18,/2005

Bob A. Montesano, New Hartford, NY
email Jan. 29, 2006, Feb. 1, 2006

The Spin On Ballroom
US News & World Report, Aug. 1, 2005

Swing Dancing Hits Campus
Ball State Daily News, undated

www.swing.com

www.northbysouth.org/1998/music/bigbands/bigbandpage.htm

www.swingmusic.net/getset.html

Craig's Big Bands & Big Names
www.bigbandsandbignames.com

Leo Walker
The Wonderful Era of the Great Big Bands (DaCapo 1990)

www.localcolorart.com/search/encyclopedia/jazz

Peter J. Levinson
Trumpet Blues: The Life of Harry James (Oxford/1999)

Gene Lees
Leader of the Band:The Life of Woody Herman (Replica/1995)

Don Berbison-Evans, History of Modern Ballroom Dancing

www.livinghistoryfarm.org/farminginthe40s/life-23.html

What Is Swing?
Randy Atlas Dancing USA Magazine, November, 1994, page 3

The President and Fellows of Harvard College, 1994

Big Band Sounds Big Line
Ken Hackett, Herald Tribune, Sarasota, FL

Ballroom Dancing is Back
Linda Murphy, Utica Observer-Dispatch, March 27, 2005

Linda Murphy
email, March 28, 2005

Celebrating Tommy Dorsey
at the Hollywood Palladium, PBS 1980s with Mel Torme

www.Kplu.org/newsinfo/ubb/Form3/HTML/000038.html
June 8, 2005

The Chesterfield Broadcasts of Glenn Miller
Vols 1 and 2 liner notes by George T. Simon, 1968

http://Library.thingquest.org/18602/history/swing/swing.html

http://discuss.washingtonpost.com/zforum/99/http://music990126.htm

1greatdancesite.com/partners2.htm
George F. Johnson Pavilion, Johnson City, NY, Oneonta Daily Star, Aug. 19, 2004

www.thehistoryNet.com/ahil/biglennmiller

David Dodrill
email 2005.

UC Roundtable, WIBX
Utica, NY Don Cantwell, Dick Robinson, March 24, 2002

Kay Weber, Browsers'
February, 2005

Utica, NY Dance Spots, Utica (NY)
Observer Dispatch, Audrey Lewis, Jan. 1, 1990.

Steve Early
email messages, 2003 undated

Popular Bands and Ballrooms
Billboard, 1940, Leo Walker's The

Wonderful Era of Great Dance Bands (DaCapo 1990)

James Ronan of Iowa
personal correspondence, Jan. 19, 2006

New York Times
Aug. 14, 1938

Battle of the Bands
www.swingmusic.net

Kevin Hoffberg
web site: www.kevinhoffberg.com/Archive/Emily1.htm
email Feb. 14, 2006

www.wikipedia.org/wiki/Bill_Haley_&_The_Comets

The Browsers', Phil Holdman, No. 92, August, 2005

Partner Waited Lifetime For Last Dance, Honolulu Advertiser, Dec. 2001

World War II Remembrances: Remembered By Walter Clarence Danison, Jeanne Worachek, 2003

Lester Lanin, Bandleader of High Society, Dies at 97, New York Times, Oct. 29, 2004.

Lester Lanin, www.spaceagepop.com/lanin.html June 4, 2006

This Week in History, Utica Observer-Dispatch, Aug. 31, 2003

Man Hopes Big Band Comes Back Swinging, Utica Observer-Dispatch, undated

Music, Popular, Folk and Jazz
Collier's Yearbook, 1965

Learning to Count, to Two
New York Times, April 21, 2005

Ella Fitzgerald, http://en.wikipedia.org/wiki/Ella_Fitgerald

"Chick Webb, "Dr. William F. Lee, "American Big Bands,"
Hal Leonard Publishing, 2005

Yahnundasis Golf Club: A Century of Tradition
1897-1997

DANCERS, BANDS FLOCKED TO EAST COAST

No one in the Midwest and South who grew up in the '30s. '40s and '50s could forget what it was like to hear the famous bands on the radio from exotic eastern places like the Glen Island Casino or Frank Dailey's Meadowbrook. The bands were legendary and the ballrooms, for a great majority of the people listening, were places to dream about if you loved dancing or socializing. . . or playing.

Some realized the dream occasionally on trips to Gotham City (before the Big Apple) . . . others who lived in the east could sample a vast range of ballrooms, hotels, roadhouses and lounges that would be packed with young, middle aged and old on any weekend. The city featured places like The Savoy, the Cotton Club, Roseland, Hotel Taft, the Roosevelt Grill, the Waldorf, The Village Vanguard, the Blue Note and dozens upon dozens of places that gained a piece of the limelight if a name band was playing and a telephone line could create a remote.

The east was not only the place where everything seemed to start (thanks to the broadcasting networks that were founded in New York City) but it was the birthing center for a great number of musicians who scattered about the country – primarily to the west coast – playing in the big bands of the day.

It's where Glenn Miller and his Orchestra took advantage of an NBC radio feed from the very popular Glen Island Casino in New Rochelle, NY to make their debut. In a year and a month before the start of his second band, Miller had created a band that could cause kids to roll up the carpets at home to fast and slow dance. He knew he couldn't "outswing" Goodman, Shaw and Dorsey but he knew kids jitterbugged to his music and his beat was right down the middle. Glen Island management took advantage of Glenn's popularity to fit its advertised slogan "Mecca for Music for Moderns."

Thanks to a friend who obtained a copy of the script for the program, here's what announcer Hugh James said as he introduced the show between 11 p.m. and midnight on the night of May 17th. In your mind, listen to the sound of "Moonlight Serenade," that melancholy Miller signature number that first night, and envision looking out over the water of Long Island sound. Then enjoy Glenn's theme as you hear Hugh take us inside the ballroom.

"Good evening ladies and gentlemen, the spotlight is on celebrities and music at the Glen Island Casino as it opens its 1939 season. . . Let's listen to the music of Glenn Miller and his Orchestra. . ."

There were slightly more than 1,800 jubilant fans at the ballroom and they continued the musical excitement shown at the band's record breaking performances in Washington, DC, the Syracuse State Fair in New York, Hershey, PA and Salem, MA.

The announcer continued. . . "Tonight, here comes the music beside the waters of Long Island sound as NBC presents Glenn Miller and his Orchestra opening for the first time at the Glen Island Casino . . . first up is 'At Sundown.'" Glenn was still fine tuning the band which featured peppy girl vocalist Marion Hutton and her male counterpart, Ray Eberle and saxophonist Hal McIntyre among others. Within weeks he added a fourth trumpet and another trombone. By Oct. 6, five months later, Glenn and the band were on the prestigious stage of Carnegie Hall and announcer Gene Buck said "They were the most popular band in the United States at the moment. . ."

Days later, Glenn and Chesterfield Cigarettes signed to broadcast weekly 15 minute shows from throughout the country which would terminate in September, 1942, when he ended his civilian band to enter the army air force.

Said archivist Ed Burke, "Many critics of the day said that the band could not play jazz. Well, all I can say is, they must not have heard the 1939 band." To me, Glenn didn't have the strongest swing band and, given his critical self-analysis of his band and his own horn playing, he'd probably agree. He was, however, a likeable crowd-pleaser without much of a personality which was uncommon in a day when bandleaders were attempting to emulate gregarious masters of ceremonies like Sammy Kaye, Ben Bernie, Rudy Vallee, Ted Lewis and Ozzie Nelson. His hits – novelty tunes like Pennsylvania 65000, Chattanooga Choo Choo, Little Brown Jug and others – were up tempo and danceable. Yet, he stayed clear of the microphone and acted like a CEO handling employees. Said his Steel Pier announcer, Lou DiSario, he was different than most leaders. "Glenn was quite shy, didn't like to talk like Guy Lombardo or Ozzie Nelson. He'd give me a quick list of the numbers for each set but didn't tell me any soloists although he'd mention a singer thank goodness. That was it. No conversation, no banter between numbers or sets. He wasn't the likeable guy some thought he was I found."

But Miller's ballroom magnetism was already golden. In 1940, Billboard produced its annual top 78 record choices by disk jockeys and while Tommy and Jimmy Dorsey were one and two, Glen Miller was third with "Imagination," fifth with "Fools Rush In" and seventh with "Pennsylvania 6-5000. "

Fifteen years later and more than a decade after Glenn's death, Billboard showed Miller's post-war band renditions of "Moonlight Serenade," "Stardust," "In The Mood," and "String of Pearls" continued in the top ten. National Public Radio named "In the Mood" by Miller's '39 band as one of America's 100 Most Important American Musical Works of the 20th Century.

Like Chicago, the number of black Americans in New York City grew by the 1930s and a good half of them lived in Harlem. There were a number of "leisure houses" to find all kinds of entertainment like the Apollo Burlesque, Brecher's Harlem Opera House and others but emcee Ralph Cooper's" Harlem's Amateur Night" at the Apollo in 1934 ignited swing bands in the city and elsewhere. Ralph's show acquired a live national radio broadcast on WMCA and it became well known wherever there was a radio set. White entertainers, especially bandleaders like Charley Barnet, Woody Herman and Harry James, took the trip uptown because of Ralph's popularity.

Meanwhile, at the Cotton Club you could hear variations of sounds and rhythms; the sophisticated and raw swing of Duke Ellington, Count Basie, Fletcher Henderson, Lionel Hampton and Chick Webb. It was the Depression, times were tough . . . but night spots were swinging and black and white dancers were letting their feet speak for them on the dance floors.

A book called "Showtime at the Apollo" (Mill Road Enterprises/2004) gave a solid account of the theater's 70 years. Said Quincy Jones: "The influence of the Apollo reaches beyond the shores of the country – it is truly the premier platform for world music. When the Beatles first came to America, they told me that the first place they wanted to go was to the world famous Apollo."

West 125th Street, Harlem. . . is where the Apollo still stands although most believe it doesn't have the reputation it had in the early days when it was considered the "world's toughest audience." It would only take minutes to boo a performer off stage. But it didn't stop top music stars from appearing. The list was the best and greatest at the time; Aretha Franklin, Nat "King" Cole, Ray Charles, Count

Basie, Dizzy Gillespie, Louis Armstrong, Duke Ellington, Chick Webb, Billy Eckstine, Moms Mabley, Sammy Davis Jr, Nancy Wilson, Redd Foxx, Flip Wilson, James Brown, Michael Jackson, Leslie Eggams and Sarah Vaughan all launched or continued careers there to name a few. And don't forget the legendary Ella Fitzgerald first sang on an Apollo amateur night. Apollo performers certainly knew what a day's work meant. You did three to five shows daily depending upon the time of year. It was the place to go. . . the place to be. It opened as a burlesque house where girls and comedians played to all-white audiences.

Aretha Franklin remembered what it was like between shows with fellow entertainers. She told the crowd that she was in a downstairs phone booth once and Count Basie came over and nearly beat the door down to get her out. "I was talking to my boyfriend and I wouldn't be rushed," she laughed. "He (Count) was in a panic on the other side of the door and I did not have any idea what was wrong with this man. I could not figure out why he was panicking the way he was until I heard later it was the time of day he played his horses . . . and numbers."

I can't think of anyone who deserved a title of "Mr. Music" more than American jazz promoter and producer George Wein.

Most aficionados have known him best as the founder of America's well known jazz festival, the Newport Jazz Festival. In the 1950s he launched a storied jazz club in Boston called Storyville and later started a record label of the same name. But he was a player first . . . and one who caught the fever as a very young unschooled teen. Here's his account of growing up playing in places that popularized the title "joint."

"I was a kid playing the piano. I mean my folks would pick me up at 1 a.m. when I was playing. . . they would be out in the car waiting for me. I was maybe 15, 16 or 17 I don't know. But there were a couple of years. . . you can't believe some of those joints in Boston. . . they were sailor joints, fights, and everything. . . and we were non-union musicians. I mean I knew about 12 songs and I was trying to play by ear. . . and I didn't really have a good ear. I did all the wrong changes. But still learning. It was a great, great period of learning."

The war and military service interrupted his life like so many of his generation. "The next thing you know I was in the army. All during the army days, I was never in a musical group. But we always played music. Whatever group became a band we really had fun playing and there were some good musicians, too. I was a combat engineer so I wasn't in an easy group. We were lucky we didn't see combat. Playing the piano saved a lot of problems for me in the army because we'd play for the officers' dances. If we'd get into trouble we'd just say to the sergeant or officer or whoever was in charge that we were to play the officers' dance on the weekend and the problem would go away. So playing the piano had its pluses," he said in the recorded oral history at the Hamilton College Jazz Archive. George offered his recollections of growing up in his book, "Myself Among Others (DaCapo Press, 2003).

Another eastern player who recalls his days getting a start in the big band business is trumpeter Joe Wilder. His father, a bandleader and bassist in Philadelphia, started him on the cornet and he got the invaluable training of studying with commercial players and Frederick Griffin who was a powerful mentor to the young cornet player. Like so many young black musicians in the 1930s, Joe realized that a career playing classical music wasn't possible regardless of talent, Ed Berger of Jazztimes said in a piece about Wilder in 2001.

He was a class guy from a young age. A longtime observer said that when Joe was with the Hampton band in the '40s, band members used to try to bribe him to say four letter words. They'd offer him $10. He never wavered and he never collected his $10 either.

Joe has fond memories of the ballroom days in New York City; "The Savoy Ballroom . . . I played the Savoy with Lucky Millender. . . and Jimmy Lunceford's band. I subbed a few times with Erskine Hawkins. . . Jimmy Rushing's band. . . I played with them a few times. The Savoy. . . quite a place. There were certain tempos that would get people going. They wanted to dance to certain tempos. Lucky was one of the guys that knew exactly what tempos and certain pieces that people would like to dance to. And he'd get people going with the 'Huckle Buck.' And you'd look out and people would be getting up out of their seats and going out on the dance floor. And the floor had a certain spring to it and when it would be full you could just see the floor floating up just a little bit. I don't know if they had some coasters or something under it but. . . to carry the vibrations of this continual dancing and everything it was something to see. . . I mean just a sea of people all up. Funny scenes out there. Oh I remember Hamp's was some kind of band, too. It was an exciting band to play in. It was an innovative band and it was a new style. . . I went overseas with Count Basie in 1954. My first time overseas. I knew a lot of people in that band. But Joe Newman was the featured trumpet soloist. He played most of the solos, not all of them, but he was working so much and he said they needed someone to take the load off . . . that's how I came to join the band. It was interesting you know . . . I was there a couple of weeks and I hadn't played any solos. And I was a little frustrated. So I wrote a little note to Count and I said 'Bas, could I play a couple of choruses of just about anything?' I signed it, ' the trumpet player second from the drums.' Basie took the note while he was playing and he stopped . . . looked up at me and said 'you want to play, go ahead. . . play.' You know he was very nice, you know." Monk Rowe, curator of the Hamilton College Jazz Archive, shared Wilder's words with a central New York radio audience in 2002. While he played in big bands all over New York City, he also spent 17 years as a staff musician at ABC.

Ralph Marterie alto saxophonist Chuz Alfred has his own memories of the east coast. He had just earned his degree at Ohio State in June 1961, begun dating the young lady who would later become his wife and gone to Buckeye Lake's (OH) Crystal Ballroom to "catch Ralph's big band. Before the night ended, Ralph had talked me into coming back on the band just until Labor Day. So I figured it would be worth delaying my first 'day job' search. We wound up at Freedomland in New York backing Paul Anka. After one week of that, I was more convinced than ever that I wanted off the road and a day gig. There were probably five thousand kids at the show, all trying to get onto the bandstand and grab Paul. Cops had a rope line in front of the bandstand (a couple feet high) and they were standing there to keep order. When we started the intro for his big hit at the time "Put Your Head On My Shoulder," Anka's manager would survey the screaming young urchins clutching for Paul, pick out the most delirious, lift her on the bandstand and bend her head onto Anka's shoulder co-incidentally as Paul sung those words whereupon she immediately collapsed and was hauled off stage on a stretcher by a couple of paramedics who just happened to be standing in the wings. . . just in case. . . and all this while Paul's still singing, the band's still playing and 4,999 other kids are still screaming and yelling that they should be so lucky. Whew! Twice a night for seven nights was more than I could handle."

*The next thing you know I was in the army.
All during the army days,
I was never in a musical group.
But we always played music.*

The Marterie band went to the Steel Pier playing for evening dances and backing the Dick Clark Show, three matinees Friday, Saturday and Sunday and Chuz saw similar crowds. "Clark had Chubby Checker on and once again, when he yelled 'Let's do the twist!' there musta been 5,000 kids twisting and shouting with Chubby! After a whole lota' shakin' and twistin' and working' his way into a gigantic sweat, Chubby would pull out a handkerchief, wipe his brow and fling the dripping sop into the frenzied throng while I sat there blowing . . . with eyes aglaze in disbelief," he recalls as he watched the arrival of the rock'n'roll age.

Yet, while players came and went, special nights attracted huge crowds to every place that had a license. Some locations became landmarks in the big band business.

New York's grand Hotel Pennsylvania was such a place. Designed by celebrated architect Sanford White, it began as the largest and most elegant hotel in the world.

For example, it introduced high-rise elevators. But, while it housed about everyone who ever took the railroad to New York City in its 2,200 rooms (it was built by the Pennsylvania Railroad in 1919 across the street from the train station), its real fame came from the big band era and one particular song; Pennsylvania 6-5-0h-0h-0h recorded by Glenn Miller in 1940. Like most of Miller's recordings, it sold quickly; over 40,000 in the first month.

The telephone number was actually established when the building was opened. According to historians, it is the oldest number in the country . . but today you better dial 1-212-73(6) to activate your call. While the "6-5000" band shout number became the song heard 'round the world,' Miller's "Tuxedo Junction" during a live remote in the summer from the hotel's famous Café Rouge gave him another hit and, according to Mike Santangelo in the New York Daily News "made the hotel a New York landmark and established its 3-year-old, 600-seat cabaret as one of the ultimate Swing Era symbols for the folks out there in the heartland."

Probably hundreds of other touring bands played there but the telephone number and the Miller pre-war band are best remembered by so many from the era who saw them or read about them. "Who could forget it? I know people who would call the number and ask for Glenn Miller," Steel Pier emcee Lou "King" DiSario laughed. "It generated plenty of demand for Miller. He and Harry James got $4 to $5 per person when they played the Steel Pier while I was there and they got a half hour intermission besides."

It was a Brooklyn born song writer named Carl Sigman who collaborated with Glenn to produce the breezy hotel tune. The Miller band was in the studio to record it April 28, 1940, less than a month after Artie Shaw had recorded his famous hit "Frenesi" and within the same period that Carl had written his first major composition for Tommy Dorsey called "Love Lies." Glenn had already vaulted beyond Artie in January, 1940, when his hit "In The Mood" took the top spot on the charts for more than 15 weeks. Downbeat Magazine, meanwhile, reported that the Miller band was the top Sweet Band in the country and Dave Garroway, then hosting an all-night radio show on Chicago's WMAQ, told his audience that Glenn Miller's theme "Moonlight Serenade" was the country's "second" national anthem.

Twenty-four months later, Glenn had voluntarily reported to military duty with the Army Air Force and Carl was drafted and served with a glider division assigned to the 82nd Airborne. Glenn's patriotism and dedication to his occupation are certainly admirable traits in a day when both are frequently ignored by young people. He understood the value of his music to his generation and recognized that, while he was over the military recruitment and draft age, he didn't have to get involved. He could, in fact, have stayed home and made money and records. Imagine a man with a wife and family today contacting the military and asking to join. He tried the

Navy Reserve but was turned down. He then wrote Brig. General Charles Young, US Army, and a month later he accepted Young's offer of the position of director of band training at the Army Air Forces Technical Training Command at the rank of captain. While Glenn didn't survive the war, Carl did and wrote the 82nd Airborne's official song "The All American Soldier." He received a Bronze Star and returned a true World War II hero in 1945.

The late trumpet player, band leader Billy May had fond memories of the Hotel Pennsylvania. A prolific arranger for Charley Barnet, Miller, Les Brown, Frank Sinatra and Capitol Records, Billy was in the trumpet section of Glenn's band for about two years and he especially remembers "taking five" between shows. "When we played the Pennsylvania Hotel—I was on the band 1940-41 and then in '42 – the bandstand was up against the wall in Café Rouge Room in the Hotel on 32nd Street and opposite that was a long hallway which exited on 33rd Street I think. It was actually a block away and you could see down that hall. So when the band would take a break we'd go to a place called Kelly's Bar. . . and when we 'd be gone 20 minutes or so Frankie D'Annolfo – he was our timekeeper – would get back on the stand and the bartender at Kelly's would look out along the bar and see him and he'd yell out 'Quick fellas . . . time for one more . . . Frankie's on the bandstand."

The Miller band's stay at the Hotel Pennsylvania was an inexpensive evening's entertainment compared with the dollars you might spend today to see nearly anybody at a hotel. Weekday cover charge to see Miller, for example, at the Café Rouge was 75 cents. And when bands played theaters in the city it was a package price (band and movie(s) at one price). The purpose, of course, was to increase crowds.

It was frenzied period for musicians, bandleaders, booking managers and ballroom owners. Monk Rowe, curator of the Hamilton College (NY) Jazz Archive, summed it years later. "Luckily for musicians, it was an era when the problem of creating more sound for larger venues was solved by adding people not amplifiers. Bands numbering up to eighteen players were everywhere. A young musician might find work with a territory band, playing dance halls and gin mills in a specific area of the country. After the on the job training, he might catch a break and land in one of the BIG big bands, crisscrossing the country in a bus or a Pullman railroad car. While singers were an important element, we had yet to arrive at a time when vocalists were backed by nameless orchestras. Each band had its fans and they knew who sat in the drum chair, who blew hot trumpet, lead alto and jazz tenor. Downbeat kept track of personnel in the top bands and broke the news if one band raided another."

Hollywood picked up on the popularity of the bands and movie directors created simple theme scripts written to include the bands, leaders and other entertainers. "Movie studios rushed to sign up the hot ensembles of the day, as directors churned out a succession of mediocre motion pictures, in which the image of the musicians, characterized in films by phony jive talk, bore little resemblance to true life. Despite their generally poor quality, however, these movies offered viewers, the performances of such bands as those of Goodman, the Dorsey Brothers, Artie Shaw, Harry James, Sammy Kaye, Woody Herman and, of course, Glenn Miller," said The History Net online.

When he looks back, Joe Wilder told Hamilton College's Rowe, he has his own wartime reminisces. He joined the Marines and served as assistant bandmaster at the Monteford Point Marine Base. "This was one of the first times they had Black Marines. And my platoon brought the number . . . to ten hundred . . .the first ten hundred Black Marines. Most of the musicians we've talked to who were in the service were able to play music."

New York was a hot town, Wilder believed "but oddly enough, and I almost hate to admit it, I never went there. I don't drink and I don't smoke, and I couldn't stand the smoke in most of the clubs you know. And I played in Birdland with Count Basie and I played in another place called Bop City with Herbie Fields' band. And I always had difficulty with the smoke in those places. "

Blues singer Joe Williams likes to remember the Benny Goodman stories that have passed from generation to generation. "There's a million Benny Goodman stories," Joe says in Hamilton College Jazz Archive's oral history. Benny was based in New York City, Joe recalls. Milt Hinton was called about a gig on the west coast and he was asked to bring some major east coast musicians out.

Milt said he would . . . he contacted Jo Jones, Claude Hopkins, Budd Johnson, Benny Morton and Roy Eldridge among others. "You couldn't get a more senior group than that. So we were going to go to California to do this concert. So Benny Goodman's going to be out there, too." . Each guy is to get $1,000. Benny, meanwhile, calls Milt to tell him that he's closing a gig and going out. He asks Milt if he wants to join his group. "Yeah, Benny, I don't mind playing with you," Milt replies. "What's the bread like?" Benny asks if $185 will be okay. "Wait a minute Benny, wait a minute," Milt retorts. " I knew that I was getting $1,000 already so I figured I'd get greedy. So I said 'if you give me $500 more I'll do it.' He hung up on me. Benny hung up the phone," an exasperated Milt replied.

Former Glenn Miller saxophonist and bandleader, the late Jerry Jerome has his own memories of days on the road with Benny and his famous "forgetfulness."

A story he tells describes Benny's singlemindedness. "I joined Benny at the Waldorf in the fall, 1938, and no sooner had I checked into a hotel then I had a call waiting from Benny. He said there was going to be a band meeting the next morning. Important. . . be there. Unfortunately, several hours later, my grandfather died and I had to rush home. I called Benny and told him I had to go home for a family funeral. Benny sounded remorseful but agreed it was an unavoidable situation. At 2 a.m. the next day . . . my hotel phone rings and it's Benny. 'Jerry, this is Benny. . . can you get out of that thing and come to the meeting this morning?'"

Jerry said that Benny was always self-conscious on the platform or stage and he remembered a night when the band was playing at Moonlite Gardens and he and Toots Mondell, another Goodman sideman, went for a stroll between sets. "We saw those parachute things that you tossed in the air and they fluttered for awhile before they came down. We bought a few and tossed them up and took them back to the bandstand. Benny called up 'One O'Clock Jump' and we got into it and Toots and I started tossing the parachutes among the sections. Benny of course was facing the crowd and in the final minutes of the number the crowd was standing around laughing at what Toots and I were doing. The number ends and Benny turns around red faced and panic-stricken and says 'Is my fly open?'"

Meanwhile Benny was always good for laughs at the parties that took place when musicians and their fans gathered. Jerome remembers when Benny and Artie Shaw attended a post-event party where the talk shifted from music to books and movies. Benny, Jerry said, wasn't much of a conversationalist or reader. But when the subject turned to the popular book of the day, "The Sword and Citadel," Artie turned to Benny and said "I'm sure you've read that book, right? " Benny said nothing for a moment and then asked "Is that the one with the red cover?" According to Jerome, Goodman and Harry James were similar when it came to small talk. Harry, he said, knew two things; the big band business and baseball. When the conversation drifted elsewhere Harry became silent.

The big band business was no different than other occupations when it came to money. Singer Frank Sinatra enjoyed working with the Harry James band but when his wife became pregnant reality set in. Tommy Dorsey offered $125 a week as compared to the $75 Harry was paying him and he joined the Sentimental Gentleman for the needed $200 more a month. Woody Herman was getting $1,500 to $3,000 or more in the mid-1940s but when he took his band to Brooklyn's Roseland Ballroom for his first gig he got $75 and his sidemen were paid $50 each.

As I reviewed a number of books and monologues, either autobiographies or as-told-to stories, about bandleaders and veteran players it was clear that one of the toughest ballroom managers among a number with business acumen at the time was former musician and bandleader Frank Dailey of the Meadowbrook. Said Road Manager Ed Gabel in his book about Stan Kenton, Dailey would pay as little as possible but dangle a national radio wire as a part of the deal to bands he thought would persuade them to widen their audiences. Miller and Kenton were among the bands who gained from such deals.

New York, of course, was a mecca for those from the heartland because of the excitement generated for entertainment palaces well advertised throughout the country. But no one should overlook Boston and New England where other large crowds gathered to hear the touring bands. . . and still come out to support good territorial bands from time to time.

Jim Calogero, a Boston Globe correspondent, wrote a fascinating piece about "When Ballrooms Bounced" that offered great nostalgia for those who lived, worked and danced in the 1930s and '40s. He took the reader to the Raymor-Playmor Ballroom, the Roseland State, Revere Beach, the Wonderland, the Oceanview and the Spanish Gables ballrooms and then set the Bostonian dreaming of the old days when he mentioned Kimball's Starlight in Lynnfield, Nuttings on the Charles in Waltham, Moseley's on the Charles in Dedham, Ala L'Air on the Worcester Turnpike, the Totem Pole at Norumbega Park in Auburndale, Narragansett Pier and Rhodes on the Pawtuxet among the ballrooms in Rhode Island and Hampton Beach Casino, Canobie Lake and Alton Bay Pavilion in New Hampshire. ". . .For the old-timers, certainly nothing exists today to match the setting in which the music of the 1930s and '40s was played," he wrote. His reminisces were exactly what New Englanders remember even though the names sound far more British or different to the rest of us.

Travel, of course, was as necessary as eating and sleeping. But bassist Rollie Bundock who played with Glenn and later spent time with Les Brown, still laughs when he thinks of what it was like. "When we went on the road it was difficult, believe me. . . . night after night on and off the bus. I tried to see my folks at least three or four times a year but I'd get home for just a few hours and then it would be off to Boston or New York or wherever it might be, " he told a mid-1980s PBS audience.

Sammy Kaye, another sweet band from the Midwest, is rarely associated with New York but it was in the Big Apple where the band's signature "So You Want to Lead A Band" audience participation feature became a hit at the Commodore Hotel's Century Room. Months earlier Sammy and his college crew were playing a nickel a dance spot on campus. Upon graduation from Ohio University with a degree in Civil Engineering, he went on a series of one-nighters in choice locations where radio remotes gave the band notoriety. By 1938, popular demand gave Sammy a chance to follow the high flying Tommy Dorsey band at the Century Room. It was a young man in the crowd who, after some prodding from his girlfriend, challenged Sammy to let him "lead" the band. "Swing and Sway" followed and the Kaye band remained at the Commodore for two years.

A militant Chicago union leader, James C. Petrillo, president of the American Federation of Musicians

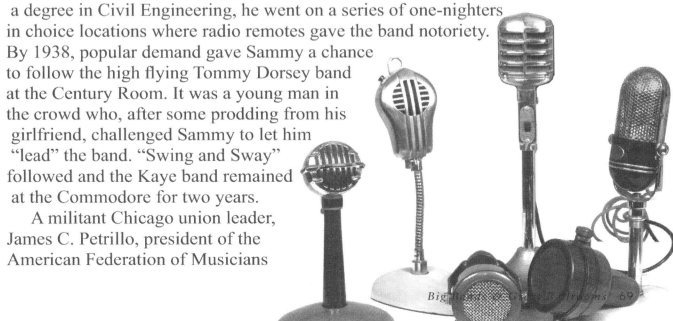

Big Bands and Ballrooms 69

(AFM) made the money issue worse for all musicians in 1942 when he began what became known as "Petrillo's War." Although the purpose was to get union musicians' royalties on recording sales, the union chief saw radio, which was generating promotion for big bands everywhere, as a serious threat to musicians who played live at hotels, restaurants and local events. Petrillo initiated a ban on all phonograph recordings other than radio broadcasts sponsored by the government – V-Discs, Treasury Department war programs, for example – and connected with the war effort. The ban lasted for more than two years and was ended when the recording companies reluctantly agreed to pay AFM fixed royalties.

Petrillo threatened another strike in 1948 as television arrived, however, recording studios were better prepared and had more product on hand. Ten years later AFM musicians rebelled at Petrillo's controversial use of union money and formed the Musicians Guild of America which won the right to negotiate with Hollywood studios and Petrillo resigned.

No question, though, Petrillo's "war" was inevitable. National Public Radio in a story and broadcast entitled "Royalties Elusive For Many Jazz Greats" by Felix Contreras explained that while reissues were a meat and potatoes issue for those in the music business, some recording industry executives used various ways to avoid paying artists what had been earned. Unscrupulous ones would pay the band leaders an advance only to maintain later that their records never sold enough to cover the advance, much less provide royalties, the NPR story reported.

Wendy Oxenhorn, executive director of the Jazz Foundation of America in New York echoes NPR's concern especially today for older musicians who were playing dates long before changes were made. Her foundation is attempting to help senior musicians who are frequently uninsured and abandoned.

Legendary big band leader and longtime saxophonist Frank Foster told Felix what many other older musicians I talked to feel; "I wasn't thinking about my future the way I should have been. The way I was living, I thought I'd just have fun while I'm here. . . I had no idea that I would live beyond 50."

An interview with saxophonist J. R. Monterose while he was an artist-in-residence at Utica College where I taught offered similar thoughts. J.R. started his career on a 1950 tour with Henry "Hot Lips" Busse's band, one of the sweet bands of the era.

He jumped to Buddy Rich which he found demanding but far more satisfying as a player. Yet, he said, your income was all you had. "There was no health plan or retirement plan or anything like that," he said, "in fact, I don't remember one band that had such things."

A great friend and former east coast ballroom emcee, singer and dance instructor, the late Lou DiSario, told me that the risks were beyond any job because "this isn't a business . . . it's a hobby that takes devotion and love with little thought of what you'd get besides applause. Whether you were a musician or a dancer or an emcee like I was in the early days, the pay was not going to pay your bills." A Philadelphian, Lou, who took the name "Lou King" which he felt could be remembered more easily, was the likeable emcee at Hamid's Million Dollar Ballroom at Atlantic City in the 1930s. He introduced bandleaders like trumpeter Charley Spivak, who became a friend; another trumpeter, Randy Brooks, and two young singers who later went on to fame in TV, Ozzie and Harriet Nelson.

He liked Tony Pastor, Sam Donahue and another trumpet player who he considered down-to-earth, Harry James. Public persona, in other words, wasn't always what it appeared backstage.

Frank Sinatra? Lou had fond memories of "ol blue eyes" when he sang with Tommy Dorsey. "I got the chance to socialize with singers like Billy Eckstine, Andy Williams, Frankie Laine, Vic Damone off and on while I was appearing with Jerry Murad and the Harmonicats of the "Peg Of My Heart" fame in Pennsylvania and other parts of the Northeast. And I always remembered this lanky Italian I met at a bar when I was working in southwestern Pennsylvania. He bought me a drink, we talked about the business, finding work and getting paid and such and he gave me tickets to his performance with Tommy Dorsey at Hershey Park. I didn't know who he was but I sure knew Tommy Dorsey. That's how I met Frank Sinatra." Lou told me.

Of course, there was the nation's oldest active bandleader, Sterling Weed of St. Albans, VT, who passed away at 104 in the summer, 2005. He was still leading his band, Weed's Imperial Orchestra, just weeks before his death. He played a sold out benefit for the Preservation Trust at the Grand Isle Lake House. He was too weak from a bladder infection to play his sax that evening. . . but he took his place in the middle of his nine piece group to perform anyhow. He totally loved what he did.

Through it all, said Ray Riegert, author of "Hidden Hawaii, "Hidden San Francisco," "Northern California" and others, in his article "New York Nostalgia: The Grand Old Hotels," "For transplanted Easterners like me, there is only one place to summon the past. It's an island wedged between two rivers, a tumbling block of territory that contains within its narrow span an expanse of personal remembrance. . . . New York's grand old hotels have been around a lot longer than (this) impressionable kid. The Plaza is approaching its 100th birthday, while the Waldorf Astoria has marked over 70 years. In the days of Dorsey and Duchin, when Big Bands roamed the earth, those hotels were king. Though not even a toddler until the 1950s, I've always lived that brassy era through my grandparents. . . The memories in these hotels hang heavy as the chandeliers. New York's grand old hotels are emblems of the city's history, symbols of its style. Every visitor to one extent or another borrows part of that history as his own."

Dancers, Bands Flocked To East Coast Bibliography

George Wein, Joe Wilder and Joe Williams
oral histories at Hamilton College Jazz Archive, Clinton, NY

www.trumpetguild.org/2000conference/saturday/s10.htm

George Wein
http://en.wikipedia.org/wiki/George_Wein

Myself Among Others
by George Wein (DaCapo Press/2003)

Same Old Stand
by Mike Santangelo, New York Daily News, June 2, 2004

Carl Sigman
Songwriters Hall of Fame, www.songwritershalloffame.org

www.ieee-virtual museum.org/collection/people.

php?taid=&id=1234680&lid=1

James Petrillo

John Behrens
Big Band Days (1stBooks/2003)

Glenn Miller
http://en.wikipedia.org/wiki/Talk:Glenn_Miller

"Royalties Elusive For Many Jazz Greats,"
Felix Contreras, NPR

www.npr.org/templates/story/story.

php?storyId=4608713

www.sammykayeorchestra.com/sammy.htm

UC Roundtable
WIBX, Utica,NY with Monk Rowe, curator, Hamilton College
Jazz Archive, Nov 10, 2002;

Lou DiSario
correspondence, March 27, 2002; April 3, 2002, April 10, 2002

Glenn Miller Band Reunion PBS
1980s Glenn Miller, http://en.wikipedia.org/wiki/GlennMiller
March 16, 2006

Hotel Pennsylvania
www.hotelpenn.com/thehotel.html January 2, 2006

Stepping Gently Out of the Sideman Shadows
Ben Ratliff, New York Times, Feb. 3, 2006

Jazz
Colliers Yearbook, 1965

www.thehistorynet.com/abi/blglennmiller.

Ed Gabel
Stan Kenton: The Early Years, 1941-1947 (Balboa Books/1993)

Showtime at the Apollo
Mill Road Enterprises, 2004

"New York Nostalgia: The Grand Old Hotels,"
Ray Riegert www.grandtimes.com/New_York_Nostalgia.html

Chuz Alfred
personal correspondence, Oct. 30, 2000; January 23, 2003

Glenn Miller and his Orchestra
Live at Glen Island Casino, May 17, 1939

Glenn Miller http://launch.yahoo.com/ar-257261-bio

Glenn-Miller
March 16, 2005

Glenn Miller
The History Net www.thehistorynet.com/ahi/blgemiller/
index1.html February 22, 2005

Glen Island Casino
www.porthalcyon.com/reviews/200411/fields.shtml
March 17, 2005

Overdue Ovation: Joe Wilder
by Ed Berger, Jazztimes, October, 2001

Touring the Apollo Theater
New York Times, March 28, 2002

**Harlem's Historic Apollo Theater Celebrates 70th
Anniversary,** undated

Jerry Jerome and his All-Stars
Pinecrest High School, Boca Raton, FL, May 19, 1998

Ray Riegert
New York Nostalgia: The Grand Old Hotels
www.grandtimes.com/New_York_Nostalgia.html

NYC's Historic Hotels
www.nycvisit.com January 2, 2006

125th Street-The 1930s: The Heyday Years
www.125thstreet.co.uk/article/articleprint/27/-1/12
May 26, 2005

When Ballrooms Bounced
The Boston Globe, March 13, 2005

**Sterling Weed: Nation's Oldest Known Active Bandleader
Dies at 104**
www.boston.com/news/local/vermont/articles/2005/09/
13nations_oldest_known_act September 15, 2005

THE ARAGON
CHICAGO'S BIG BAND PALACE

It never got the attention that New York and Los Angeles received when talking about the big bands but America's third largest city, located on the southern shore of Lake Michigan, was as important to the big band era as any US music or entertainment community. It was frequently ignored by the national media which were headquartered on the two coasts.

Chicago. What a hellava town! And what a city to find a choice group of dancing, eating and listening places. In the early years there was Midway Gardens, Byrd Ballroom, White City Ballroom, the Trianon Ballroom, the Marigold Ballroom, the Rainbow Gardens, the Majestic, The Paradise and the Deamland Ballroom and later add the Blackhawk Restaurant, the Palmer House, the Drake and dozens of nearby spots. Said Leo Walker, who wrote the fascinating story of a number of big bands called "The Wonderful Era of the Great Dance Bands." "The city of Chicago was the only one which could really compete with New York as a band building area and there are many music people who rate it as having been the more important of the two. It moved into that position in the early twenties and maintained it well into the mid-thirties."

It's also the city that gave us one of the musicians most associated with the beginning of swing; Benny Goodman. While Benny's success came in California and moved east to New York City, no Chicagoan will let you forget he was born and discovered in the city. And for good reason. Benny returned in 1976 and

The Aragon Ballroom, New Year's Eve 1949.   Photo courtesy of Dick Jurgens Jr. web site

participated in a lecture at the University of Chicago. He inspired the Department of Music to gather other materials to create an archive that focused on the birth of jazz in Chicago from 1910 to 1920. The music program had been successful without a jazz curriculum but it started a collection of 78 recordings.

But it was a north side Chicago ballroom that became bigger than life because of its size and because of its longevity. The Aragon Ballroom, which celebrated its 80th birthday in 2006, became a beacon to many bandleaders seeking larger crowds and the necessary radio remotes to connect with the rest of the country. It was built to hold nearly 8,000 people. The goal of the owners, Andrew and William Karzas, was unique in a day when contractors built places to simply attract crowds and generate a profit. The brothers certainly wanted profit but they were thought to have coupled their business interest with social purposes for a dance hall in uptown Chicago. The Karzas family had made money in nickelodeons and movie theaters and then built the very elaborate Trianon Ballroom on the South Side four years earlier.

I didn't see it during its heyday but what a place it must have been. I got there in the early 1950s and I remember things like a castle with turrets, some palm trees scattered about, Middle Eastern murals and giant swords. I also recall, as a musician would, a distinct echo out front of the bandstand probably caused by the size of the band on the platform that left more than half the stage bare.

The Aragon, said its owners, was an elegant place for men and especially women to feel at home. Some of the city's other dance spots were looked upon as unhealthy places that caused women to worry about their reputation when they entered or left. Good families didn't let their daughters or sisters go to certain places, it was said. Add to that, the official ban on alcohol and bootlegging which much of the nation thought was centered in Chicago and you can understand the city's political and cultural climate in the 1920s.

The new ballroom was going to be different. "With its stylish interior décor, its courteous but watchful staff, and its strict policies against alcohol consumption, the Aragon was intended to impress critics and convince them that public dancing need not always be considered a bad thing. As much as such policies helped win the patronage of middle-class youths, the regular booking of the nation's top jazz bands was equally important in helping the ballroom attract huge crowds on a nightly basis," said Jazz Age Chicago.

Aragon management offered Chicagoans a word picture of what it would offer in an advertisement in the Chicago Evening American, on the opening day: "Beauty so exquisite that it transcends the loftiest imagery of the most poetic mind – immensity providing diversion and conveniences of unmatched variety. . . . What a spectacle of joyous memory it will be! A soft glow of opalescent color – stars twinkling in blue Mediterranean skies that gently enfold quaint patios and scent-filled balconades

– enchanted throngs dancing under the spell of old world romance, wafted through a golden, glamorous sphere touched by the magic world of illusion. . . . Rare tapestries, bizarre Chinese plates, statuettes, orange trees astonishingly real in the simulation of tropical verdure, appointments breathing the spirit of Castilian grandeur. Here is the flaming beauty, the romantic glory of old Spain. Commodious checkrooms for both men and women, a handsomely appointed grande mirror salon for the convenience of milady, a clean wholesome refectory where appetizing refreshments are served by charming senoritas, carefully selected attendants who are guided in their contact with visitors by the creed, 'Every patron an honored guest.'"

On a summer day in an era of opulence although not air-conditioned I can't think of anything that could have been added to this 80,000 square foot block of Spain in Chicago.

Walker recalled how the Russo-Ted FioRito Orchestra came from Detroit to open the Aragon, July 15, 1926. The Coon-Sanders Band was playing at the popular Blackhawk Restaurant and doing a remote nightly. Said Leo: "Although many of them may have originated elsewhere, there were probably more Negro bands steadily employed around Chicago during the span of the twenties than in any other American city. . . it was also in Chicago about 1927 that Louis Armstrong had the first band under his own name, playing for awhile at the Sunset Café. "

During the 1960s the Aragon went through a name change (it became the "Cheetah Club") and ownership transfers and a musical transformation at the same time. Rock performers and psychedelic paint pushed the sophisticates out the door and new sounds changed the place. Several years later, owner Emerson Whitney spent a considerable fortune refurbishing to create a nostalgic revival. It brought a short flurry of interest but nothing long term. In the 1970s more ownership transfers continued and rock'n'roll returned along with ethnic parties and even wrestling matches every other Friday to stem the red ink. That, of course, was later. An earlier period was much different.

Music historians speculate one reason might have been the population growing in and around Chicago in the early years of the 20th century. World War I brought nearly 50,000 African-American families from the South to the Windy City to take jobs in the city's manufacturing and munitions plants. The south side black entertainment district, known as the "Stroll," was home for many who typical of their southern hospitality, took in touring black entertainers without a thought about rent money or paying for "grits." These were genuine northern homesteaders who were eager to see friends and meet new ones. I visited the district – which extended at the time from 31st to 35th Streets – and I remember there was still music coming from homes years later. It was a great place to stroll and hear the blues and jazz. Not far away was another early Chicago landmark for black musicians and dancers. Paddy Harmon's Arcadia Ballroom, an uptown entertainment spot that broke the color line prevalent

The Aragon Ballroom, Chicago, one of the midwest's largest and picturesque ballrooms.

Photo courtesy Dick Jurgens Jr. web site

among other ballrooms at the time. Paddy cheerfully hired all black jazz groups for predominantly white audiences playing a mixture of their own music and popular numbers of the day. Competition with the Aragon caused a decline in the Arcadia crowds and, while boxing matches and other sporting events kept it in business, the building deteriorated and in the 1950s it burned and was torn down.

Guy Lombardo would always have a special feeling about Chicago, especially in the late 1920s. He worked in Cleveland, OH for nothing in the early days of his career to get air time. His first break as a bandleader came when he played the Grenada Café on the South Side of Chicago. It was a mob-managed night spot with a pistol range in the basement and gambling upstairs. But the pay was good. The Lombardo band left Cleveland for $300 a week more in Chicago. Later, he used to tell the story that the café was right across from a cemetery "not exactly the audience I thought I'd start with."

Sure enough, his first nights were disastrous. Few came to hear a group of Canadians, whether they were "royal" or not. Weeks of virtually no business caused the band and club to wonder about the decision. But Guy knew that radio remotes were successful at places like the Blackhawk so he paid $75 of the $100 charge for the wire to the Grenada. The first show was broadcast on WBBM in November, 1927. Fifteen minutes was all the Lombardo band got but it was the exposure the band needed. Shortly after the

NAT TOWLES
and his Orchestra
Management
HOWARD WHITE
1506 Spring Street
OMAHA, NEBRASKA

We don't know whether the band played the Aragon but Nat Towles and his Orchestra were "spiffy" enough to play anywhere. Notice the white buck shoes. Photo courtesy of James Ronan Collection, IA

show was aired, calls came into the café and the station. People wanted to hear more. In fact, the station wanted the band to play all night! The Grenada Café, meanwhile, had a transfusion of new customers. When Guy and his band returned within 24 hours there was an SRO crowd and the next morning he had two sponsors for the radio show. Even Al Jolson, riding the success of his movie "The Jazz Singer," showed up one night. Several days more and Guy was the talk of the city. The Lombardo band seemed to have a knack for turning things around, too. Two years later, Guy, his brothers and the band went to New York City to open an engagement at the Roosevelt Grill. . . just before the momentous stock market crash and the beginning of the Great Depression and the closing of more than 1,300 banks.

While the era ended a number of successful bands and caused thousands of musicians to seek other work, it was the beginning of big things for Guy. The short term engagement at the Roosevelt Grill continued for 33 years ! The Royal Canadians introduced more than 500 hit songs during Guy's tenure. It also was the beginning of a tradition that Americans associated with New Year's Eve. Guy Lombardo and the Royal Canadians celebrated the new year on radio and later television shows on CBS and NBC for 48 years, For years, I heard or watched the Lombardo band play "Auld Lang Syne" at the stroke of midnight. Like millions of revelers, we'd always find a TV set to ring in the new year with Guy.

But Chicago was the melting pot for the band business, big and small. Said Walker in his book about great bands, "The potency of Chicago grew steadily in the last half of the twenties. Doubtless the beginning of Music Corporation of America (booking agency) in that city was a strong factor in attracting bands to the area and contributed to the build-up which they received . . . Chicago had by now (1929) become identified as the hottest spot in the nation for band-building via radio."

It was a year earlier, Jules Stein and Billy Goodheart started what became the largest band booking agency in Chicago called Music Corporation of America (MCA). Its success was meteoric. Lombardo, Coon-Sanders, Isham Jones, Ted Weems and the waltz king, Wayne King, all became MCA bands and reaped success from arrangement.

Obviously, bandleaders and musicians also benefited from the bootleggers and the mob too. Mob enterprises controlled by Al Capone, Bugs Moran and others owned or "influenced" a number of the Chicago clubs and speakeasies of the era and for years everyone looked the other way and enjoyed the excitement of the good years especially musicians who were earning more money than they had seen in other cities. But there were drawbacks. Bandleader Woody Herman told audiences years later of the time he was shot in the leg while traveling in a car that was stopped by gangsters. He was 16 years old, he said, and it showed him how the dangerous city streets could be.

Lombardo remembered tangling with a rowdy guest at the Grenada who tried to wrestle the mike away from him and the bandleader shoved him away. Later, he discovered the intruder on his bandshell was connected to Moran's gang. Friends told him had not the man left his pistol in his car . . . Guy might have been history, too.

Yet, while the city's music seemed to be dominated by the exciting sounds of bandleaders like ragtime clarinetist Wilbur Sweatman, who could play three instruments at once and led a vaudeville band, Charley Straight, who was called the man who gave us the swing sound, Kid Oliver who came from New Orleans in the early 1900s to offer the raw jazz numbers and a number of others, it was the sweet and mellow dance bands that Chicagoans seemed to enjoy most. Lombardo, fellow Canadian Jan Garber, and Ted Weems discovered Chicago was a city that enjoyed ballads. . . even the old fashioned waltz was given a new treatment.

A popular Savannah, IL native who rose to fame quickly thanks to his very elegant dance music and smart business acumen was Wayne King, known as the "Waltz King." Like every leader of the era striving to find that commercially successful "sound," Wayne focused on waltzes, novelty numbers and the sentimental songs of a decade steeped in economic ruin and despair. But King didn't ignore his big swing band friends either. Benny Goodman, Duke Ellington, Louis Armstrong, Count Basie and Glenn Miller's charts influenced his music too, he said. A long-running contract with Lady Esther Serenade on radio and Victor recordings gave him identity and popularity but to Chicagoans. . . his first night at the Aragon Ballroom in 1927 became the beginning of decades of work at the dance pavilion. And King and the Aragon both gained. By 1935 with radios in about 23 million homes and an audience of 91 million across the country, bandleaders like King could name their venue.

Another sweet band of the same vintage, Californian Dick Jurgens, also became a popular name to city residents. Radio transformed Jurgens' music from a little known band from the west coast to respectability especially in Chicago.

Listen to Annie Freeman, wife of Jurgens' longtime trombonist Virgil Freeman, on going from California to Chicago. "The . . .orchestra was very popular at the Aragon. . . on the north side of Chicago. I learned that the band was unique. I'm sure every one had a bad image of musicians in the early years, including myself. I was happy at the fact that when Virgil was released after four years in the armed forces along with Dick from the Marines, he had a call from Dick to join the band at the Aragon. Virgil also had a call from Eddie Howard who had left the Jurgens Orchestra to form his own orchestra. Virgil chose Dick. . . those were happy days. It was fun to travel with the band. They had the appearance of a very clean cut band on the road. No scandal, no drugs, no heavy drinking. When any drinking was done at all it was made clear that it had to be after working hours or you were fired. A few tried it and were replaced. It was Dick's policy to hold the band together with the same men as long as possible. He didn't believe in changes. He encouraged the men to bring wives and children along when on long locations such as Berkeley, CA at the Hotel Claremont where we spent three months every year and always at Christmas."

Annie offered an interesting vignette about what it was like to be a traveling spouse with a touring bandleader. "Our excitement through the band travel days were a newspaper, once in awhile a movie and anything that was free from museums and zoos to parks on the days off from Hollywood to New York. Exercising was something else we tried to do. Walking was free too," she smiled.

Her wedding to the Jurgens' trombonist came during an Aragon engagement, she remembered. "Virgil and I scheduled our wedding for his day off. . . a Monday. He flew to Pittsburgh late Sunday night after the job and with my dad driving . . . he asked if we could get married. My dad was so shocked he went the wrong way on a one way street! My aunt donated a wedding cake. The wedding went off as scheduled. Being Hungarian, we had a custom that anyone wanting to dance with the bride at the reception had to pay. Man, the money poured in but my feet hurt. When the groom thinks there is enough money he claims the bride and off they go to count the money. After the dance, it's back to the airport because Virgil had to work the next night. No honeymoon."

Early July, 2006, Virgil was honored by his community of Newhall, IA and his memorabilia was placed in the Newhall Alumni Hall of Fame. His wife Annie was at the event and told Belle Plaine Union/South Benton Star-Press (IL) publisher Don

Jack Joker and the Aces
Presenting their old and New time Rhythms
BOOKING ADDRESS:- LANESBORO, MINN.

Musicians had to find "shticks" even in the early days to catch attention. Here's Jack Joker and the "Aces" from the 1930s. Besides the catchy playing card bandstand, Jack said his music "presented old and new time rhythms."

Photo courtesy of James Ronan Collection, IA

Magdefrau of their years together during those big band days. Virgil, it seems, only missed one opening theme song. He forgot his suit one evening and they had to drive 100 miles back home to get it. According to Annie, Virgil got to the gig late and told her he and leader Jurgens didn't make eye contact the whole night. The Aragon was special to the Freemans for another reason; it's where Jurgens ask Virgil to meet for a tryout.

Virgil, just home from the service, was working with his father "Gussi" as a carpenter installing a floor in a new house when the call came from Dick in Chicago.

Jurgens introduced a very popular singer to Chicagoans too. Eddie Howard became a fixture with the band until he started his own orchestra and was also booked at the Aragon. In three years (1945-48) Eddie produced 11 one million (gold) records (who from the era can forget "To Each His Own"?) . . . a feat few singers before or after him surpassed. Howard represented the kind of musician/singer of the era that is rarely found today. The story that circulated about him was that he auditioned with Dick Jurgens as a trombone player and he was unable to read notes. He memorized the audition tunes to get the job. He later played guitar with the Jurgens band.

Another bandleader who owed his future to Chicago ballrooms and audiences was southerner Kay Kyser. His standard "Evenin' Folks. . . How y'all. . ." and Kollege of Musical Knowledge was a fixture on his radio show and gave NBC one of the top

EARL GARDNER & HIS ORCHESTRA THE BAND WITH A MILLION FRIENDS

MANAGEMENT—NATIONAL ORCHESTRA SERVICE—OMAHA & MINNEAPOLIS

Earl Gardner and his Orchestra and their instruments traveled through the midwest winter and summer in this traveling van. The band was based in Omaha and Minneapolis. The band's motto? "The band with a Million Friends."

Photo courtesy of James Ronan Collection, IA

ten shows for 10 of its 11 years.

A North Carolinian, James Kern Kyser, who decided that a stage name like "Kay" was far better than his real name James Kern, got his start as a leader not as a musician when Hal Kemp, also a student at University of North Carolina along with Kay, asked the "ol professor" to take over his college group when he left. The Tarheel band barely made it out of college, friends report, but in 1933, Kay, along with sax player/vocalist Sully Mason, went on the road. Times were even tougher out of the shadows of the college campus, fraternity dances and community events.

But Kemp didn't forget his college friend. He recommended the Kay Kyser Orchestra to the manager of the Blackhawk Restaurant in Chicago. Kay, meanwhile, hired perky Ginny Simms on the strength of the new contract and the band scored with a Brunswick recording agreement. He recorded his theme "Thinking Of You" and months later hired several others who added more popularity to the band, vocalist Harry Babbitt, and a trumpet playing business manager named Merwyn Bogue who became the silly looking, dippy vocalist named "Ish Kabibble." To add to the fun-loving which increased crowds at the Blackhawk especially on slow days like Monday, Kay started an amateur night routine called "Kay's Klass." Mutual Broadcasting aired a regional version and, within months, Lucky Strike bought the show and moved it to New York City. Sully is credited with coming up with the name, "Kollege of Musical Knowledge" and Kay as the "Ol' Professor." The show format offered a music related quiz with songs and comedy. Winners got diplomas.

Twelve years later, a very successful Kay Kyser who starred in seven feature films and had 11 number one hits, walked away from the band business and went home.

Horace Heidt, another Californian, started a second band and journeyed to Chicago to open at the Drake Theater in 1936 and find his own "Pot O' Gold." A pianist, he became a far better showman and launched a program at the Drake which led to national fame on radio and television. His talent show offered chances for such later stars such as Dick Contino, Al Hirt and a number of other show business and musical personalities. A large number of musicians owe their careers to work with Heidt. Jess Stacy, Warren Covington, Shorty Sherock, Frankie Carle, Joe Rushton, Glenn Miller, Bobby Hackett, Red Nichols, Bill Finnegan, Gene Krupa, Lionel Hampton, Pete Condoli, Benny Carter and Pete Fountain were among the list of sidemen who played with Heidt's "Musical Knights."

Several other bandleaders made names for themselves and were great attractions at the Aragon as the 1930s became the 1940s. No one from the era or the Windy City could forget Ben Pollack who, some insist to this day, had one of the best jazz/swing bands of the period.

Pollack, like so many drummers of the 1930s, 40s and 50s, was a self-taught percussionist. He went on the road at probably 18 and was good enough to join the New Orleans Rhythm Kings, a top jazz band of the early 1920s. Like Charley Barnett, he came from a well-to-do family so money wasn't necessarily needed to eat and pay the bills. But it was Ben's ability to find talent like Benny Goodman, Jack Teagarden, Glenn Miller, Jimmy McPartland and Harry James to drop a few names that gave his band an all-star quality. The band did a number of recordings and Ben, who became more enamored of his leading than his drumming, hired a great young drummer named Ray Bauduc to handle the throne behind the bass drum.

The stock market crash was difficult for Pollack, his family and his future. He struggled in the 1930s and '40s and although he reorganized the band several more times and even tried becoming a record executive and a restaurant owner, the good life never returned. Fifteen days before his 68th birthday, he hung himself.

Bandleader Freddie Martin of Cleveland, OH who began work as a musical instrument salesman, was another Aragon success story. His start, of course, was due to a competitor who became a longtime friend, Guy Lombardo. Martin tried to persuade Lombardo to buy some saxophones. He was unsuccessful in selling the saxes but Guy did hear Freddy's band and when the Royal Canadians couldn't do a gig he recommended the Martin band. And the rest was big band history.

Chicagoans were enthralled with their newest ballroom when it opened during the "Roaring Twenties." Said the "Jazz Age Chicago" in reviewing the big night: "Thousands of eager dancers, including Mayor 'Big Bill' Thompson, attended the opening event. Many were astounded by the ballroom's extravagant interior design. The second-level dance floor was reached by a thickly carpeted grand staircase guarded by large plaster dragons."

It was, said many in letters to the editor in Chicago papers, a different kind of world from other dance halls or ballrooms. It certainly was to me. I had never seen a ballroom with men's smoking rooms or bathrooms that size. The Karzas brothers had created a theme palace as well as a place to dance. It was designed like a Moorish castle courtyard, complete with palm trees and thousands of tiny lights in the ceiling that gave it a surreal feeling of a Mediterranean night overhead. The dance floor was all maple with a cork cushion, felt and springs that offered vibrations to the music of the bands. It had to be the most opulent place in Chicago really. Oil paintings and draperies adorned the walls of two very large promenades on the sides of the ballroom. A grand salon was on one end and three stages were at the opposite end.

WGN radio broadcast dance music six nights a week from 10:05 p.m. until 11 but it hardly diminished the crowds. The ballroom routinely topped 18,000 a week from the 1920s into the 1940s. It was one of my father's favorite radio programs on our old Philco and he would wake me up if I fell asleep to make sure I heard any number of bands from the Aragon. If there was inclement weather, static would interrupt from time to time. . . but you NEVER tuned out until it finished.

But those who look back at its beginning believe that bands and décor were just a part of the success of this ballroom. Social behavior was another and perhaps as powerful a factor in making the Aragon something most places lost by the end of the era. For example, men were expected to wear jackets and ties, women semi-formal evening wear. Smoking was prohibited even at a time when it was vogue.

Tuxedoed floorwalkers cruised the floors to ensure that couples close dancing abided by inches apart rules and jitterbugging wasn't like the gyrations they saw in other dance halls. One Chicagoan told me if you wanted to see or be involved in such "wild dancing . . . you were told to join the young crowd at the Arcadia Ballroom not far away."

The owners thought about transportation, too. The Aragon was close to the "L" which brought in people from throughout the city, not just the North Side.

Anna Idol remembers what it was like to "go downtown" in the mid-1950s. "I used to double date with Ann Margret (her name then was Olson) and we would dance to bands in the Aragon," she says. "I still use some of the steps she taught me. Her parents and mine let us go on double dates because we were good Scandinavian girls (Ann Margret is Swedish, I'm Norwegian) and we would not get into trouble with the boys. That was also the era in which no one smoked, drank, and good girls behaved themselves. We had a wonderful time and didn't realize that anything was missing

JACK and RUSSELL and their MUSIC — A RADIO BAND WITH A MILLION FRIENDS

MANAGEMENT—NATIONAL ORCHESTRA SERVICE—OMAHA & MINNEAPOLIS

Not to be out done with friends, Jack and Russell and their Music, also from Omaha, told bookers and listeners that they had "a radio band with a million friends." Wally Way was the director and vocalist.

Photo courtesy of James Ronan Collection, IA

from the experience. It's too bad that that age of innocence has ended for teenagers."

Chicago in the early 1940s; Hemingway's "For Whom The Bells Toll" was popular, Pogo and Sad Sack cartoon strips gave readers a lift during somber and distressing war news from abroad and, at the stately Aragon, jitterbugging, while frowned on, was gaining popularity as a dance form.

Touring big bands visiting Chicago ballrooms and dancing pavilions were paid from $1,500 to $4,000 and much less for the territorial groups during the 1940s.. Today? Not much has changed really. A review of the Gigmasters web site shows that a big band can be paid $1,000 to nearly $3,000 but contracts are much more defined these days.

Television, younger families with different tastes and interests and the decline in the neighborhood forced management to make the fateful decision on weekly dancing. Consequently, dancing under the stars and among the palm trees ended Feb. 9, 1964. Chicagoans knew the final days were in the mid-1950s.

Here's how the Aragon described it in response to my question:

"Eras have a way of ending. By 1955 an era in which an estimated 50 million people had danced at the Aragon to the very best of America's orchestras was in decline. They danced through Prohibition and danced during the Depression. In 1958 the Normandy Cocktail Lounge, located next door to the Aragon, caught fire and an

Think waiting in line is bad today? Here's a line waiting to see the Dick Jurgens Orchestra at the Aragon in the 1940s.
Photo submitted by Dick Jurgens Jr. web site

explosion erupted. The blast, probably set off by pressure from heat generated by the fire, ripped the glass and brick storefront of the saloon, hurled bar stools, glass and shreds of fancy draperies across the street and punched a huge hole into the wall that separated it from the foyer of the ballroom. Damage to the Aragon was estimated at $50,000. . . .No one was injured. Consequently, the Aragon closed for a few months in order to repair the lobby. When it reopened, attendance dwindled."

Yet, the Aragon brings memories to many in the midwest. The Chicago Sun-Times, July 9, 2006, published the recollections of a number of those who had visited the ballroom over the years. Beth Bretell recalled seeing and hearing great salsa music and she remembered how the Aragon was one of the few places where Puerto Rican bands visited. Rita Witowski has memories of the one hour and a half trip from south side Chicago to north side that she actually looked forward to every week because it was a very special place where big bands played. And the price of admission? Seventy-five cents to one dollar!

To Julia Galas, she always remember that Glenn Miller packed in quite a crowd in 1941 but Kay Kyser actually had a larger crowd when she was there.

Today, the ballroom continues to operate and host such events as wrestling matches, roller skating, rock concerts and disco nights.

On occasion, though, it returns to that luster it once had.

Chuz Alfred of Columbus, OH was a member of bandleader Ralph Marterie's saxophone section and remembers the band's visit to the Aragon five years before it changed its venue.

"I'll never forget one afternoon about 3 in Chicago in '59 when the bus pulled up to the Aragon Ballroom so we could unload and get set up for the night. It was sunny but cold and windy outside and we'd been traveling through the dark of night and most of day's light. There was no chattering or chiding. . . just the dull, clicking of shoe leather on marble as we silently shuffled by the gigantic marble pillars one after another, toward the band room behind center stage. I suddenly stopped dead in my tracks. As I stood there soaking up heat from the dusty sunlight streaming in, I was instantly overcome by the spirit and sound of all those who'd been there before. The band's performance would mark one of the last to be offered in that hallowed hall of another age. I was beat, and tired of one-nighters, and getting tired of the whole damn scene, but as I stood there in the echo of those silent sounds, I knew way back in my soul that the night would be special. . . that the band was going to swing its butt off for sure that night."

A newsletter that evolved from a popular radio show called "The Browsers" continues to demonstrate how Chicago perpetuates a love affair with big bands, their musicians and the magical music that was played. Phil Holdman, a former record salesman from the 1940s, put together a show on WAIT radio when he returned from World War II and it kept big band music alive. "The Browsers" was the name given to a group of big band experts who would try to out-guess one another on the program. His free newsletter of the same name is available today by writing him and sending along self-addressed envelopes with appropriate postage so you can get on the mailing list. Phil, who is legally blind, his wife Alberta and a number of friends offer all kinds of stories of Chicago and the days when bands dominated the city's social calendar. The vignettes are the stuff legends are made of and the letters to the editor tell you how much Phil and his wife have meant to those who listened to his broadcasts and read his publication.

Not long ago, Phil told a great story about the famous Chicago "coin toss." Thanks to a clerical error, Don Roth, the late owner of the Black Hawk Restaurant and dancing spot, had booked Glenn Miller and Jack Teagarden Bands . . . the same night. At the "toss," Glenn shouted "heads," and it came up tails. Teagarden got the week at the Blackhawk . . . and Glenn ended up at the Panther Room of the Hotel Sherman.

Chicago, of course, was home for a number of top musicians of the big band era too. As a drummer, I felt a kinship to Gene Krupa who I met later at a much smaller ballroom in the middle of Ohio. But any number of others should be remembered too. People like bandleader Sig Myer, a prizefighter who became a drummer, Bernie Cummins, tenor saxophonist Paul Biese who you could find frequently at the Edgewater Beach Hotel, Don Bestor who went on to back a young Jack Benny on radio in 1934, trumpeter Jimmy McPartland, Hal Leonard, Mugsy Spanier, Ralph Marterie who opened in 1946 at the Melody Mill, Chicagoan Abe Lyman and his Californians who co-led a band with Gus Arnheim, Art Kassel, also of Chicago and Al Trace, another Chicago drummer who was remembered for working the World's Fair in the Windy City. Of course, it was also the hometown of popular singer Lou Rawls.

And, during an age when men dominated the band business there was a diminutive Ina Rae Hutton who led an all-girl orchestra that competed with Phil Spitalny who also led an orchestra of women musicians.

The city has taken the leadership in music professionalism, too. In 1978, band leaders and those involved with conducting orchestras former a not-for-profit corporation called the Association of Professional Orchestra Leaders, based in Westmont, IL. The organization abides by the APOL's Code of Ethics and Professional Standards which encourages the highest level of professional conduct and musical standards. Among its activities are a music scholarship and monthly meetings to formulate programs to improve the value of live musical entertainment. Yet it was the palace called The Aragon that ignited the city.

In retrospect, says Aragon Manager Liz Varney: "This place in the '50s and '60s was really popular for ballroom dancing. This place actually is a big turning point for a lot of groups. If you can fill a place with 4,500 people, the next step is pretty big. " My one visit told me how right she is. The Aragon today, however, is more likely to feature a concert by Ministry, Primus or Alanis Morisette where no dancing is allowed. Signs tell you don't try stage diving or body surfing. Such tactics didn't exist generations ago.

Has Chicago slipped as a jazz and big band capital over the years? Don't even jest about it to Chicagoans!

In the summer 2001, the Chicago Jazz Festival drew about 300,000 fans and it was broadcast over more than 100 radio stations.

And a loyal big band devotee from South Holland who began with virtually a short wave radio station from his home, John R. Ghrist, still keeps the flame burning for that special music from an era before his time. His station came from one of those kits that transform your radio speaker into broadcast user friendly.

Five years ago he returned to his music from the formal setting of the campus of the College of DuPage student station (WDCB-FM 90.9). Every Saturday supper time he has an hour to broadcast his show, "Midwest Ballroom." He says that '40 big bands like James, Goodman, Miller, Shaw and others still consume a good part of the hour but he also makes sure that Chicagoans hear area bands like Teddy Lee and his Orchestra, Frank Young and a number of others.

I know the feeling. I hosted a program called "UC Roundtable" on WIBX, CBS affiliate in the Mohawk Valley from Utica College, NY every Sunday morning at a time that took all my listeners could do to get up on winter days: 6:30 a.m. But we drew an audience and for 10 years we did 1,500 programs featuring every area and national band we could. Engineer Bill Parker, whose death in 2004, ended a wonderful partnership, always chuckled at the faculty member who called the radio station and the college early on a Sunday morning trying to talk to us "while we were on the air." He became agitated and argumentative when operators at both locations told him the show was taped!

The Aragon: Chicago's Big Band Palace Bibliography

Association of Professional Orchestra Leaders

www.bandleaders.org

New York Times
Aug. 28, 2001

Wonderful Era of the Great Dance Bands
Leo Walker (DaCapo Press, 1990)

Annie Freeman
Dick Jurgens web site www.dickjurgens.com
Dick Jurgens Jr emails February 8, 2002; February 20, 2002;
January 8, 2003

Wikipedia.org

Rise In Popularity of Big Band Music
www.swingmusic.net/getstart.html

Society Orchestras, '30s, '40s, '50s
www.society.html

Explore Big Bands
www.allmusic.com/cg

www.swingmusic.net/getset.html

www.kaykyser.net/kay.html

swing
http:llen.wikipedia.org/wiki/swing December 11, 2005

Jazz Age Chicago
http://chicago.urban-history.org/ven/dhs/dh_ar11.shtm1

The Aragon
1106 W. Lawrence, http://centerstage.net/music/clubs/
aragon-ballroom.html

Aragon Entertainment Center History
University of Chicago Magazine, April, 2001

Browsers'
No. 90, April, 2005

The Last Mogul
Lew Wasserman

Freddy Martin
//en.wikipedia.org/wiki/Freddy_Martin

Jazz Age Chicago
Urban Leisure from 1893 to 1945
http://chicago.urb-history.org/ven/dhs/aragon.shtml

www.bigbandsandbignames.com

www.mmguide.musicmatch.com

Trumpet Blues: The Life of Harry James
Peter J. Levinson (Oxford/1999)

Radio Host Keeps Big Band Sounds Alive
Feb. 11, 2005, George Haas, Daily Southtown, www.
southtown.com

The Golden Age of Television
Video Images, 1978

The Browsers, Phil & Alberta Holdman
3000 West Hood Ave., Chicago, IL 60659

Anna Ido
Chicago, email 2/25/05
http://metromix.chicagotribune.com/usic/29768,1,1584642.location?

Aragon Ballroom
Chuz Alfred, personal correspondence, Oct. 30, 2000;
January 23, 2003
http://chicago.urban-history.org/sites/ballroom/arcadia.htm

Aragon Entertainment Center
History, February, 2005

Newhall Alumni Remember Freeman
Don Magdefrau, The Belle Plaine Union/The South Benton
Star-Press, July 5, 2006

Your Aragon Memories
Chicago Sun-Times, July 9, 2006, www.suntimes.com/
output/rock/sho-sunday-aragon09b.html

Guy Lombardo
http://members.aol.com/famemgt/fame/lombardo.thm

January 19, 2006

THE PLAYGROUND OF OHIO
BUCKEYE LAKE'S BALLROOMS

It opened in 1901 and closed 69 years later but Buckeye Lake Park and its two ballrooms – the Pier and Crystal – were powerful drawing cards to a tiny man made lake that didn't have the allure and attractions of an Ohio River Coney Island or Lake Erie's Cedar Point.

To those who lived in the center of the state, it was THE recreational site for the family, dancers, swimmers, skiers, boaters and those who fished. "The park" was your destination of choice every summer in good and even bad weather. I doubt if those who artificially flooded 3,500 acres in 1825 ever envisioned its impact in later years. Summer cottages that rented for $35 a week or were owned by families throughout the midwest realized the lake's value in the century that followed.

The leap in its popularity, of course, came during the swing era. It also ended like so many other amusement parks across America when the music stopped.

"With the end of the Big Band Era, fewer people visited the park. By the 1960s, the park was in decline. Parks all over the country failed. People stopped dancing. There was a new lifestyle," said Chance Brockway, a legendary Buckeye Lake historian in an article in the Lancaster (OH) Eagle-Gazette.

The good times, he added, came when Crystal Ballroom and swimming pool were built in 1931. The second dance hall was the Lake Breeze Pier which stretched out over the water and was rebuilt in the mid-1930s after fire gutted the first dance pavilion.

What gave the two ballrooms their magnetism even though they were next door to Columbus, the state capital, which boasted its own dance halls and plush hotels with ballrooms?

Buckeye Lake native and longtime resident, Paula Kirk, offers a personal vignette that speaks for many Central Ohioans who endured the Depression in the 1930s and the world war that followed. "The Pier, in particular, was special to me. I was 18 just home from a year at Ohio University and I was working behind the refreshment stand at the ballroom. I was introduced to a handsome, blond soldier of 19 who was on leave after being wounded in France. We fell in love . . . we married in 1947, had two children, three grandchildren and five great-grandchildren. Our love continued through those years and we were together 56 years at the time of his death. But it all began at the Pier Ballroom . . ."

Like other states in the Midwest, ballrooms at one time were in all four corners of Ohio. You could find SRO crowds at a place like Moonlite Gardens down on the Ohio River where young teenage singers like Doris Day and the Clooney Sisters sang with local bandleader and talent developer, Barney Rapp. A Cincinnati Post column by Nick Clooney offered an explanation. "In 1946, the band names were familiar and included Johnny Long and Glen Gray. There was also Clyde Trask, who became something of a 'house band' that year, appearing 10 of the 17 weeks of the season. Drew good crowds, too," Nick reported. But it was Ralph Martiere six years later who set the attendance record at the Gardens. On July 25, 1952, the Martiere band played for 5,564 dancers.

Columbus offered local dancing favorites like the Valley Dale, and a great restaurant dance spot, the Grandview Inn, which drew crowds. More than 100 miles north on Lake Erie, couples from Michigan, Indiana, Illinois and elsewhere joined Ohio dancers at the Cedar Point Ballroom.

Musician Chuz Alfred, who summered on Buckeye Lake most of his young adult life, remembers Buckeye had different venues offering music at both ends of the lake. "Back in the Roaring '20s, the Alfred Melody Syncopaters played to capacity crowds at the Summerland Beach Hotel and Dance Pavilion. They even had a road manager and chief ticket taker; my mom's brother, Uncle Oscar. Ted Alfred, my uncle, was inspired by his reminiscences of a Lancaster (OH) High School Assembly program where the Melody Syncopaters played all decked out in clown garb.

"Then in the '40s, Thee, dad (George) and Tom (Mithoff) would get together at Thee's cottage at the lake at 10 or 11 in the morning and have a jam session that would cause a stir up and down the line of cottages," he recalls.

In her book, "My Buckeye Lake Story," Donna Fisher Braig offers a picture of the nightly entertainment sandwiched between big band appearances. Chuck Selby was a popular house band that played Sunday matinees featuring singer Anita Hutch. So was Wayne Martin of nearby Newark who started his own band at 15 and played the park's dancing spots. Midwest orchestra leader Carl "Deacon" Moore and his wife,

BAND STAND   PIER BALLROOM   BUCKEYE LAKE, OHIO

The bandstand at the Pier Ballroom, Buckeye Lake, OH where Vaughn Monroe and his entourage (front cover) packed the small platform with NBC radio remote equipment to do the "Camel Caravan" shows.

Photo courtesy of Paula Kirk, Newark, OH

the band's singer, Marge Hudson, were favorites at the Pier. Meanwhile at the Lake Breeze Hotel, just steps from the Pier Ballroom, Tony Sacco and accordionist Mitzi Joyce and later, organist Lenny Dee, would headline the entertainment at the Mayfair Room. It wasn't uncommon for the park to attract 50,000 people on a special day.

Donna remembers that the ballrooms used two dance plans. The Social Plan sold tickets in advance and for the price of the ticket, people could dance all evening. This plan was used for name bands and it certainly was a saving considering the cost of performers today. You could see Guy Lombardo for 90 cents at the Crystal, Jimmy or Tommy Dorsey for a $1 and Gene Krupa for ninety-eight cents when they came to the Pier.

The Park Plan sold tickets for 10 cents a dance set. I remember serving as a volunteer usher letting dancers on and off the floor at the Pier in my early teens. People would buy tickets for dances and then return to the roped areas and wait for the next dance. The floor cleared and the process started again. For me, there was more excitement when I went to the boat dock at Crab Baker's to head back seven miles across the lake to our cottage. My canvas deck racing hull was old and leaked like a sieve and my 5

Baritone saxophonist Jim Booker of Lancaster, OH (shown here at left with the US Army's 44th Division Dance Band in 1954) played with a number of big bands. Photo courtesy of Jim Booker.

horse Johnson didn't generate much speed. I think I weighed as much as the boat. The previous owner had actually painted the boat with orange polka dots on the bow area. He said he wanted to be seen under water if he went down! Night after night I'd find the boat nearly sunk at the dock at 1 a.m. and I'd bail enough that I was only up to my ankles in water. Crab watched out for me. He left a hand pump on the dock and told me "you have to buy one or one day you're not going to make it." What he didn't know was that my parents DIDN'T know the boat leaked and I wasn't about to tell them because I thought I'd lose the boat and my free ushering gig at the Pier!

"The ballrooms were big, but they tried not to let more than one hundred dancers on the floor at one time. There were no tables or chairs then, just benches along the wall. If you did not want to dance you could come in and listen for no charge. This made playing for dancers rough, as the band had to play twelve sets an hour with a fast and slow song having to be played every five minutes. There were no 'breaks' for the band, no intermissions. Band members could get a five minute break but the band 'played on'. . . . Never a lull in the music. Eventually, the ballrooms . . . switched to the Social Plan and put in tables and chairs," Donna remembers.

Shortly after the ballrooms opened you could buy six dances for a quarter and Mondays were special evenings between 6 p.m. and 8 p.m. for kids.

Both ballrooms were far less fashionable than their city counterparts. They were sparsely decorated as compared to Chicago's Aragon, for example. Yet both took on a different glimmer and glow at night when large mirrored balls hanging from their ceilings reflected a myriad of colored lights produced by spotlights. There were sideboards around the outside walls so that both could benefit from lake breezes when the weather was warm. No question the breeze let the music waft onto the lake and sidewalks and brought people to the facilities too.

George Dale McFarland of Hebron, OH, can close his eyes and see it like it was yesterday. "I really enjoyed dancing at the Crystal and the Lake Breeze dance halls at Buckeye Lake. But I missed many of the big bands when I was in the Air Force from 1942 to 1945. I do remember dancing to Deacon Moore's band. Those were great days," he told me.

Like so many Central Ohioans, George's mind keeps a clear memory of what Buckeye Lake Park was like. "Even though the physical park is gone, it still lives in the pictures and very vivid memories of those of us whose lives were enriched by its presence. If you close your eyes, you can still hear the sounds of the roller coaster, the shrieks of the riders, the big band sounds floating over the summer breezes, the boats on the lake and the laughter of the crowds," he wrote.

I hear the same sounds.

The music came from some of the best of the traveling big bands, too. Henry Jerome, who gained notoriety in the 1930s and '40s at the Edison Hotel and remotes with ABC, stopped by on a string of one nighters. He reorganized his band in 1944 and his new band, which actually featured some bop arrangements thanks to Johnny Mandel, may have had two later White House appointments playing in the sax section. Former Chairman of the Federal Reserve Alan Greenspan once played bass clarinet and ex-Richard Nixon White House counsel Leonard Garment played sax in the Jerome band.

Trumpeter Ray Anthony brought his big band to the Crystal and Pier a number of times during the 1940s and '50s. After spending four years leading a Navy band, Ray came back to start a Glenn Miller sounding band and parlay hits like "Peter Gunn," "The Bunny Hop" and "Harbor Lights" as well as a swinging version of the popular TV show theme "Dragnet" into more success. He continued as a big band leader long after the era was over.

I had a brief interview with Ray in early 2002 and he told me that he couldn't "remember a time when music wasn't a part of my life. Music puts wings on the human soul. Nothing can touch people the way music can. And every day is a new opportunity to create, change, stretch and reach for new heights doing something that I absolutely love – entertaining people through great music."

His life offers plenty of proof. He began playing in the family orchestra in Cleveland at 5, was 1st trumpet in the young Glenn Miller band at 18 and 5 years after WWII, his band, which included his brother Leo, was voted the number one dance band in the United States by all the trade polls from 1950 to 1955.

A leader more amused with his success and his big band career was Blue Barron who graduated from nearby Ohio State. He started as a booking agent but noted the success of leaders like Guy Lombardo, Sammy Kaye and Kay Kyser and in '36, formed his own band. His music styling was called "Music of Yesterday and Today, Styled the Blue Barron Way." His major hit came in 1949 when I saw the band at the Pier and I think it played "Cruisin' Down the River" at least a dozen times that evening. The number was in the top slot on the Hit Parade for seven weeks and helped him keep a lucrative deal with RCA and MGM records. About six years later, Harry Friedland – aka Blue Barron – disbanded but worked from time to time in the early 1960s.

Johnny Long's sweet, smooth sounding band was pleasing to Central Ohio dancers in the 1940s and '50s, too. Long came from Duke as did Les Brown but they had little relationship to one another. Les organized the Blue Devil band while Johnny helped create and later led a band called The Duke Collegians. Long's band actually replaced The Blue Devils and stayed intact when they graduated. Everyone remembers the story, I'm sure. Johnny was the victim of a farming accident near his Parkersburg, WVA home at 6 and he lost two fingers from his right hand. It would have ended his violin playing years had it not been for a violin teacher who worked with him to reconfigure his playing to his left hand. The Long Orchestra was a society pleaser from its first appearance without a name on a Friday evening in October, 1931 at the Alspaugh Dormitory Open House on the Duke campus. As the war years created more demand for soft, danceable music with vocals by Bob Houston and Helen Young, the band, which formed the famous Long Glee Club, produced several big hits including the world famous "The White Star of Sigma Nu" theme which made it a popular collegiate band and the peppy "In A Shanty in Old Shanty Town" which was the band's signature until Johnny retired from the business in the 1960s. However, it was a quirky songwriter named Norridge Mayhams who probably catapulted the Long band up the ladder. Mayhams wrote a song entitled "We'll Build a Bungalow" (with war bonds and stamps) in 1942, according to the Amateur Song Poem Music Archives, and Johnny's band recorded the number in 1949 with changes to meet post-war United States. By early 1950, the tune went to number 22 on the Billboard list.

While some critics and reviews that I've read claim Johnny's sound was both swing and sweet, I'd suggest that his popularity at Buckeye Lake was definitely as a sweet band that could offer some novelty numbers but it certainly didn't give Benny Goodman, Woody Herman or other swing bands much competition.

The band got a great career launch in 1939 when it appeared on the national radio program The Fitch Summer Bandwagon Show. The Old Shanty number recorded for Decca followed in 1940 and the Long group was considered a band with a future. In the early days, Johnny attracted talent from Jack Teagarden, Goodman and a stack of arrangements from Miller arranger Jerry Gray just after he left the service.

Chuz Alfred of Lancaster, OH was a popular bandleader in Central Ohio. Here's Chuz (far left) on the cover of his album "Jazz Young Blood."

During his frequent appearances at Buckeye Lake's two ballrooms Johnny was promoting a new career besides leading a band. In 1941 and '42 he did some Hollywood musical shorts with other name bandleaders entitled "Meet the Bandleaders" and he did some lines in these 15 minute films. In movies like "Swingin' at the Séance" and "RKO Jamboree" he played himself and his band offered the musical backdrop. Jamboree was re-issued in 1947 and I saw the band at the Pier the same week I saw the short feature at a hometown theater.

He became an actor-bandleader in 1943 with the release of "Hit the Ice" with Bud Abbott, Los Costello and Ginny Simms, an unrated plotless 89 minutes of typical Abbott/Costello mayhem that gave Long a few lines. Later the same year he returned to Hollywood with his band to do a patriotic movie called "Follies Girl" and, once again, a few lines on camera. Like Glenn Miller, he played himself in all the movies in which he appeared. Unlike Glenn, however, his movies received little attention after release dates and remained unrated. But Johnny Long's image as a clean cut college band fit Buckeye Lake's growing crowd of college age and military service dancers.

Buckeye Lake dancers enjoyed several other bands with distinctive soft sounds although both could easily play up tempo numbers. Trumpeter Charlie Spivak, an immigrant from Kiev, Ukraine, brought his band to the lake to play both the Pier and the Crystal in the 1940s and '50s. Charley had played with the Dorseys and Ben Pollack, Bob Crosby and while lead trumpeter for Tommy Dorsey, Glenn Miller urged him to organize his own band. Like Benny Goodman who financed Harry

Louie Armstrong played and sang with his signature handkerchief at Buckeye Lake's Skateland to a crowd of more listeners than dancers in 1960.
Photo Courtesy of Great Buckeye Lake Museum

James, Glenn backed Charley and while the first band folded . . . the second struck a chord with ballrooms and dancers. When I saw him in the early 1950s, the band had trombonist Urbie Green, Charley's wife, singer Irene Daye and Nelson Riddle. Drummer Davey Tough had been with the band, so were Les and Larry Elgart at one time. I can still hear Charley's trumpet standing outside the Crystal on one of his popular numbers "Stardreams."

Ralph Flanagan, a pianist-arranger, led another popular Buckeye Lake band as the big band era began to slide. To many, Flanagan merely copied the Miller sound . . . but his work and connections (he arranged for Blue Barron, Alvino Rey, Boyd Raeburn, Gene Krupa, Tony Pastor among many others) and the strong backing of Victor and Bluebird record companies gave him a quick promotional lift few bands received in the early 1950s. He gave us Miller likenesses "Harbor Lights" and "Nevertheless" and he created pop numbers that caught the public's attention such as "Slow Poke," "Rag Mop," "Hot Toddy" and "Flanagan's Boogie." He could entertain a crowd as he did the night I saw him at the Crystal. And from time to time, I remember he mentioned his Buckeye roots were in Lorraine, OH in the eastern part of the state.

In fact, Ohio may have had it all in those days. It had musical celebrity Ted Lewis of nearby Circleville ("Is Everybody Happy?") who led bands in Ohio from 1910 to 1915 and played Buckeye Lake before my days and then left to make far bigger money in New York City and elsewhere. His crazy antics, his battered top hat and clarinet styling made him the Spike Jones novelty band of the early dance era.

Cedar Point was a top dancing spot and so was King's Island, Cincinnati too. In 2005, Theme Parks Magazine rated the two locations one and two in a readers' choice contest. Band bookers I talked to said that during the 1940s agencies would try to get Cedar Point on Lake Erie and Cincinnati locations for weekends and add Buckeye Lake's Pier and Crystal Ballrooms late in week or a follow up night after an appearance in the state.

One of the first big bands I saw at the lake was a dapper trumpet player who was considered a terrific horn man leading a powerful, swinging band. Harry James, a former circus trumpet player who was taught by his bandmaster father, drew crowds throughout the 1940s whether his gorgeous wife with the great legs, Betty Grable, was in town or not. James had one of those loud bands that could play soft . . .but could bring dancers to the floor with a powerful beat . . . and minutes later, he could offer a ballad that could sooth as easily as a Jan Garber, Freddie Martin or others. His hits like "You Made Me Love You," "You Turned the Tables On Me," "How Deep Is the Ocean" and "These Foolish Things" could be balanced on any one-nighter with good beat numbers like "Back Beat Boogie," "Ultra," "One O'Clock Jump" and jitterbuggers swarmed on the floor. Harry's sense of the beat was quickly noted. He started as a drummer in his father's circus group. Later, rumor was that Harry actually set the tempo from the trumpet section for Benny Goodman when he was with the Goodman band in the 1930s.

The Albany, GA native and his band appropriately called the "Merry Makers" caught CBS' attention when airchecks gave the network positive feedback on the west coast. During the winter of 1948-49, the James Band was spotlighted at the Hollywood Palladium. Veteran trumpet player Neal Hefti told a reporter that "I played the Palladium twice with Harry James, twice with Woody Herman, twice with Charley Spivak and once with Ziggy Elman – all good solid bands – and nobody drew more than Harry."

The reason? While schmaltzy to some, James was one of the top commercially successful bands in the business. In 1942, the band broke crowd records at both the Palladium on the west coast and Meadowbrook in the east. George T. Simon, the legendary jazz and big band critic of the era, raved about Harry's magnetism with crowds. According to George ". . . the day it was to open a $12,500 a week engagement at New York's Paramount Theater was a nasty, rainy one. The doors were to open at a quarter of ten. At five in the morning the lines began forming, and if a batch of extra police hadn't arrived there could have been a riot." The same year Harry took Glenn Miller's title as America's Number One orchestra on Martin Block's popular "Make Believe Ballroom."

While Harry was praised by critics for having one of the best if not the best swing bands of the 1940s, he had mood swings far beyond his music. James band members found him fiscally tight although it was generally reported he spent lavishly on himself . . . even when times were bad. Like so many bandleaders of the era, Harry was said to have started his band with a meager $400 in his bank account and loan of several thousand from a bandleader known to be as tight with money, Benny Goodman. He became obsessed with baseball, teams, players and his own pick-up team which would play anyone, anywhere to win. Some said he'd continually ask new musicians "what do you play?" He wasn't talking about instruments. . . he wanted to know what position on the field! One pick up game the day of an engagement caused the band bus to get stuck in the mud and never get to the night's performance.

Every time I saw him I expected to see Betty Grable too. Didn't happen. Betty was a big band singer, of course, but she sang for Ted Fio Rito not Harry.

Tenor saxophonist Jim Booker vividly remembers what it was like to be a musician playing a gig at the lake. "In the summer of 1952 or '53, I played on the Dick Buntz Band, house band at the Pier. I was pleased to be on the band that played the lake but I was a bit of an outsider. At least three or four were from Ohio University and they rented a house or cabin at the lake and lived there that summer. . . I drove to the lake from Lancaster daily to rehearse . . . I remember that Dick wrote the arrangements for the band and that he had played with a 'name' or 'semi-name' band. . . Clyde McCoy, I think."

With the excitement of playing a "lake gig," came the reality of the business, he added. "The engagement was to be for the summer but after a month or two Pier management decided we were not drawing a big enough crowd and the engagement ended."

Like others, Jim felt the ambiance of the ballrooms went beyond the dance floor. "I have fond memories of the great sounds of some of those big bands. One night I was with a group of high school friends at a park across the lake from the Pier Ballroom and the sounds of the band floated across to us. Apparently coming across the water made the music sound even better because I cannot remember big band music sounding more beautiful."

The Pier received national notoriety when Billboard magazine asked ballroom operators and big band promoters around the country to select the best bands in 1940. Manager Doc Perkins and his associates chose Ben Bernie, Deacon Moore and Jan Garber and said that Garber, Ace Brigode and Russ Morgan drew good crowds, too. Park management at both ballrooms knew one thing for sure; a young crowd that came to dance was a crowd that spent money. Big bands typically drew about 2,000 a night when they appeared and I was one of a number of "volunteer" helpers who was eager to

Buckeye Lake's Grand Opening at Danceland brought Benny Goodman for one night in June. You couldn't beat the price. . . . 75 cents plus tax in advance at Heaton's Varsity Drug Store.

Photo courtesy of the Greater Buckeye Lake Museum

work wherever they wanted me and that kept the number of paid employees low at the ballrooms. . . and profits certainly reasonable.

I played a Crystal engagement with another familiar Central Ohio band, Dick Trimble, in the early 1950s. I remember it because I thought it had a bigger bandshell than the Pier. I also remember it for another reason. . . I went to the ballroom by myself in the only car that could carry a set of Slingerlands drums – my fire engine red 1950s Dodge convertible – but I didn't have my Palm Beach white sports jacket on that Dick's band wore at the time. Consequently, the ticket taker wouldn't let me in without paying. Someone finally got a hold of a band member . . . and he vouched for my player status. Uniforms could be your ID in larger places although those of us who played at the territorial level didn't have many sports coats or pants outfits. Certainly nothing to top Jimmy Lunceford's touring big band. Jazz critic Stanley Dance once reported that Willie Smith, a great alto saxophonist with Lunceford, told him that if the band did seven shows in a day. . . it changed uniforms seven times! Not just coats either. Ties, pants, socks and even shoes.

NPR's David Miller of Swingin' Down the Lane fame believed that uniforms

Here's a posterboard of the big bands that visited Buckeye Lake's ballrooms during the early 1950s.
Photo courtesy of the Greater Buckeye Lake Museum

were a must for touring big bands and certainly an added expense, too. "It was just taken for granted that the band would dress up for a gig just as a college marching band does. The antics were few and far between and I don't think they did anything except add a bit of pizzazz to the band's presentation. Lunceford was a past master at the visual effect of section men moving their instruments in intricate patterns and it had to add to the appeal of the band from a visual standpoint. Ditto Glenn Miller who borrowed the idea from Lunceford." Trombone players in Miller's band did complain years later that tossing their instruments in the air while holding the slide could be dangerous. Ralph Martiere once had a baritone sax player who, while playing a honking solo, got down on his back and played his horn while holding it with his feet. Showmanship was vogue.

I also remembered a not too subtle sign by the Crystal Ballroom ticket and pool ticket office that said "Caucasians Only." Over the years I've thought about that placard and the "Negro Nights" when some great music came to Buckeye Lake and its ballrooms. Like so many counties, towns and amusement parks in America, Buckeye Lake was caught in the racism of the time. And it took time to heal. One of the lake's nightmares occurred in August, 1928 when the Muskingum Colored Elks #82 held its day at the Lake Breeze Hotel and Pier and the ballroom collapsed drowning seven and injuring dozens.

My gig at the lake that summer brought me back the next night when Woody Herman and the Third Herd was scheduled to play. I had a date with a young lady I had talked to the night before. We agreed to meet at the ballroom (my transportation was boat not a car at the time) because all I knew was that her home was in nearby Thornville and she had her own car and worked at the park. She "dug" the Herman band unlike other dates. She knew the names of soloists and she even hummed the "shout phrases" the band used on numbers like "Apple Honey," "Calidonia," "Wildroot" and "Bijou" and other fabled Herman charts. We danced and talked through Woody's closing theme "Blue Flame" and then we took a ride in my boat (always a show stopper for young women, a young guy with his own cruiser).

The Herman band was my kind of musicians; drummer Art Mardigan, bassist Red Kelly who had replaced Chubby Jackson and pianist Nat Pierce. What made them different? None of them read music and yet they played with fluency on every number. I loved Woody's comment later. He was asked why he would hire sidemen who weren't readers. "I don't hire my rhythm section to read. I hire'em to swing," he told Gene Lees in his book, "The Leader of the Band: The Life of Woody Herman" (Replica Books, 1995)

Years later, Woody told PBS more about his philosophy as a bandleader. His first band was actually five members of popular leader Isham Jones' band which folded in the mid-1930s.

"Isham wasn't a stickler for much. You could come on (the bandstand) with the wrong uniform or out of it but boy you better not hit no wrong notes or it's you and me out back!" he said. Isham impressed the young Milwaukee clarinetist because, he said, there were leaders out there who were more into rules than music. Woody continued Isham's commitment to the performance not social conduct during his years on the stand. Among the great talent he acquired were problem players, too. One young and gifted trumpet player was hired on the third Herd in 1950 with a solo salary of $400 a week – big money in that day – but his alcohol abuse forced even Woody to have to let him go when he showed up so smashed he virtually collapsed on the stand.

"We started out with nothing but charts. It was so bad that we gave guys stock in the band just to join us – if you were nutty enough – and we didn't know where the next gig would come from," Woody laughed. He wasn't satisfied with his own playing but he respected good players and tried to keep them. "I was never happy with my playing and later with my store bought teeth it didn't get better either."

But the crowd "dug" him and his band like my Crystal Ballroom date did one summer night in 1949. Ten years after he started at the Roseland Ballroom in Brooklyn,

NY, the band grossed a cool million. Sadly, Woody Herman died virtually penniless.

Booker has memories of dancing and just being among the crowds that squeezed into the ballrooms when the bands were in town. "I remember the pleasure of hearing big band music, dancing and socializing with girls. I can remember standing up close to the bandstand to listen to the music and watching the musicians. They looked 'cool' to an aspiring young musician. And, although people came to those dances from a number of different cities and towns I don't remember that there ever any unpleasantries even when it was crowded," he said.

The 1950s were the twilight period for the big bands but there were a number of great bands playing and it wasn't unusual for one name band to be at the Pier and another at the Crystal the same evening.

I never thought anyone but my friends and I would find someone fondly remembering Buckeye Lake's ballrooms but I recall my trip on a military transport flying from Seoul, Korea, to Tachikawa Air Force Base, Japan, in 1957-58 accompanying Les Brown, his band, Bob Hope and Jerry Colonna. In a quick exchange of pleasantries he asked where I was from and I told him Ohio and then mentioned I had seen the Band of Renown at Buckeye Lake. "Buckeye Lake. . . hey, guys," he said to several sitting near him, "remember the Pier? That was a fun night. . . I remember Buckeye Lake. We had to squeeze to get 16 guys and our singers on that bandstand. Great crowd though," he told me.

Carolyn Walters Ziebell of California has her own memories of the bands at Buckeye Lake but for different reasons. "I especially remember Keely Smith and Louis Prima. Also the great sounds of Ray Anthony. We would dance for hours and be soaking wet. . . but such fun! I literally danced my way through college.

"Being one of the 'older' sisters at Ohio University, I was often asked to chaperone. I loved it when the featured band would do the Bunny Hop. Everyone could participate. My parents were pretty strict during high school days and didn't approve of my going out of town on a date. Of course, I was guilty of not always telling them where I went either. "

No question, Ohioans loved to dance. Not long before her death, 112-year-old Mary Margaret Smith, who was the oldest Ohioan and the 6th oldest American in 2006, told The Associated Press reporters who interviewed her that her long life was the result of years on the dance floors. The Ashtabula (OH) Star-Beacon reported that Smith and her husband frequently attended dances in the region and they were winners of dancing contests during their younger days. Her comments echoed the excitement my mother, Dorothy Pairan, would demonstrate when the conversation turned to music. Before her marriage, Dorothy worked weekdays to enjoy Friday and Saturday nights dancing sometimes until dawn at fraternity and college functions. "We didn't have much money during the Depression and my friends and I didn't go drinking like the men did. We spent our time learning all the new Tin Pan Alley numbers so we could sing them as well as dance to them. We'd get a table and nurse a soft drink among us for hours to dance," she laughed.

Betty Perkins Mercer, daughter of the Lake Breeze Hotel and Pier Ballroom Manager Doc Perkins, enjoyed meeting the musical celebrities. While working as a coat check girl she remembers Glenn Miller's petite young singer Betty Hutton. "While we waited for the band to start playing one night a young lady walked by. She had plenty of makeup and her hair was blond. I remember her dress looked like it needed a wash. That was Betty Hutton. . . and could she sing! It was such a great place to grow up. . . because I loved to dance. . . and I still do. . ."

John "Red" Imhoff of Florida recalls moments that had more to do with the celebrities than the music, too. "I remember a time at the Crystal when I was two or three tables behind the bandstand and I heard Billy May and Tommy Dorsey talking. They were discussing an arrangement and I was fascinated as a guy who played trumpet would be listening to two brass players. Another time I remember I sneaked into the Crystal one afternoon when Johnny Bothwell (Boswell) was rehearsing the full band," he says.

Not long before her death, 112-year-old Mary Margaret Smith, told Associated Press reporters that her long life was the result of years on the dance floors.

I was there when Sammy Kaye, then a name bandleader who had grown up in Cleveland and gone to college at Ohio University, was at the Pier for a one nighter. He was always associated with the mickey mouse bands touring in the '40s but Kaye had gained a national reputation for hits like "Harbor Lights," 1937; "Daddy," 1941 and "There Will Never Be Another You," 1942. He was different from other bandleaders I had observed just feet away from the bandstand. Claude Thornhill was much more distant, I thought, so was Vaughn Monroe although the night I saw his band he was surrounded by others and he disappeared off the bandshell from time to time. Monroe did his Camel Caravan radio show coast to coast from the lake thanks to Cincinnati's WLW radio station. And I paid $2 to see Monroe and only $1 to watch either one of the Dorseys! Buckeye Lake was among those early ballrooms to do the famous radio remotes that you heard from the major city sites like Glen Island Casino, the Meadowbrook in New York and New Jersey, the Aragon in Chicago or the Hollywood Palladium in California, thanks to Cincinnati's WLW and NBC. The broadcasts were done four nights a week from June until after Labor Day at the Pier Ballroom.

Monroe was originally from Akron, OH when his father worked at a rubber processing factory but the family moved to Cudahy, WI and later to Pennsylvania. Like a few other bandleaders he started college after he was voted the high school senior "most likely to succeed" at the prom. But he also won a trumpet contest at the same time. While he wanted a professional career and toyed with engineering he enrolled at Carnegie Tech's School of Music and later took vocal training at the New England Conservatory of Music in Boston.

He worked with several territorial bands before he got married and promptly started rehearsing a Vaughn Monroe band. He opened in April, 1940, and with the band's first radio broadcast from Siler's Ten Acres in New England, RCA-Victor signed him to a record contract. His voice and his trumpet and trombone playing never caused him to look back.

Kaye was a likeable leader with a collegiate attitude really. He formed his own band at Ohio University while studying civil engineering and washing dishes at a girls' dormitory. He had to make enough to add to his track scholarship to pay for his public education. He played football and went on to become an engineering graduate, kept his band and never returned to his college major. He was a decent saxophone player and clarinetist but didn't appear interested in featuring himself when I saw the band.

Imhoff remembers that Monroe made it clear a gig was a gig. "I remember watching him walking into the Pier Ballroom at 9:30 p.m. carrying a full set of golf clubs. And he sang until midnight and then picked up the golf clubs and marched out."

Drummer Gene Krupa who played both the Pier and Crystal a number of times during the '40s was nice enough to buy me a Coke and demonstrate how different he was off the bandshell. A very affable, diminutive guy I found him rather shy considering his show business image at the time. Said Donna Braig in her book, the Krupa band and Gene loved to swim in the Crystal Pool behind the ballroom. Sometimes, she said, permission was given to open the pool after 1 a.m. for the band.

Donna remembers the rumor and buzz that two music celebrities supposedly honeymooned at Buckeye Lake after playing a gig at the Crystal. Ozzie and Harriet Nelson, who more than a decade later became the first family of ABC TV with their own show, played the lake but, said ABC publicists, were unlikely to have honeymooned in the Midwest after their marriage Oct. 8, 1935 in Hackensack, NJ. The park would have been closed after Labor Day, they theorized. Furthermore, the Nelsons were riding a crest of popularity at the time and would have been unlikely to leave the Northeast in the fall or winter with a busy schedule of gigs and recordings for an off-season trip to the Midwest, the publicity people said.

Meanwhile, Marty Frankenbery has that special memory of one who grew up on the north shore of Buckeye. "I remember the All in One Restaurant situated next to the entrance to the Dips. At 15, I was the grill cook then. I was really too young to work (as many of us were) at the park so when state inspectors came around, the park office sent an employee to tell me to take a walk. From as early as I can remember I could hear the bands from my bedroom window on a summer night. All of us (Paula Kirk, Betty Perkins and I) worked at the Pier and we saw all the big bands when they came each summer." Today Marty is among those who volunteer at the Greater Buckeye Lake Museum which offers visitors' scenes and memorabilia of a past none of us will forget.

Some visitors remember the beginning of lifetime relationships at the park's dance pavilions in the early to mid 20th century. "Who can guess how many romances began as couples danced to the lilting strains of Guy Lombardo and his Royal Canadians, (or) the Tommy and Jimmy Dorsey Orchestras. . . . One thing is certain, though, and that is that the Pier Ballroom . . . and the beautiful Crystal Ballroom were the symbols of a bygone age when dancing was a favorite form. . . of recreation. Thousands of couples from Licking, Franklin, and cities like Columbus, Zanesville, Newark, Lancaster, Coshocton, Mount Vernon and towns in surrounding states came to Buckeye Lake during the 1930s, 40s into the early 1970s," David Shinn wrote in an article entitled "Buckeye Lake Glory Days" in the May, 1998, issue of Licking Countian.

Shinn added that park officials believed that "some 10,000 people passed through the gates . . . daily in its heyday during the 1940s."

Buckeye Lake veterans recall that while the park appeared to be one happy family to visitors, it was a competitive place to those who worked there. The Pier Ballroom, for example, was owned by Carl Carlin and James Gratziano and it was managed by Perkins. A.M. Brown managed the Crystal and local bandleaders knew the punishment for crossing either one. If you did gigs at the Pier it wasn't wise to solicit work at the Crystal. The same was true if you worked the Crystal. One bandleader said it was like an imaginary line drawn through the park. You knew instinctively when you crossed it.

By the late 1960s any visitor from the past would have known the end was near.

The place along the lake once called the "Playground of Ohio" was a debris filled collection of acres. Today it is an empty field.

Playground of Ohio: Buckeye Lake's Two Ballrooms Bibliography

Chuz Alfred
letter, Jan. 23, 2003

Chuz Alfred
"Dick Trimble and His Bands: 1948-1951" no date

Donna Braig
My Buckeye Lake Story (New Concord Press, 2002)

Carolyn Ziebell
email March 6, 2005

Ray Anthony
www.parabrisis.com/d_anthonyr.php

Henry Jerome
www.parabrisis.com/d_jeromeh.php

Blue Barron
www.parabrisis.com/d_barronb.php

Jim Booker
letters, March 26, 2005; April 28, 2005

Betty Perkins Mercer
undated letter, 2005

Paula Kirk, letter
Feb. 7, 2005

"Dancing . . . Beach to Beach,"
Sherry Beck Paprocki, Country Living, May, 1998

Buckeye Lake's Glory Days
Dave Shinn, Licking Countain, undated

The Halycon Daily Review
Shep Fields Novelty, Sweet Band, undated

Buckeye Lake Then and Now
Lancaster Eagle-Gazette, July 30, 1991

Dick Trimble's Band Uniforms
Lancaster Eagle-Gazette, undated

George Dale McFarland
letter, Feb, 9, 2005
http://gmcnow.www5.50megs.com/buckeyelake/id6.htm

Aircheck tapes,
WHOK, 1949-52 Dick Westbrook, Lancaster, OH

John "Red" Imhoff
email, 3.27/2005

"Magic of Buckeye Lake Park Lives on in the Hearts and Memories of Thousands,"
Dale McFarland, undated story

Marty Frankenbery
letters, 5/02/04; 3/17/2005

"Swing and Sway Started Right There,"
Lakewood Sun Post, Dec. 21, 1989

Sammy Kaye
www.sammykayeorchestra.com February, 22, 2006

Peter J. Levinson
"Trumpet Blues:The Life of Harry James" (Oxford Press, 1999

David Miller
Swingin' Down the Lane, email undated

"Big Bands Found Home at Coney,"
by Nick Clooney, The Cincinnati Post, OH Feb. 28, 2000.

http://nfo.net/usa/12.html
American Big Bands Database (Johnny Long)

www.rottentomatoes.com/m/follies_girl
(Johnny Long films)

"Life's Dance Ends for Oldest Ohioan,"
AP, The Canton (OH) Repository, May 25, 2006

"Leader of the Band: The Life of Woody Herman,"
Gene Lees, Replica Books, 1995

www.songpoemmusic.com/labels/mayhams.htm

www.answers.com Johnny Long

The Story of Vaughn Monroe,
1945 promotional from the Vaughn Monroe Society
www.vaughnmonroesociety.org

Paul Miller,
"Lancaster (OH); What A Town, What a Time!" Naneare Publishing, 2000

Songs of World War II
Big Band Database http://64.33.34.112/WWW/ww2.html

Vaughn Monroe Big Band Era Singer
www.vaughnmonroesociety.org

Farming in the 1940s

www.Livinghistoryfarm.org March 18, 2005

THE PALLADIUM
WHERE EVERYONE WANTED TO PLAY

If you look over a roster of big bands and noted players from the 1930s to the 1950s, you'll get the feeling that every other musician on the West Coast was from some place in the East or Midwest. The westward migration editor Horace Greeley talked about a century earlier took a while . . . but it happened.

Listen to Bud Shank, a talented saxophonist with a number of great bands from the era and a leader himself, describe how he finally made his way from a farm in Dayton, OH:

"From the time I was fourteen until I entered college we moved around a lot as my father was in the army at that time. . .up until maybe 1963, I was always working with a group of my own, on the road or in Los Angeles. . . In the early fifties when I first became a professional musician and went to Los Angeles jazz musicians across the board were not permitted to be on a film score. I guess it was the period 1973-74 that whole thing turned around; there was new interest in what jazz musicians were, especially guys who had been around in the fifties. . . . In the late forties, the jam session was a big thing with clubs around here. Clubs would hire a rhythm section then have the horn players come by and sit in. You could almost do it five or six days a week, traveling all over the area. You never got paid for it but you sure did play a lot."

What made the West Coast the mecca?

Bud said the whole West Coast jazz thing in the 1950s had a connection to the Stan Kenton band. Shorty Rogers, Shelly Manne, Bob Cooper were in Los Angeles and everything and everybody gravitated around working at the Lighthouse with Howard Rumsey. There was more sophistication among jazz musicians and what they were attempting to do at the time.

The difference between the two coasts as he witnessed it?

"In New York, things were a little bit more fiery and less regimented. I hate to say less sophisticated because it was still sophisticated in its own way. There was an obvious difference between what was going on in Los Angeles and what was going on in New York."

There were a few significant differences for musically inclined youngsters of my generation living in the Midwest. The coasts, Downbeat Magazine showed us, had exciting cities like New York City and Los Angeles filled with opportunities (later we discovered that was a myth) and just a bus, train or car trip away. Of course, if you didn't find work of some kind waiting for your chance (or after you had your chance and failed) how could you go home and face the folks? I convinced myself that my father would have changed the locks on the doors and accepted no long distance calls had I left. That rationale and a reality check kept a good number of us home. It shelved my dreams.

Yet, trombonist Frank Rosolino is one of those gifted few who let music be his guide after his military service in World War II. His gift was seen at Cass Tech High School in Detroit, a school that took only the exceptional students from throughout the city. In a biography of the late horn man he told how he joined the bands of Bob Chester and Glen Gray and, in 1948, was among the bop-influenced musicians playing with Gene Krupa. He later joined Kenton for several years. In 1954, he decided to settle in California and divide his time between studio and jazz work.

Said Gene Lees in his book "Meet Me At Jim's & Andy's" (Oxford Press) "Frank was among the best-loved men in jazz. One of the finest trombone players in the history of the instrument, he had a superb tone, astonishing facility, a deep Italianate lyricism and rich invention. Frank was very simply, a sensational player." And he was a very funny guy too. Which made his self-inflicted death at 52 in his Van Nuys home in late November, 1978, so tragic and still unexplained to his friends and the police.

Los Angeles, Hollywood, good weather most of any year, friends and enough glitter to last anyone a lifetime could be as powerful as any addiction.

It remains so today and has so many alluring attractions.

There's that sign HOLLYWOOD that still greets people either on television or when you get into the city and look up into the hills. It has its own story, too.

The web site, "Frankie Goes to Hollywood." (www.midnightinsanity.com/Hollywood/HollywoodSites.htm says the sign was originally constructed in the 1920s to promote a housing development called Hollywoodland. But it not only promoted promise for the rich and famous . . . it also brought death for those who didn't find a future. A struggling actress leaped to her death and "sparked a rash of suicides by

The famous Palladium Ballroom in Hollywood, CA where every major touring band played at some time or another during the big band years. It was home for the Lawrence Welk television show for more than a decade.

Photo from Palladium web page

failed starlets" in the 1930s. You can't tell from a distance but the letters that spell out the sign are 45 feet tall and 30 feet wide. It became such a tarnished image and an embarrassment (repairs were discontinued in 1939) that the Chamber of Commerce authorized restoration and a number of people including legends like Gene Autry. Hugh Hefner and Andy Williams helped pay the $252,000 ($28,000 a letter) bill.

Certainly another fixture for me and a company I spent probably several thousands of dollars buying records to support was Capitol Records at 1750 North Vine Street.

Most of my favorite recording artists from the 1940s and '50s were on Capitol. In fact, I probably spent more because I bought replacement 45s when I wore out Kenton, Johnny Mercer. Freddy Slack and Ella Mae Morse vinyls.

Talk about a small business going gold! Songwriter Johnny Mercer got financial help from movie producer Buddy DeSylva and they enlisted the business knowledge of the biggest record store owner in Los Angeles, Glenn Wallichs, and opened, Capitol, the first West Coast label to compete with New York City-based giants like RCA-Victor, Columbia and Decca in 1942. In the middle of a global conflict with shortages of everything possible. . . starting a recording studio had to give investors heartburn!

The excitement, of course, was in their newly hired artists. First records were made with Paul Whiteman, still the established "King of Jazz," singers Martha Tilton and Ella Mae Morse. The first Capitol gold – Ella Mae's recording of "Cow Cow Boogie" – followed Glenn Miller's gold recording of "Chattanooga Choo Choo."

Ella and Freddie Slack teamed to do the number called "Cow Cow Boogie" and it sold seven figures plus. Freddie had just signed with the recording company and was desperately trying to keep a band together as the draft took key players, a shortage of gasoline cut into road tours and James C. Petrillo threatened a ban on recordings. Boogies were big thanks to Slack, trombonist Will Bradley and drummer Ray McKinley who put together every kind of boogie tune you could think of. There was "Boogie Woogie Maxixe," "Beat Me Daddy Eight to the Bar," "Rock-A-Bye the Boogie," "Scrub Me Mama with a Boogie Beat," "I Boogied When I Should Have Woogied," "Boogie Woogie Conga" and a few others when he played with Bradley's band. But "Cow Cow Boogie" wasn't his . . . Benny Carter wrote it. And what a difference it made for Freddie.

The ditty caught the public's attention, which, in turn, led his studio band to a series of national tours and gigs at Frank Dailey's Meadowbrook on the east coast.

In four years, Capitol sold 42 million and had such name stars as Les Baxter, Bing Crosby, Peggy Lee, Les Brown, Frank Sinatra and Nat "King" Cole. In a year, Judy Garland, The Andrew Sisters, Jackie Gleason, Ray Anthony, Andy Griffith, Martin Denny, The Kingston Trio, The Four Freshmen, Al Martino and Nancy Wilson along with the famous "Rat Pack" had signed. It got bigger and better, too. The Beach Boys, The Beatles, Jimi Hendrix, Bobby Darin, Pink Floyd, Linda Ronstadt, Grand Funk Railroad made the 1960s dwarf the early years.

The popularity of the company made the building that housed it more of an attraction. The Capitol Tower, built in 1956 by the company's new owner EMI of England, catches your attention immediately even in the neo everything landscape of Los Angeles. Supposedly Nat "King" Cole and Mercer suggested the building look like a stack of 45 records on a turntable. And it does. . . complete with curved awnings on windows of each of its 13 stories. When it was first built the light at the top blinked the Morse code "Hollywood." To celebrate its 50th birthday in 1992 it flashed "Capitol 50" in Morse Code but today it's back to "Hollywood." But the architecturally different looking building has made big band history nationally. . . not just in California.

The Hollywood Palladium, a ballroom that has a long history of big events, witnessed the great stars and the greatest big bands since it opened on October 29, 1940 just 66 years ago.

And the opening act in this Deco/Acro-modern dancing palace was a blockbuster at the time. The popular Tommy Dorsey Band with Frank Sinatra, Buddy Rich, Connie Haines filled the 40,700 square foot pavilion with a fire marshal sized crowd of 6,500 attending each show that night and spilling from the dining area to the dance floor to the mezzanine. Connie would never forget her 21st birthday celebrated at the Palladium either. No one said anything during the evening show and she and Jackie Cooper were planning to spend the evening together. Dorsey told the band and singers not to leave because they had to rehearse some new numbers right after the evening show. Lonely and unhappy about her aborted evening plans she went from her dressing room to the stage, Tommy led the band in "Happy Birthday" to her delight and there was a surprise party with a cake, friends like Lana Turner and others to help her celebrate "the kind of day and night one doesn't easily forget."

But it was Harry James in an eight-week engagement that began in April, 1942, who set an attendance and financial record, said Peter J. Levinson in his fascinating book, "Trumpet Blues: The Life of Harry James" (Oxford/1999). The James band drew 160,000 and made $88,000.

That had to have made Harry happy; he had borrowed $1,900 from Benny Goodman to start his band just a few years earlier . . . and paid him back with interest, $2,600 he told an interviewer in the 1970s.

Like other large dinner/dancing spots The Palladium had a great location. It was nestled between NBC and CBS studios which made it a terrific photo op for movie and television stars to drop by . . . and they did. You could probably find Ty Power, Lana Turner or Betty Grable among the crowd. And the prices were fire sale variety compared to today's $85 to $125 to see Jay-Z and Friends. For a $1 you could dine and dance and listen to the Dorsey band that historic Halloween evening. Woody Herman loved it, however, for another reason. Woody like to schedule The Palladium near the holidays so he could live at home and go to work like other people. He had bought Humphrey Bogart's home in the Hollywood Hills and he loved the commute and time with his family.

The Palladium had a great location ...
For a $1 you could dine and dance and
listen to the Dorsey band ...

Like its Chicago competitor the Aragon, the décor is of a historical era today but it still boasts an expansive powder room for ladies and a sizable gentlemen's lounge for men. Incidentally, don't confuse ballrooms called Palladium. The granddaddy was the London Palladium built in 1926, the New York City Palladium on 126th Street and the Manhattan Palladium on 53rd Street and there were probably several

Denver's Rainbow Ballroom was a frequent stop for major big bands on their way from the east to the west and return trips. Here's a popular band in the 1930s, Al Sky and his Musical Stars playing at the Rainbow.

Photo courtesy of James Ronan Collection, IA

hundred of the same name throughout the country at one time.

During World War II days, soldiers, sailors and airmen stationed at military bases near Hollywood were the envy of their peers. For 50 cents you could go to the Hollywood Canteen steps away and dance to live music by Glenn Miller, Artie Shaw, Les Brown, Harry James, Stan Kenton or a hundred or so other big bands

The radio broadcasts brought millions of others like me to the Palladium's 11,000 square foot dance floor vicariously.

The largest one night crowd? Says the Palladium web site: "Even after the war, when big bands began to lose their popularity, the Palladium still drew in a record 6,750 eager dancers to the January, 1947 opening night performance of Tex Beneke and the Glenn Miller Orchestra – an event enthusiastically covered by Life Magazine." Of course, not everyone shared the excitement once they got to the ballroom. Said one exasperated dancer: "It was fun but so smoky and loud that I didn't enjoy it that much. It was impossible to get close to the bandstand and that was a real disappointment."

Earlier the same year, Tex and the Glenn Miller band lit up the attendance meter in August when dancers at Moonlite Gardens, Cincinnati, paid $2 each to crowd the Ohio River ballroom. The band set record on that Friday evening with 4,728 people.

Beneke's talent as a tenor saxophonist and vocalist and his popular personality were showcased from the time he joined Miller's pre-war orchestra in the spring of 1938. They made him a natural choice to lead the post-war Miller band. Even Glenn wife's Helen agreed. There were others equally suitable like arranger Jerry Gray, drummer Ray McKinley, trumpeters Ray Anthony and Billy May who had been with Glenn but they weren't necessarily close to him.

Beneke, of course, didn't follow Glenn when he volunteered for military duty in the army air corps. Tex joined Horace Heidt when the Miller band folded and then enlisted in the US Navy and spent his service years leading a navy dance band in land locked Oklahoma.

The reorganization of the Miller band after the war with remnants of the military band was a shrewd business move although it was a calculated risk, too. The big band business was slipping fast as ballrooms closed. Beneke took over in late 1946, at New York City's Capital Theater and financial backers had their fingers crossed.

It was a different Miller band than stateside fans heard before the war. From 1938 to '42, Glenn had 15 to 16 pieces, a conventional band for the era. After the war, the band became one of the few largest traveling organizations (Harry James had the other) with 31 players including 13 violinists.

Tex, however, had more problems than he anticipated. Working with the Miller Estate became difficult. Helen and her lawyers wanted Glenn's reed-dominated sound perpetuated exactly as it was. "Something old, something new, something borrowed and something blue" became a haunting echo of the past. Tex wanted to innovate as did some band members. He even wanted to experiment with bop flavorings in the arrangements something he insisted Glenn told a number of people he wanted to do after the war. Richard Jessen in a web feature entitled "Glenn Miller: The Godfather of Bop?" claims that the popular bandleader recorded the first evidence of what would become "be-bop" in 1939 in a song written by Eddie Durham and "Taps" Miller called "Wham Re-Bop, Boom, Bam!"

Miller recorded it on the B side of a Bluebird label in August, 1939 long before Dizzy Gillespie and Charley Parker collaborated on a bop immortal "Salt Peanuts."

No question the sellout Palladium crowd for the '47 Miller band came to hear the traditional Miller sound. Yet, it forced Tex to make a choice in career directions. He left the Miller band a year later. Sadly, the estate responded in a less courteous manner. Tex was omitted from the 1954 movie, "The Glenn Miller Story." He had been a member of the band who was seen in both "Sun Valley Serenade" and "Orchestra Wives." In Sun Valley, Tex sang the famous "Chattanooga Choo Choo" with the Modernaires which, in fact, won the best song? In "Orchestra Wives" Tex sang "I've Got A Gal In Kalamazoo" with Marion Hutton and the Modernaires, a number singled out as the top original number in a film nominated for an Academy Award for Best Music.

To be left out of the band he had played a major role with while other Miller musicians and celebrities he knew such as Louie Armstrong, Gene Krupa, Ben Pollack, the Modernaires, Paula Kelly, Barney Bigard, Marty Napoleon, Arvell Shaw, Cozy Cole and Babe Russin who played themselves in the movie had to hurt.

Leo McElroy remembers The Palladium years later as an announcer for KFI radio when he worked the "Saturday Night Dance Party" broadcast on a regional network.

"It was mid to late 1960s, I guess, I got assigned to do the 9 p.m. live half-hour pick-up of Lawrence Welk from the Palladium. Then, while colleague Dick Sinclair did the 10 p.m. pick-up of Freddy Martin from the Coconut Grove of the Ambassador Hotel, I drove like hell to Glendora on the outskirts to do the 11 p.m. pick-up of Johnny Catron's big band from Glendora Palms. . . which was far and away the best live music of the night," he recalls.

"Doing Welk didn't take much skill. I would introduce the maestro, get off the stage, grab a bite to eat (free!) and I was back on stage in time to sign off. The musicians I talked to griped a lot about Welk's shlocky arrangements but it was steady work and they accepted the paychecks, " he remembers. " At the Glendora Palms, though, it was much more fun. I introduced the numbers and I was up with the band throughout the evening. We did that Saturday night gig for a couple of years as I guess. How did I get my training? Doing live pick-ups on CBS New Year's Eve parties in 1961-62 with Freddy Martin and Russ Morgan."

The '60s are also special memories for Leo.

"I was assigned by CBS to do a West Coast midnight pickup of Freddy Martin at the Santa Monica Pier on New Year's, 1962. I got there, checked with my engineer, checked the time, and as air time approached . . . I start getting nervous because I don't see Freddy. Five minutes to air and the band is on break. I ask where Freddy is and I'm directed to his dressing room where he's having a Scotch. He doesn't seem excited about the time at all. I go back out on stage and grab a musician begging him to get his buddies back on the stand. We're on the air now in less than a minute! Five seconds to air time, almost half of the orchestra is in place without Freddy and they strike up a very raggedly opener as I holler into my mike 'Live from the Aragon Ballroom at the Santa Monica Pier in Southern California. . . it's Freddy Martin and his Orchestra!' Seconds seem like minutes go by when Freddy strolls out mid-song, baton in hand, and begins leading the band like nothing had ever been in doubt. . . . I went to the bar and forestalled a nervous breakdown with a tall drink!"

The next year, Leo worked the Long Beach Hotel where Russ Morgan and 'Music in the Morgan Manner' were playing New Year's Eve. "Russ had a reputation for not wanting anyone but himself to talk but when I checked in, he's just finished listening to an East Coast bandleader and decided he had talked too much. So, I'm tapped to introduce most of the numbers. It's a small ballroom and a smaller bandstand so

Russ and I have to stand on the dance floor to do the show."

Working territory band pick-ups gave him a chance to listen to some fine music, too, Leo said. "By the mid-'60s I'm working at another station and doing Saturday nights with Welk and Johnny Catron. Catron was no household name but he was a fine bandleader with solid big band arrangements and top musicians who liked playing the good charts. Johnny was a Volkswagen dealer who ran the band and the nightclub on the side. A great guy, he drew lots of celebs out to Glendora to enjoy his music."

While Welk wasn't necessarily popular among swing musicians, he enjoyed their music and made sure later in his television shows to salute the big band leaders who had already disappeared from the scene. His "Champagne Music" gave him tremendous popularity as the decade of the 1960s began. He signed a lifetime contract with the Hollywood Palladium in 1961 and within 10 years was syndicated across North America. He had been a regular earlier at the old Aragon Ballroom off the coast and he considered it a tragic loss when the place burned down in 1970.

What made his truly American story so impressive was that he was a grade school dropout from an immigrant German family who had to work on the family farm until he repaid his father for the $400 accordion he bought mail-order. He kept his word.

His lack of musical training didn't diminish his optimism or enthusiasm.

An estimated 14,000 people came during his first two evenings at the Palladium. His popular TV show was done from the Palladium over the next years. And his commitment to his band and staff demonstrated the kind of person he was, too. When ABC cancelled his TV show in 1971, Lawrence, in his late 60s, refused to end the program and put over 200 people out of work. He became the show's producer and lined up more stations than ABC offered him before he left. The final program was completed in 1982.

The Palladium also provided us with great sounds for posterity, too. In the early 1950s crude monaural single track but very bulky tape recorders were appearing and just before the Labor Day weekend of 1953 Les Brown took his band to the Palladium bandstand for a three-week engagement. Gerry MacDonald, meanwhile, had built a stereo sound system unlike others and he persuaded Les to let him tape the Band of Renown's appearances. Les agreed and a historical moment came years later when Coral Records released a boxed two LP 33 1/3 album of the results of those Hollywood nights at the ballroom. But it was thanks to Bob Thiele that this first-ever recording of a live performance was produced from the actual format of the evenings. Unlike other recordings which cut soloists to

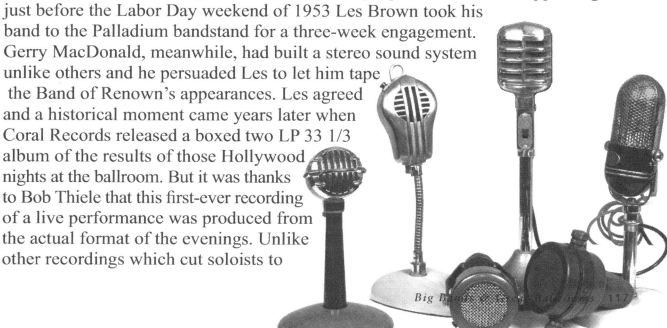

Big Bands and Great Ballrooms 117

brief passages and numbers to abbreviated songs, Thiele put no restrictions on the length of solos and the resounding enthusiasm of the audience.

Said Leonard Feather in his liner notes of the Brown Palladium nights:

"Through the entire (Big Band) era, Les . . . alone has continued to move along smoothly in a straight line. His changes in style and personnel have been minor; his popularity has persisted unflaggingly. Yet he has never had the allegiance of the type of fan cult that has elevated the Goodmans, the Kentons, and Hermans to prizewinning pinnacles. . . For the first time, the Les Brown band comes into focus not only as a great dance band, but as a superlative jazz orchestra with several top-grade soloists. This album, presenting 'Les Brown at the Hollywood Palladium' should do much to rectify the situation."

The personnel was much the same as the USO Brown band I saw four years later when I accompanied them in Japan and Korea with the special Bob Hope holiday show. Trombonists Ray Sims and Les' brother Stumpy, tenor saxophonist Dave Pell, trumpeter Wes Hensel, bassist Rolly Bundock, alto saxophonist Ronnie Lang and drummer Jack Sperling were featured.

A review I did of the taped Palladium show gave it the four star appraisal it deserved. "The band at the time was composed of solid West Coast players you might find at Howard Rumsey's Lighthouse sitting in any night. It was so good I have kept the static filled 33 just to absorb the tremendous sound of players handling great arrangements in front of people who loved every note. It doesn't get any better."

George Simon once told the story of how accidental some numbers were to the success of touring bands because either the songs didn't get plugged or they were forgotten. That happened to Les Brown with one of his most famous numbers, "Sentimental Journey. "

The first time the band played the number it was doing a gig at the Hotel Pennsylvania. Doris Day said she remembered that it was late at night and there was little reaction. In fact, Les didn't plan to record the number. When it was featured on several band broadcasts, however, the mail poured in. That made it a hit. But that wasn't as bad as what happened to one of the band's biggest instrumental hits, "I've Got My Love To Keep Me Warm." Les remembered years later that it was a number the band zipped through in 15 minutes. It was done and put in the can for later release. About five years later, Les pulled it up for a Bob Hope Show and, after the show, Columbia executives called and told him to get the band into the studio to record the number. Les smiled as he told them "look in your files."

Similar to the east, California was a mecca for bands and musicians during the 1930s, '40s and early '50s because of the opportunities it offered. Yet it had other strengths for the progressive wing of swing as well as lighter side of sweet.

Anyone in the big band business was cheering former Freddy Martin band singer and television personality Merv Griffin in 1998 when he tried to re-create the excitement and fun of the 1930s and '40s by opening The Coconut Club in the Beverly Hilton Hotel. His hope and dream was to match the great times he and others had at the original Cocoanut Grove. The Coconut Club had a 900 foot dance floor in a tropical setting with gold and silver palm trees. Neon monkeys added a different twist! Why the Coconut Club? Nostalgia, really. Merv's big hit was "I've Got A Lovely Bunch of Coconuts." While he put everything imaginable into building a successful return to a great age and equally great dance music. . . the Coconut Club closed a few years later.

The Palomar, which virtually launched the big band swing era in 1935 with Goodman, continued to be a drawing card to tourists and regulars. Meanwhile off the coast some island ballrooms, like the Rendevous on Balboa Beach which featured Stan Kenton, were popular as were the sentimental and novelty bands like Kay Kyser, Freddy Martin and Dick Jurgens which played at the Avalon Casino Ballroom overlooking Avalon Bay at Catalina Island.

Jurgens' theme song, "Daydreams Come True At Night," which he wrote in a music course while attending Sacramento Junior College, was an interesting parallel to his life. Said a longtime friend at his funeral, "People got a lot of joy from his music. It was pleasant, happy sounding music. . . full-bodied music that was very harmonious. " Band members recall Dick cared for his musicians and as the Jurgens group gained popularity he tried to make sure that the band could celebrate the holidays with their families. Consequently, the band was booked at the plush Avalon Casino on Santa Catalina for a month or more at Christmas and New Year's. During his lifetime, Dick, who was also a regular at the Aragon in Chicago, recorded more than 250 selections on 78s, 80 numbers on long playing 33's and he wrote or collaborated with others on more than 12 songs.

A longtime friend, Harry Teasdall, who remembered Dick in high school at an afternoon dance for "Senior Ditch Day" (seems like every high school had such informal skip days in the 1930s and '40s) at California's Wilson High School in Long Beach, summed up Dick Jurgens' appeal the best:

"When the band opened with "Day Dreams Come True At Night" . . . what a band it was! We had all heard other prominent bands of that era, but there was something about the Jurgens band which set it apart from the others and WOW! those vocals by Eddie Howard, Ronnie Kemper and later by Harry Cool."

Those are testimonials from the heart.

Certainly Catalina, 22 miles off the coast, a sports fisherman's Shangri-la has always drawn people from all parts of the globe. During the heydays of the big bands Catalina offered the best of the best musical groups. The bands appeared at a place built by chewing gum czar William Wrigley Jr. who purchased it in 1919 and built a casino on a beautiful spot called Sugarloaf Point which looks down on Avalon Bay. The upper floor featured the top bands and among them was the very popular

Canadian, Jan Garber. From 1934-37, Garber was a CBS favorite who drew crowds of 5,000. Those who heard the broadcasts remember Don McBain beginning each radio program telling listeners "From the beautiful Casino Ballroom, overlooking Avalon Bay at Catalina Island, we bring you the music of ". . . Kay Kyser, Garber and a number of other bands of the time.

Today more than 90 years later, the casino, for the most part, remains unchanged and still welcomes dancers to the ballroom.

The Palladium: Where Everyone Wanted to Play Bibliography

Band Leader Dick Jurgens, 85;
Toured, Had Several Hit Songs, undated

The Hollywood Palladium
web site: www.hollywoodpalladium.com/history

"Hollywood Palladium Lives Up To Its Namesake,"
The University of Southern California Daily Trojan, Online, Nov. 11, 2004

Lawrence Welk
www.parabrisas.com/d_welk1.php

Frankie Goes To Hollywood
www.midnightinsanity.com/Hollywood/HollywoodSites.htm

Frank Rosolino
www.jazzmasters.nl/rosolino.htm

Leo McElroy
email 2/28/05; 3/1/2005

Capitol Records
www.answers.com/topic/capitol -records

Capitol Records
en.wikipedia.org/wiki/Capitol_Records +

Richard Jessen
"Glenn Miller: The Godfather of Bop?" www.anyswinggoes.com/features/108758116111926.shtml

Morrissey Charms Fans
Hollywood Review, Reuters, Dec. 17, 1999

The Dick Jurgens Orchestra
www.dickjurgens.com

Dick Jurgens Jr.
email February 7, 2002

The Timely Emergence of Bud Shank
undated

Harry Teasdall letter to Dick Jurgens
undated Dick Jurgens web site.

Connie Haines
web site www.conniehaines.com

Trumpet Blues: The Life of Harry James
Peter J. Levinson (Oxford/1999)

Santa Catalina Island
www.away.com/primedia/pol

Glenn Miller's Greatest Hits
with Larry O'Brien and the Glenn Miller Orchestra, PBS Special, 1995

www.swingerhead.com/Bios/the_band.htm
(The Coconut Club, LA)

Tex Beneke
www.answers.com/topic/tex-beneke

NEVER HOME FOR THE HOLIDAYS

One of the unfortunate truths of the band business is that seasonal holidays, special events in your life . . . you'll spend "working" whether you're talented or can play well enough to be dangerous!

During my last two high school years I was playing for proms in the spring and, during the summer, I played as many weekend dances as I could get. From Thanksgiving until mid January there were usually good paying gigs you certainly didn't want to miss. It was always the busy season. However, you did miss out on the social scene, the dancing and the fun that friends, family and neighbors were enjoying.

Touring big band drummer Jack Sperling was working his 4th Christmas Holiday thousands of miles from home with the Bob Hope USO Tour. The band left the states in late November, did one nighters in Japan, Korea in various hot spots near the DMZ for the troops and later entertained the Marines on Okinawa.

The US Air Force returned them stateside in January.

"Every job has some problems. . . and, believe me, it's tough for most musicians to spend the holidays waiting for phone calls to play somewhere. Anywhere some years. You get used to it because it's the busy time of the year," he told me when the Les Brown Band and entourage played for 8th Army/Seoul Area Command Headquarters in Seoul during the holiday season 1957-58.

During the '30s, '40s, '50s and most of the '60s, young and old adults liked to dress up in glamorous gowns, suits, and their fancy best to go dancing and sampling hor d'oeuvres from Thanksgiving to Christmas. And New Year's would finish the year (or start it depending upon when you got home) the "right" way even if you were sick! I experienced all those situations in my six years as a player.

While very few musicians I knew ever worked Christmas Eve (aside from those who sang or played in church services) the local country clubs, Elks, American Legion and charitable organizations stacked enough gigs into their social calendars that community pick up bands had to be assembled because it was rare for a touring big band to make the Midwest during the holidays. Most had already secured far better paying longer term engagements in hotels usually in the major cities. New York's famous society bandleader Lester Lanin actually found so much work, he started stand-in bands under his name. You got Lester's band without Lester but nobody seemed to mind.

Any musician who had an "axe," 'skins or played piano and had a union card as well as a telephone could be working for one or more bands in that 31 day window of valuable playing time. I spent one holiday working for three bands in a month and friends I knew worked for more.

But you had better be available to take the call. There were no answering machines at the time and good gigs (country clubs, Elks, Legions events) went quickly.

Regardless of the planning it was usually the time for improvisation, too. I'm not talking about the music either although that could be a problem too. I got a call to join an 18-piece group during the holidays, 1954, and felt comfortable with my big Slingerland drum set (if it was good enough for Gene Krupa, I thought, it certainly could handle any job). What I didn't know as a drummer who played by ear was that the leader had gotten a Les Brown arrangement of the Nutcracker Suite which called for tympani effect near the end of a more difficult number and I only had a small tom-tom . Fortunately, I showed up early and, after struggling through a rehearsal with a few members of the band, I figured out a way to use a tom-tom (I untightened the drumhead) to meet the leader's standards.

If you were on a national touring band, holidays were just another travel day or layover in a hotel. Unless, of course, you were a member of Dick Jurgens' band.

Jurgens, said several of his longtime musicians, "encouraged the men to bring the wives and children along when on long locations such as Berkeley, CA at the Hotel Claremont where we spent 3 months every year, and always at Christmas. Also at the Aragon Ballroom, Chicago also 3 weeks or longer at Elitches Garden in Denver, CO. The band would only do 48 or so one nighters a year; he didn't enjoy the packing every night."

The Claremont has had a fascinating 100 year old history since it was finally completed in 1915. In the early days, it had to prohibit sale of liquor because of its one mile radius of the University of California. The hotel was built on the borderline of Berkeley and Oakland and was assumed to be within the radius. It was one of the few hotels without a bar in 1936. A female student at UC seized the moment however. According to the History of the Claremont Resort and Spa, she and her friends "measured the shortest route from the UC campus to the front steps. The result of their efforts found that the Claremont was a few feet over the one mile radius which meant that a bar could be opened (now called the Terrace Bar!). The woman responsible for these findings was given free drinks at the Claremont for the rest of her life!"

Touring bands had more difficulties that couldn't always be fixed as easily.

The Stan Kenton Band had crossed into Canada during December playing such remote spots as Kitchener, London, Peterboro and cities like Ottawa and Montreal. The band was used to playing in normally cold auditoriums but at Peterboro the road manager found the impossible. With temperatures hovering at -48 the band would be playing that night in a hockey rink with wooden planks covering the ice! Making matters worse, the event promoters had overhead gas fired heating units that were so loud nobody could hear the band beyond a few feet out in front of the bandstand. Stan had to give the brass players the night off because of the fear their lips would freeze to the instruments. Kenton was furious. . . but like good troupers. . . the show went on.

Band leader Monk Rowe of Central New York says that the audience can put a damper on fun sometimes without realizing it. "I remember a number of New Year's Eves where people kept asking for "Auld Lang Syne" over and over far before midnight as well as after it. Enough is enough even of a good thing," he laughs.

By holiday time, 1939, Harry James was so financially strapped he wasn't sure where the money would come from to pay for the band bus. Greyhound, in fact, had sent liquidators to get the bus back. Harry and band members spent time each week traveling back roads and parking the bus in places where it wouldn't be seen. Two years later, the James Band had new management and was signing contracts like the one with the Paramount Theater, NY, for $17,000 a week!

Even a band all America loved during the 1940s – Glenn Miller – faced difficult times at holidays. The band was going to get $200 for a seven hour dance date on New Year's Eve in Valencia Ballroom, York, PA., but that was the least of his worries. In getting to the gig on bad, snow-covered roads, one of his musicians had totaled his car, two trumpet players went on drinking binges and the remaining two cars broke down which stranded half of his rhythm and sax sections. He played the gig with those who could finally make it, paid the band off. . . and started 1938 virtually broke!

Glen Gray and the popular Casa Loma Band

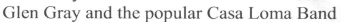

felt Glenn's pain four years later. As the holidays approached Glen had arranged a lucrative New York City show to play for several nights. The struggle was finding musicians. Selective Service had taken several of his band prior to the dates. Add to that, some arrangements were considered less than inspiring to the band or the leader. But the last straw, Glen said, came when a new upcoming singer named Andy Russell was on stage with the band. In a two night show, the band actually played three numbers by itself. His band folded several weeks later.

Yet, the holiday time could be bizarre too for musicians. One time I played a Country Club and shortly after we started a musician friend of the leader came up and talked to him about sitting in on the drums. The leader asked me if I minded and I said no problem – an 18 year-old listening to 40-somethings who had played together before how could I refuse? We had a four-hour gig and I played exactly one set that night, ate his delicious dinner, danced with his wife . . . and got paid for four hours! Great way to make a living I thought!

Internal politics in a band, though, could make things very tense sometimes. A singer I worked with found it didn't pay to be too ambitious. She was used to taking several numbers a set and when she felt there was a chance to plug her self . . . she would do so. A delegation of the band told the leader he HAD to do something about it. A consensus said she should be fired. The lead saxophonist usually put the charts together for the sets we played and one night between Thanksgiving and Christmas she sat on the stage the whole night with no songs to sing. She finally stomped off stage at the second intermission. The band applauded which definitely confused the audience!

Bassist Chubby Jackson, a fun-loving guy on the Woody Herman Band, used to tell a story about a female singer who also wasn't popular with band members.

During a holiday gig in the late 1940s, trombonist Bill Harris felt she didn't fit and went back stage where workers had earlier been painting props, came back on stage and attempted to paint her name off the large poster along side the band on stage! She left in tears. . . while the band howled in delight.

In 1946, Kenton was on a tour close to home at the San Francisco Civic Auditorium, which at the time was home to the San Francisco Symphony. The band arrived at 6 p.m. for an 8:30 p.m. concert the day before Thanksgiving. Instead of 18 chairs, a piano and drums set up on the stage. . . there were 36 chairs, two pianos and two sets of drums! Why? The union contract at the auditorium called for a backup band to be on duty if a traveling group was playing. Stan argued for several hours that the band didn't want a backup band, had not asked for one and finally, he threatened not to play unless the changes he requested were made. He was told that he would have to forfeit his advance of $1,500 if he didn't play.

The concert went on . . . with two bands playing the Star Spangled Banner and the second band sat through the three hour concert without sounding a note. Both bands were paid!

Kenton band manager Ed Gabel remembers the Christmas of 1946 when he played more gin rummy and poker than slept. The Kenton band was playing an important two month engagement at the Paramount Theater in New York City which meant steady paychecks for awhile. But there was a downside, too. The band did two stage shows daily, seven days a week. That meant finding something to do during the breaks. Cards became the answer when you weren't sleeping on one of the cots that were backstage for exhausted musicians. In the midst of the Paramount gig, Kenton was asked to play for a special UN fund raising affair to help the new state of Israel at the Waldorf Astoria. It was a logistical nightmare, Ed said. The band stand at the Paramount had to be dismantled and taken to the hotel and then on a tight schedule several hours later dismantled again and taken back to the Paramount. It was such a tight schedule New York City's finest had to escort the band back to the theater.

Holidays brought some limitations on music selections during the big band era of the 1930s to the 1960s. Christmas carols were not played in the dance bands I belonged to during the late 1940s and early '50s. Carols were sacred music written by clergy and organists of earlier centuries and there seemed an unwritten code of many bandleaders that playing such music would offend their audiences. But two Russian Jews brought happiness to a war-torn America and the world during the era and both went on to musical success because of their contributions. Irving Berlin wrote the tune "White Christmas" which Bing Crosby sang in the movie "Holiday Inn" in 1942 and it gave bands as popular a hit as Lombardo's "Auld Lang Syne" for Christmas season dances. Most bands use it today and the demand causes it to be played a number of times in an evening. Mel Torme followed in 1946 with a wonderful number called the "Christmas Song" which he wrote on one of the hottest days in the San Fernando Valley, July 1945. It became a national classic the next year when Nat "King" Cole recorded it as a holiday number. It's also in nearly every band's list of "to do" numbers during the holidays. Jule Styne wrote the "Christmas Waltz" in 1954 to add to the Christmas numbers. Jule's hit came two years after comic bandleader Spike Jones gave us "I Saw Mommy Kissing Santa Claus."

Yet I can still remember doing a gig with a 12-piece band for a pre-Christmas club dance in northern Ohio where the piano player had put together a clever medley of such Christmas carols as "Deck the Halls," "Hark the Herald Angels Sing" and a few others which we played. Moments later the club manager came over to the leader noticeably angry telling him to stop playing "holy music . . . people are here to drink and dance!"

Embarrassing moments could come because of a familiar local face in a national touring band, oddly enough. Utica (NY) Symphony Orchestra trumpet player and big band musician in New York and Florida, the late Frank Galime told me his experience when the Warren Covington Band played a one-nighter in Utica. "Warren needed a few musicians for the gig and called Utica College and talked to music professor Lou Angelini. He wanted musicians who could sight read the arrangements and not embarrass his band in the performance. Lou called me and I signed on. Warren later told us absolutely DON'T SHAKE HANDS with other band members because he didn't want people coming to the dance thinking he had a pick-up band of local musicians . . . they came to hear Warren Covington he said. Well, when we started to play some of the dancers knew us and were surprised to see us and started waving and shouting our names. I had a solo and stood to do it and several people shouted 'Hey Frank . . . good job.' I sat down and Warren didn't smile when he looked at me. I discovered that image is everything when your price is higher than local bands," Frank laughed.

...I can still remember doing a gig ... where the piano player put together a medley of such Christmas carols as "Deck the Halls," "Hark the Herald Angels Sing" and a few others ... the club manager came over to the leader noticeably angry telling him to stop playing "holy music . . . people are here to drink and dance!"

Jazz and big band trumpet player Marion "Doc" Holladay thinks music is far too universal to be barred because of religious overtones. Doc is a Baha'i member and he gave young jazz musicians and others his thoughts at a lecture at North Texas State University in February, 2001. He played with Tommy Dorsey, Duke Ellington, Dizzy Gillespie and Quincy Jones during his touring years. "Being a Baha'i doesn't affect my music; that is what I was all along. The teachings regarding music were what I believed all along. It was a confirmation of what I thought was right. If you watched the Ken Burns Jazz documentary on television, I am going to tell you what was missing. . . If you want to understand a culture, get acquainted with its music. The world equates American culture with jazz; that is how the world sees us. It isn't European, it isn't African . . . it's American. It embraces both European and African characteristics . . . but it created a culture of its own. And it's ours," he explained to students.

What kind of power does music have on an audience? Listen to Rui Zhv, a marketing professor and researcher at Rice University, who found that young listeners associate classical music with benevolent paternalism and consider contemporary music unique and original. "Simply the sound of a particular piece of music can evoke favorable or unfavorable impressions. On the other hand, that same music can elicit feelings or thoughts consumers associate with specific events or experiences such as childhood, or concepts and emotions like frivolity, calm and fear," he says and you can understand more why the music of Glenn Miller, Guy Lombardo and many others from an era now gone can live on when they are heard.

Richard Duffy wrote an interesting article entitled "Big Band – What's Big?" in which he tried to explain that big bands went through an evolutionary process. Yet he noted that there are good reasons that Miller's sound continues to reverberate today and why most people over 50 can recognize Lombardo's heavy saxophone vibrato on "Auld Lang Syne." The sound Miller got is very distinctive, he says. "The reed section; the clarinet plays the lead, while two altos and one tenor are in block harmony close to the clarinet, all within the same octave. The second tenor plays lead with the clarinet, one octave below; the most unique and rich in quality reed sound existent." The average person doesn't know how and what the horns do. . . but they loved the sound then . . . and they continue to love it today.

Young and old respond to such pleasurable listening. A professor of jazz history at the University of Nebraska interviewed by the Daily Nebraskan summed it best a few years ago: "Music strikes people so emotionally. That's what makes the history of jazz so fascinating. My parents have a connection with jazz. When you play Benny Goodman, they're right there. That's their music." Don't forget the episode of "Everybody Loves Raymond" on television when Robert and Ray were accused by their Korean War veteran father, Frank Barone, of destroying his vinyl LPs of great swing and jazz numbers. Frank wouldn't accept the CD renditions they bought to "replace" his old music. . . he wanted his "real" records back.

Because it returns in nearly the same form each year, Christmas music would appear to have a built in reminder factor that musicians can rely on commercially. David Miller who hosts a popular web site and radio big band program, says that big bands didn't really see holiday music as exploitable during the swing years. "I don't think big bands had any special affinity for holiday songs. The leaders put out a holiday record for commercial reasons probably . . . and they sold even back in the days of 78s. RCA put out one with Benny Goodman playing "Jingle Bells" and Tommy Dorsey playing "Santa Claus Is Coming to Town" (Victor 25145) on the other. You can be assured they did it only for the money," he says.

But some leaders today take a different view and express it in arrangements of what once wasn't considered "dance music." Trombonist Rob McConnell always wanted to express his musical thoughts on the traditional music. In the late 1990s he created his own Christmas sounds. In the album liner of his popular CD "Big Band Christmas," Rob says: "I have always enjoyed Christmas music and haven't done many arrangements of same until now. I grew up singing in church choirs with my family and remember that time of year with Handel's Messiah and all the carols with love. At one time – very early '40s – all of our family was in the choir at St. George's United Church in Toronto. . . Very fond memories." His album of nostalgia contains renditions of "Away In A Manger," "O Little Town of Bethlehem," "Joy to the World," "It Came Upon A Midnight Clear" and one no band in my era would have been brave enough to try, "Silent Night." Of course no big band in my era had a recording studio and 20 musicians to give it such a rich sound either.

"If people can hum it . . . that's what I'm after. When a tune is done whether mine or anybody's I like to have them remember it," Central New York bandleader Monk Rowe explains. Certainly big band Christmas numbers approach that level daily as retailers and consumers push the season every year.

Yet, memorability shows something else. Smithsonian experts claim that the most listened to songs are Hoagy Carmichael and Mitchell Parish's "Star Dust" with more than 1,500 recorded versions and the Beatles' John Lennon and Paul McCartney's "Yesterday" which has 2,500 variations available.

While holiday seasons were once great opportunities for musicians, times change. Territorial bandleader Joe Enroughty says that November to January, 2005 wasn't where he wanted it to be. "I did not have a very busy schedule during the 2005 holiday. I worked some but. . . the demand for smaller groups that cost less than a big band is what people are interested in. I like playing holiday events not only because people are always festive but we get to sprinkle in Christmas Carols through our regular program of dance music. I wish we did get more work around the holidays. But that hasn't stopped me from working my band either. Yet I find that we get most of our work in warmer weather. I have a lot of private events throughout the year and that seems to keep the band working steadily."

One thing for sure, said Scott Frampton, a contributing editor of O:The Oprah Magazine, some of the newer kinds of holiday music turn the season sour right from the first notes. "I think people start going wrong when they bring out "Grandma Got Run Over By A Reindeer" and those kind of novelty hits because they wear on people. "

But said a Verve Record executive Dahlia Ambach-Caplin to the Associated Press: "Everywhere you go during the holidays you hear Christmas music ad nauseam. Not everyone wants to listen to Christmas all day all the time."

I disagree, Dahlia, and I think others do, too.

Never Home For The Holidays Bibliography

Frank Galime correspondence
Nov. 2, 2003

Ed Gabel, Stan Kenton: The Early Years
1941-47 (Balboa Books)

Joe Enroughty
email 5/6/05

"Big Band — What's Big?"
Richard Duffy

"A History of the Claremont Resort and Spa,"
http://spas.about.com/library/blank12.htm

www.dickjurgens.com/bandstories.htm

BALLROOMS IN AMERICA
DANCING IS BACK

Ballroom dancing dead? Hardly! Stories from newspapers, magazines and web sites around the country show that dancing is very much alive as are a number of ballrooms that once were being considered for the wrecker's ball or renovation as a bowling alleys.

A documentary called "Mad Hot Ballroom," which grossed over $8 million, offers proof of the return of this recreation that combines so many social pleasures and interaction. "Everyone has certain strengths," says Nolan Devor of Salt Lake City, a teacher of ballroom classes for students from 10 to 12. "In ballroom, you have to be able to listen, to lead and to follow. You might not be valedictorian or a cheerleader. But you could excel at ballroom."

The TV program, "Dancing with the Stars," and the movie that followed may have been inspiration for the popularity, explains Martin Voight in an article called "Social Dancing Makes A Comeback in the AARP web site and he insists that ballrooms can offer young people good alternatives.

"Any community arts program that exposes you to mentors, and role models can make a difference." Certainly the legendary Arthur Murray Dance Studios know the power of such community assets. Number one in teaching and marketing social dancing, the Murray franchisees were up in dancers and reached an unheard of pace of 20 percent. Arhur Murray's marketing director, Thomas Murdock, believes media actually created the return of dancing.

Brian McDonald, president of the National Dance Council of America, says the younger set sees it as different; artistic and yet a competitive activity too. Consider that the Dance Council has seen competitions in ballroom dancing go from 25 a year to more than 90.

But this isn't simply a form of new competition. There's much more to it than that. An excellent blend of older and younger dancers, eager to learn new steps comes to the venerable Century Ballroom in Seattle every Sunday and Wednesday night. The 2,000 square foot dance floor is packed frequently both nights. A swing half hour dance lesson opens the evening and then it's a casual night of dancing until after midnight.

And it's mostly students interested in the latest dance steps from the east to the west coast. "Some of my closest friends now are people I met at Century," said one. The Century Ballroom, which is a 1920s vintage dance pavilion with chandeliers, dark lighting and hardwood floor, is on the second floor and it features live bands. It's got a cozy, Flapper Era feeling, dancers say. The best part, students add, is the price; it only costs $5.

A larger and more national approach to dancing takes place at the United States Amateur Ballroom Dancers Assn (USABDA) chapter sessions throughout the country. Says USABDA at its web site: "While all dancing has its value, there will be several completely memorable dances in one's life. A time when the partner, the music, the movement all come together in a sense of achievement and pleasure that stays in memory. Dancing with a partner in harmony with good music will help you develop a more open, understanding, responsive and supportive relationship with your partner and with others. Your outlook on life will become more positive. Words cannot explain the joy of ballroom dancing. It must be experienced!"

The return of its popularity, says USABDA, speaks for millions of Americans. Certainly formal weddings call for a return to the dance floor if you haven't been there in a while. It also demands that you find a way to learn more than just your vows at the altar, too. Christina Hansen in the Kansas State Collegian noted that couples feel a spike in pressure in the traditional church marriage/reception to have a memorable first dance. It's expected even though some don't turn out as well as either partner wants. It can be remembered fondly . . . or with disappointment. Ask any number of older married couples. Since movies like "Shall We Dance?" and the TV series "Dancing With The Stars" guys have had to take the heat and try to learn to dance. They don't want to embarrass themselves. Says Christina: "A way for couples to prepare for the first dance is to choose a favorite song and practice dancing together at home, well in advance of the wedding."

Seasons of the year appeal to dancers, too. New Year's Eve for many is the night to join the multitude whirling away the evening and early morning dancing to tunes you can hum. In an earlier era, there were no sober ride free taxi services like those offered in the Washington DC and other areas today. And drinking was certainly a serious matter then as it is today although I don't think it was as pronounced among the musicians as the revelers on the floor. My memories are colorful, though. One New Year's playing a ballroom dance, a woman became infatuated with my drums (not me) as the evening wore on. As I took the set apart to leave she was still dancing on the floor to jukebox music and as I moved to the exit she went along with me trying to "help" me hold on to a very heavy bass drum. I arrived at curbside on the hilly street outside and attempted to put the drum case in the car. The bass was left for the moment. Next thing I knew she had launched it down Main Street hill and it was picking up speed on the way. I caught up with it at the bottom after I set a new 100 yard dash track record. No damage but extra anxiety.

Here are the ballrooms, according to the National Ballroom & Entertainers Association, still operating today:

FLORIDA

• Coliseum
535 4th Ave, St. Petersburg, FL, 33701
Telephone 727-892-5202
web: www.stpete.org/coliseum

ILLINOIS

• Aragon Ballroom
1106 W. Lawrence Ave., Chicago, IL 60640-5026
Telephone 773-561-9500

• Cliffbreakers Renaissance Ballroom
700 W. Riverside Blvd., Rockford, IL 61103

• Crystal Ballroom
20631 Staunton Rd, PO Box 276,
Staunton, IL 62088
Telephone 618-635-3506
web: www.crystalballroom.net

• Hecker Community Center
230 E. Washington, PO Box 112,
Hecker, IL 62248
Telephone 618-473-2708

• Hub Ballroom
2708 Main St., PO Box 86, Edelstein, IL 61526.
web: www.hubballroom.com
Telephone 618-249-2482

• Lindendale Park Ballroom
PO Box 86, Highland, IL 62499
2005 Park Hill Dr., Highland, IL 62249
Telephone 618-654-9753

• Pla-Mor Dance Land
1300 E. 3rd St., PO Box 416, Pana, IL 62557
Telephone 217-562-2422

• Willowbrook Ballroom
8900 Archer Ave, Willow Springs, IL 60480
Web: www.willowbrookballroom.com
Telephone 708-839-1000

IOWA

• Col Ballroom
1012 W. 4th St., Davenport, IA 52802
Telephone 563-322-4431

• Dance-Mor Inc
77 2nd St., Swisher, IA 52338
Telephone 319-857-4205

• Dubuque County Fairgrounds Ballroom
14583 Old Highway Rd., Dubuque, IA, 52002
Telephone 563-588-1406

• Fairyland Park Ballroom Lunch &
Supper Club 18800-315th St, Long
Grove, IA 52756

Telephone 563-285-9195; 563-759-8200

• Hotel Fort Des Moines Ballroom
1000 Walnut St., Des Moines, IA 50309-3489
Telephone 800-532-1466; 515-243-1161

• Grand Ballroom
14569 Old Highway Rd, Dubuque, IA 52002
Telephone 800-532-1466; 515-243-1161
web: www.dbqfair.com

• Inwood Pavilion
16 Bridge St., Spillville, IA 52168
Telephone 563-562-3135

• Lake Robbins Ballroom
2642 150th St., Woodward, IA 50276
Telephone 515-438-2305

• Lakewood Ballroom
414 Lakewood Dr., Lake View, IA 51450
Telephone 712-657-2462

• Let's Dance Cedar Rapids
4444 1st Ave NE. Cedar Rapids, IA 52402
Telephone 319-981-1812
email: letscanceer@aol.com

• Minden Community Club
102 Broadway, Box 276, Minden, IA 51553
Telephone 712-483-2611

• Opera House
110 First Ave SW, Tripoli, IA 50676
Telephone 319-882-3675
email: jraxon@netins.net

• Ponderosa Ballroom
195 1st St. So. Walford, IA 50676
Telephone 319-846-2944

• Riviera Ballroom
Old Highway, 218, Janesville, IA
Telephone 319-984-5601

• Surf Ballroom
460 N. Shore Dr., Clear Lake, IA 50428

Telephone 641-357-6151.

• Val Air Ballroom
301 Ashworth Rd, PO Box 65338,
West Des Moines, IA 50266
Telephone 515-233-6152
email: ValAirBal@aol.com

KANSAS

• Caprice Ballroom
19906 W. Kellogg, Goddard, KS 67219
Telephone 316-838-7758
web: www.dance-at-the-caprice.com
email: dance-at-the-caprice@prodigy.net

• Cotillion
11120 W. Kellogg, Wichita, KS 67209
Telephone 316-722-4201
web: www.thecotillion.com

MASSACHUSETTS

• Mosley's On The Charles
50 Bridge St., Dedham, MA 02026
Telephone 781-326-3075
web: www.mosleyonthecharles.com

MINNESOTA

• Blue Note Ballroom
PO Box 847, 320 3rd St. S., Winsted, MN 55395
Telephone 507-485-9698

• Kato Entertainment Center
200 Chestnut St., Mankato, MN 56001
Telephone 507-625-7553
web: www.mboa.com

• Medina Entertainment Center
500 Highway 55, Hamel, MN 55340
Telephone 763-478-6661
web: www.medinaentertainment.com
email: medinarec@aol.com

• Gibbon Ballroom

HWY 19, Gibbon, MN 55335
Telephone 507-354-7112

• Golden Eagle
Co RD 103, Burtrum, MN 56318
Telephone 320-285-4541

• Iron World Discovery Center
Hwy 169, W-Box 392, Chisolm, MN 55719
Telephone 800-372-6437; 218-254-3321
web: www.ironworld.com

• Island Ballroom
Hwy 212 E. Bird Island, MN 55310
Telephone 612-365-9997

• Kato Ballroom
500 Highway-55 W, Mankato, MN 56001
Telephone 507-625-7553

• Lakeside Ballroom
500 Lakeshore Drive, Glenwood, MN 56334

• Park Ballroom
300 Lexington Ave S, PO Box 113
New Prague, MN 56071
Telephone 952-758-4603

• Pla Mor Ballroom
1913 E. 9th St., Glencoe, MN 55904
Telephone 320-864-4119

• Pla-Mor Ballroom
2045 Highway E 4th Ave
Rochester, MN 55904
Telephone 507-282-5244

• Shakopee Ballroom
2400 E. 4th Ave, Shakopee, MN 55379
Telephone 612-445-0412

• Waconia Lakeside Ballroom
PO Box 374, 8155 Paradise Lane
Waconia, MN 55387-0374
Telephone 952-442-4844

MISSOURI

• Casa Loma Ballroom
3354 Iowa Ave., St. Louis, MO 63118
314-664-8000
web: www.casalomaballroom.com

MARYLAND

• Hollywood Ballroom
2126 Industrial Parkway
Silver Spring, MD 20904
Telephone 301-622-5494
web: www.hollywoodballroom.com

NEBRASKA

• Flying V Ballroom
385 D Street, Utica, NE 68456

• Oak Ballroom
175 Higgins Drive, Schuyler, NE 68661
Telephone 402-352-9972

• Peony Park
PO Box 1919, 1620 County Rd 'L'
Wahoo, NE 68066-1919
Telephone 402-391-6253
email: PEONYPARK@aol.com

• Pla Mor Ballroom
6600 West 'O' Street, Lincoln, NE 68528
Telephone 402-475-4030

NEW HAMPSHIRE

• Rockingham Ballroom
22 Ash Swamp Rd, Newmarket, NH 03857
Telephone 603-749-9040
web: www.rockinghamballroom.com
email: rockballrm@aol.com

NEW YORK

• Roseland Ballroom
239 W. 52nd Street, New York, NY 10019
Telephone212-247-0200

OHIO

• Bavarian Club
PO Box 171, Deshler, OH 43516
Telephone 419-278-1871

• Meadowbrook Park Ballroom
5430 W. Tiffin St, Bascom, OH 44809
Telephone 419-937-2242

• Springvale Ballroom
5871 Canterbury, North Olmstead, OH
44070-3129
5200 Dover Center Rd, North
Olmstead, OH 44070
Telephone 440-777-0161

PENN

• Paso Doble Ballroom
4501 New Falls Rd, Levittown, PA
19056-3004
Telephone 215-547-2311

TEXAS

• Armadillo Ballroom

7100 CR 400 Brazoria, TX 77422
Telephone 979-798-8500

• Fiesta Ballroom
735 E I H 10, Sequin, TX 78155

WISCONSIN

• Laack's Ballroom
W 4302 CTY JM, Sheboygen Falls, WI 53085
Telephone 920-467-4591

• Park Ponderosa
5100 Erling Ave, PO Box 5
McFarland, WI 53558
Telephone 608-838-8123

• Riverside Ballroom
115 Newhall St, Green Bay, WI 54302.
Telephone 920-432-5518
web: www.riversideballroom.com
email: riversideballroom@msn.com

• Schmidt's Ballroom
7085 Highway A, Wausau, WI 54401
Telephone 715-675-2868

AMERICA'S BALLROOM PAST

Ballrooms. They were the places to go and places where special things happened as early as the 1920s and they continued until touring big bands and an apathetic public stop coming in the 1960s. America's ballrooms, whether spacious city buildings some a block long or vintage architecture near a lake, brought happiness, listening pleasure, the joy of dancing and hours of fun from a long economic depression in the 1930s to the horrors of war and loss of loved ones during World War II.

Some ballroom names were so popular in an earlier day they needed no explanation beside the title. They were the local beacons for fun. There were a number of Trianons, Aragons, Crystals, Piers, Pavilions and Palladiums scattered among Hippodromes, Savoys, and Rivieras from coast to coast. All had loyal fans especially when the big bands were in town.

Thanks to the National Ballroom & Entertainers Association, we have a list of many of the ballrooms past that brought us such enjoyment. You'll probably find one of your favorites among the following state by state chronology.

The NBEA suggests that if you know of other ballrooms that have closed it would appreciate your cooperation by contacting it at email address nbea@oneonta.net

CALIFORNIA
Balboa:
Rendezvous Ballroom
Los Angeles:
Palomar Night Club
Coconut Grove
The Palladium
Oakland:
Ali Baba Ballroom
Ocean Park:
Casino Gardens
San Diego

Mission Beach Dance Casino
Pacific Square
San Francisco:
Avalon, Balconades
Wolohans
El Patio, Palamara
Shalimar
The Pergola
Trianon/Primalon
Ballrooms
Santa Monica:
Aragon Ballroom

COLORADO

Denver:
Elitch Gardens
Rainbow, El Patio
Trocadero Ballroom
Lakes Amusement Park

CONNECTICUT

Bridgeport:
Pleasure Beach
Amusement Park
Ritz Ballroom

FLORIDA

Miami:
Flager Gardens Ballroom

GEORGIA

Tybee Island:
Tybrisa Ballroom

IDAHO

Boise:
Miramar Ballroom

ILLINOIS

Aurora:
Blue Moon
Benid:
Coliseum Ballroom

Chicago:
Allegro Ballroom
Aragon
Boston Club
Boulevard Ballroom
Edgewater
Embassy Ballroom
Green Hill
Holiday Ballroom
Lion's Ballroom
Majestic Ballroom
Melody Mill
Milford Ballroom
Palladium
Paradise Ballroom
Pilsen Park
Savoy Ballroom Shutter
Brothers Ballroom
Trianon Ballroom
Galesburg:
Arcade Roof Gardens
Macomb-Roof Gardens
Joliet:
Dellwood Park Dance Pavilion
Pioneer Gardens
North Riverside
Peoria:
Ingleterra Ballroom
Westchester:
Edens Ballroom

INDIANA

Bass Lake:
Crystal Ballroom
Cedar Lake:
Midway Ballroom
Michigan City:
Indiana Oasis
Whiting:
Madura's Danceland

IOWA

Cedar Lake:
Warehouse
Cedar Rapids:
Danceland
Clinton:
Modernistic Ballroom
German Hall
Shad Oak
Creston:
Aronda
Decorah:
Matter's Ballroom,
Des Moines:
Riveria Ballroom,
Sycamore Ballroom
Tromar Ballroom
Dubuque:
Melody Mill
Independence:
Gala Ballroom
Janesville:
Riveria Ballroom
Marion:
Armar Ballroom
Oelwein:
Coliseum Ballroom
Prairieburg:
Prairie Moon
Riverside:
Highland Palace
Sioux City:
Rigadoon
Tombs
Skylon
Spirit Lake:
Arnold's Park
Storm Lake:

Cobblestone Ballroom

Waterville:
Rainbow Gardens

KANSAS

Wichita:
Ritz Ballroom
Trig Ballroom
New Moon Ballroom

KENTUCKY

Henderson:
Trocadero

Louisville:
Madrid Ballroom

MAINE

Old Orchard Beach:
Palace Ballroom
Pier Casino Ballroom

MARYLAND

Baltimore:
Famous Ballroom
Alcazar Ballroom

Auburndale:
The Totem Pole

MASSACHUSETTS

Boston:
Raymor Ballroom
Roseland State
Ballroom
Symphony Ballroom

Lowell:
Commodore Ballroom

Springfield:
Butterfly Ballroom

Tyngsboro:
Lake View Ballroom

Waltham:

Nuttings-On-The-Charles,

MICHIGAN

Colona:
Crystal Palace Ballroom

Detroit:
Aragon
Arcadia
Campus
Castle
Eastwood Garden
Grand Terrace
Graystone Ballrooms
New Danceland
Vanity Ballroom

Manitov Beach:
Manitov Beach Ballroom

Paw Paw:
Crystal Ballroom

Saugatuck:
Big Pavilion

St. Joseph:
Shadowland Pavilion

Walled Lake:
Walled Lake Casino

MINNESOTA

Austin:
Terp

Brownton:
Lake Marion Ballroom

Cottage Grove:
Majestic Ballroom

Lake Jefferson:
Hardeggers Ballroom

Minneapolis:
Arcadia Ballroom,
Marigold Ballroom

Montevideo:
Fiesta Ballroom

Gladys Ballroom

Moundsview:
Bel Rae Ballroom

Princeton:
Princeton Ballroom

St. Paul:
The Prom

Worthington:
The Coliseum

MISSOURI

Kansas City:
El Torreon Ballroom
LaFietta Ballroom
Pla Mor Ballroom

St. Louis:
Tunetown

NEBRASKA

Arcadia:
Owl's Roost

Bee:
State Ballroom

Havens:
Clarks

Skylon:
Harrington

Hastings:
Winter Garden

Lincoln:
Turnpike Ballroom

Long Pine
Hidden Paradise

Norfolk:
Kings Ballroom

Omaha:
Royal Terrace Ballroom
Peony Park
Sokol Underground

Music Box
Sargent:
Oscar's Palladium
Sioux City:
Kings Ballroom
Mr. Tunes

NEW HAMPSHIRE
Manchester:
The Arcadia

NEW JERSEY
Almonesson:
Sunset Beach Ballroom
Atlantic City:
Million Dollar Pier
Steel Pier
Marine Ballroom, ;
Cape May:
Convention Hall Ballroom
Cedar Grove:
Frank Dailey's Meadowbrook
Pennsauken:
Ivystone Ballroom
Wildwood:
Starlite Ballroom

NEW YORK
Buffalo:
Dellwood
Crystal Ballroom
Johnson City:
George F. Johnson Pavilion
Sylvan Beach:
Russells Danceland
Utica:
Graystone Ballroom
New York City:
Fiesta Danceteria
Savoy Ballroom

Stardust

NEVADA
Reno:
El Patio Ballroom

OHIO
Akron:
Summit Beach
Park Ballroom
Buckeye Lake:
Pier Ballroom
Crystal Ballroom
Summerland Beach
Hotel Ballroom
Canton:
Moonlight Ballroom
Cincinnati:
Castle Farm
Moonlite Garden
Cleveland:
Aragon Ballroom
Euclid Beach Ballroom
Chipawa Ballroom
Circle Ballroom
Puritas Springs
Amusement Park Ballroom
Trianon Ballroom
Columbia Station
Columbia Ballroom
Columbus:
Valley Dale
Lakewood:
Homestead Ballroom
Lorain:
Banater Hall
Rootstown:
Maples Ballroom
Sandusky:
Cedar Point Amusement

Park Ballroom
Toledo:
Trianon Ballroom
Youngstown:
Idora Park Ballroom

OKLAHOMA
Maud:
White May Ballroom
Muskogee:
Gibson's Ballroom
Oakmulge:
The Hippodrome
Shawnee:
The Bluebird

OREGON
Salem:
Crystal Gardens Ballroom

PENNSYLVANIA
Allentown:
Castle Garden Ballroom
Carrolltown:
Sunset Pavilion
Hershey:
Starlight Ballroom
Mahanoy City:
Danceland Westview Park
Lakewood Pavilion
Philadelphia:
Brookline on the Blvd
Elite Ballroom
Garden Ballroom
Oakes Ballroom
Met Ballroom
Raburn Plaza
Trianon Ballroom
Wagner Hall Ballroom
Pittsburgh:

Bill Green's Casino
Cottage Inn
Garden Plantation
The Jitterbug Savoy
The Grotto
Syrian Mosque

Pottstown:
Sunnybrook Ballroom

Sommerton:
Sommerton Springs Ballroom

Upper Darby:
Covered Wagon Ballroom

Willowgrove:
Willowgrove Park Ballroom

York:
Valencia Ballroom

RHODE ISLAND

Providence:
Arcadia Ballroom

TENNESSEE

Memphis:
Casino Ballroom

TEXAS

Galveston:
Pleasure Pier

San Antonio:
Roaring 20's

UTAH

Salt Lake City:
Saltaire Amusement Park

VIRGINIA

Richmond:
Tantilla Ballroom

Virginia Beach:
Seaside Park Ballroom

WASHINGTON

Seattle/Tacoma:
Spanish Castle

Seattle:
Parker's Ballroom
Trianon Ballroom

Spokane:
Natatorium Ballroom

Tacoma:
Century Ballroom

WISCONSIN

Appleton:
Cinderella Ballroom

Lake Delaven:
Dutch Mill

Lake Geneva:
Riviera Ballroom

Milwaukee:
Wisconsin Roof Ballroom

by John "Jack" Behrens

WILL THERE BE BIG BANDS FOREVER?

Big Band music will continue, the CDs, dusty tapes and old 33 1/3 albums will persist in homes, garage sales and on E-bay . . . and a good number of musicians and bandleaders are convinced that it can continue to recycle itself from decade to decade thanks to more music education, dedicated players and a public not necessarily satisfied with current fads.

"I think I'll keep doing this all my life," Pete Jacobs told me. He leads the Wartime Radio Revue and plays gigs up and down the West Coast. "I love everything about it. I think people are picking up on my love of swing and they love it too. Certainly more women are involved, too. I have several in my band and I have three singing."

Richard Machuzak of the Big Band Theory, the band of NASA technicians and employees at Pasadena, CA, agrees. "There does seem to be an interest among the younger set so hopefully the music will continue to gain popularity. Perhaps some of it has to do with the 'music' that is being played on the radio nowadays. People enjoy hearing music with an actual melody and lush harmonies. We provide a beautiful alternative, I think."

Where did the name "Big Band Theory" come from? For a dance band with PhDs and scientific types who play the 1940 music of Goodman, Dorsey, Ellington and Basie and who use the vocal stylings of Sinatra and Ella, it came down to a play on words;

"The Big Bang Theory," a plausible scientific explanation for the birth of the universe. Says the band's web site: www.bigbandtheory.com "In this case, the scientific minds of the Big Band Theory give birth to music of the spheres. When Big Band Theory is in the house it is truly an out-of-this-world experience to be showered with the shockwaves emanating from all those horns . . . spend time relaxing to the sound of Space Jazz!"

James Bazen who heads three different territorial bands in Washington, DC thinks the big band "future is past. 'In the Mood' will never go away. However, there are a number of younger bands that tap into the past in a contemporary way. It started with Brian Setzer and was taken up by groups like 'Cherry Poppin' Daddies.' They combine the swing rhythms with a rock attitude. However, even now they seem to have faded a bit and we are drifting back to Glenn Miller and the standards. Movies will play a big role . . .like the movie 'S' Wonderful' about Cole Porter which featured contemporary artists singing his tunes. Almost immediately I started getting requests for 'Night and Day' and 'I've Got You Under My Skin.'. Certainly people like Dr. John, Natalie Cole, Rod Stewart and Linda Ronstadt have all done very successful swing/standard recordings with full orchestrations. Maybe that's the future really. Aging rock stars re-inventing themselves as crooners."

Vocalist Dorsey Tippett who sings with perhaps the oldest college affiliated band in the country, the Auburn Knights, thinks that big bands playing music from the '30s to the '50s with some later hits sprinkled at dances won't go away. "The future of our band is very promising. I believe our standards are classic and will always be around and people will always have a desire to hear them. It seems unlikely for someone my age – 20 – to like this sort of music I know. But I have enjoyed listening to swing ever since I was a little girl. I love it! I believe that is the way it will be for others in the future," she says emphatically. Certainly the band's past can make a pessimist a believer. In 1930 at a time when going to college was a tremendous financial struggle and finding part-time work was equally difficult, the Auburn Knights Orchestra was formed as the fall term at the University of Auburn opened. Earlier ventures had failed and quality was a major concern. Said the band's web site: "It was then that a number of student musicians agreed an acceptable band could be built if the best available people were invited to join and were willing to work hard for at least a semester without recognition." The band was strong enough and talented enough to attract Chicago-based Music Corporation of America (MCA) to book gigs for its summer vacations. Later, another booking agency, Holt-Pumphrey of Richmond, VA gave the band engagements in Myrtle Beach and other resorts up and down the South and North Carolina coasts.

The Internet chatter continues daily to offer differing views about the death, near death or the life and vitality of big bands as a vocation or avocation . . and the views of a great number of people who enjoy the great sounds of the "music of their lives." Like every society, icons come and go, trends rise and vanish and change forces us to make concessions to new ideas.

The era of the big bands, which started more than seventy-five years ago, continues in a different way than Benny Goodman, Glenn Miller, Harry James, Gene Krupa, Guy Lombardo and a host of others could have envisioned. Even Stan Kenton, the great innovator, who was introduced as the "bandleader ahead of his times," would be mildly surprised, I think.

In virtually every state in the union swing and big band concerts and dances continue to be held. Although there are no definitive statistics, my review over two years shows it's likely that there are actually more dances, more concerts and more performances by big bands now than there were in the 1940s.

Equally important, there are far, far more opportunities to study and play big band charts than during the 1950s when I attended a major Midwestern university where we had no chance to study the field let alone use practice rooms to improve ourselves. You either studied with private tutors or taught yourself. It's much different at most universities today as well as a great number of private campuses. Listen to Dr. Lou Fischer of Capital University, Columbus, OH, a former member of University of North Texas' famed " One O'Clock Band " and a participant in the Columbus Jazz Orchestra.

"I really do not believe there is a future in only 'big band music' per se. I see the ensemble programs of our universities and schools as training grounds for all music in general, teaching students 'how to survive in the music industry.' We teach many styles of music here at Capital in our contemporary Music Studies program and teach from a perspective that much of popular culture music is rooted in jazz theory and jazz theory rooted all the way back to Bach! There are many types/genres of popular music these days and jazz truly absorbs all of them and we as teachers of music must embrace them. . ."

Dr. Lou should know. He went to the oldest and one of the most proclaimed jazz education colleges in the country but he wasn't aware of it at the time.

"I did not know I was going to a school with such a program. Just happenstance that I went on a tuba scholarship. It didn't take me long to realize what I wanted to do once I heard the internationally renowned One O'clock Band which incidentally I played in for three years. From there it was a hop skip and jump to tour with Woody Herman, Toshiko Akiyoshi, Les Hooper, Louis Bellson, etc. However, those bands were not doing dance gigs by that time. . . a few with the Herman band but most of the work were concerts."

But study and degree programs in jazz or big bands don't translate into gigs upon graduation. Ballrooms at one time accounted for a healthy percentage of any big band tour either from the west

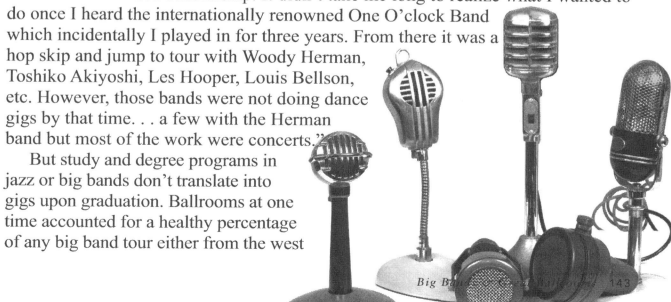

coast headed east or the east coast going to the Midwest or west. Big band historians know that the country might not have had a big band future beyond 1935 if Benny Goodman chose to close down his band the night of the fateful Palomar Ballroom dance. Goodman was despondent over the lack of enthusiasm and crowds as he turned a disastrous tour from the east around outside of Los Angeles and headed back to Chicago and New York City. He was going to make the decision Glenn Miller did a few years later when on New Year's Eve, 1938, he shut his band down to make sure he could pay his musicians their final paychecks. Two months later, of course, Glenn was back with a band that went on to become one of the nation's most successful in the annals of the big band industry.

To demonstrate how crowd sensitive this issue was at the time, Benny was stunned by the rousing excitement that came from the second set of the evening when he inserted Fletcher Henderson's arrangements and gave soloists a chance to get in some licks. Youngsters went wild and the enthusiasm spread eastward. The spark ignited good fortunes for Benny and big bands throughout the country.

Said the web site "Listener's Space Age Pop Music Guide" there has always been enterprise, discipline and musicians eager to be "keepers of the flame."

"A few refused to give up the faith, though. . . continuing to line up gigs and support for a 16-man payroll when their competition had become groups of 4 pimply-faced teenagers flailing away on guitars. Or some slick guy with a tux, an organ and smooth line of patter. And what's even more remarkable, they still managed to find labels interested enough to put their vinyls up against the Beatles. . . Usually, it was just a case of business – marginal business, maybe, but business nonetheless. Some buyers want that Polynesian-tiki bar stuff, some want those foreign groups playing those funny instruments, and some want to hear those old farts play new hits. Money talks, nobody walks."

A veteran territorial bandleader, musician and former high school band director, Don Cantwell of Utica, NY, sees big bands either creating audiences to listen and dance to them or fading from the scene. " It's keep them or lose them," he says about audiences today. "As long as the quality of the band is tops then I think it makes the band more desirable to listen to. If the band is sub par then people who've been enticed to go to hear them will be somewhat turned off. And they probably won't return. That's a reasonable assumption. Quality of musicianship thanks to college scene and the teaching of jazz have got to rise. One of the ironies is that the level of music that is exposed to young people has diminished in quality, I think. That's because there are groups that aren't up to professional standards," he says.

Monk Rowe, curator of the Hamilton College Jazz Archive and a musician, arranger and music educator, says the changes have opened doors but the field continues to be competitive because of the fewer number of paying venues.

"Traditionally you went to music schools to study classical music, " he told a Central

New York radio audience several years ago. "The last 15 to 20 years there have been significant changes. You can now go to school to become a jazz musician or a jazz teacher; golly, there are classes on rock'n'roll and all kinds of things really. Some of the people I've interviewed for the Archive said they did go to music schools but in the practice rooms were signs saying 'no jazz playing allowed.' Now jazz music has been institutionalized as well as the learning of it. I guess the days of the traveling bands and jam sessions and all the venues to play have greatly diminished. Jazz is looked upon as a legitimate art form so that it is justifiable to study it. You have places that offer a doctorate in jazz and you can dissect the music to pass it on. Actually, though, it's a two-edged sword; I think of jazz as an art form but I hope it doesn't become music only heard in a concrete setting or that's put above the listening audience because it always was a music that was free form created in low settings. It doesn't have to stay there but we don't want to lose the vitality of such music, either."

Big band sideman Chuz Alfred, now of Columbus, OH recognized in 1961 after nearly a decade touring he wanted to get "off the road for good." Yet, he has great reminisces from his days on the road. "We (the Ralph Marterie band) ended up in Texas doing a Debutante Ball in Houston which was quite an affair and wound up at the musicians' union hall for a jam that lasted 'til dawn and then went on to Dallas to play a Petroleum Club Party. Huge ballroom at the Statler-Hilton with a revolving bandstand at one end and stationary risers at the other. We alternated sets on the revolving stand with Shep Fields and the hall was so big that we could barely hear Leon Merion's big band at the other end featuring the swingin' Charlie Shavers. Believe me, there was whole lotta trumpetin' goin' on that night with Ralph, Leon and Charlie. But the real stars of the night were the guests themselves. The men in latest formal attire and their significant others all decked out in themes of color, fusia, yellow, blue, green, orange, you name it. . . whatta a night," he said.

Back home in Columbus after changing careers and becoming a Realtor, Chuz thoroughly enjoyed a night some 25 years after his traveling days. It was one of those calls that musicians love to get: from some place distant about a gathering of names you like to be with, playing what you love to play.

"I got a call at my office from a great trumpet player from Chicago, Tommy Sanders. Tommy was coming to Columbus with the New McKinney Cottonpickers for the band's first appearance at the Valley Dale. Tommy said their jazz tenor man was sick and couldn't make the trip. Would I consider doing the gig? The band, at one time all black, consisted of five saxes, three trumpets, one bone, piano, bass, drums and banjo so I knew it would be a heavy read. . . something I hadn't done in 25 years. I told him I'd think about it and call him back. I no sooner hung up when the phone rang again and this time it was Chuck Robinette, who'd played piano on the Marterie band who said he was 'ramroddin' the Cottonpickers and, no buts about it, you're gonna do this gig!

We did. . . a total blast. . . tough charts but a lot of solo work. . . and a steamboat load of kicks and licks. . . . Maybe it was the heat and humidity, or that smokey little stage room later or playing with Robinette again but I think surrealism 'sat in' during the first break when I was rappin' with one of the distinguished trumpet players, a white haired black gentleman named Charles Victor Moore. . . blew me away! He played Valley Dale in '34 when my mom and dad were trippin' the light fantastic on the old floor."

The memorable dates, people and places never really go away. In fact, such memories are what made the business something many couldn't leave, said Louis "Lou King" DiSario a year before his death. He was a proud member of the American Guild of Variety Artists for 30 years – 1946 to 1976 – and he thought it was just in "his blood." Unlike today, he told me, celebrities were far more accessible. "I played a place called the Merry-Go-Round Night Club in Steubenville, OH where I socialized with Billy Eckstine, Andy Williams and his brothers and Vic Damone. Sometime earlier, I was working Walker's Café in Steubenville and a guy comes to see the show. The bartender tells me he was Dean Martin, the 'stickman" for the gambling house club. The stickman pulled the dice back on the table. After my act, he introduced himself and we spent the night talking about the business. This was before Dean worked with partner Jerry Lewis. Think about it. . . Dean came to see me . . . and we talked about places and nights. I never forgot it."

But the business side of big bands is a reality that can overwhelm even the best intentions. Bruce Raeburn, son of once famous bandleader and saxophonist Boyd and curator of the William Ransom Hogan Jazz Archives at Tulane University, saw it up close and personal.

"I have mixed feelings about the future of this business. As the son of bandleader Boyd Raeburn, and vocalist Ginny Powell (who was featured with Raeburn, Jerry Wald, Gene Krupa, Charlie Barnet and Harry James) I have come to appreciate what a huge logistical undertaking the organization and maintenance of a big band actually is. Boyd made many sacrifices to keep his bands together especially from 1942-58, and yet when one hears the music that was made possible as a result of these efforts, I have to agree that it was all worth it. What the big bands accomplished from late 1920s through the late 1950s (and, in some cases, beyond) is one of the greatest accomplishments in the history of American music in the 20th century. Yet, today it is difficult, if not impossible, to keep a big band together. Most of what I see now are efforts which are only partially successful because band chemistry is something that does not occur with a few rehearsals. The great virtuosos of the big band era, musicians who had technique plus something more – too numerous to name – have passed from the scene and these are voices that cannot be replaced. Even when the section work is happening, solos are too often a disappointment. Thank goodness these bands of the past recorded prolifically making it possible for young people to learn about a musical age that has, in fact, become a part of history. But who knows what surprises await us in the future?"

There is a new twist, of course, which goes beyond the music. Exercise to swing and jazz called jazz exercise. . . which Richard Simmons featured with his "sweating to the oldies" exercise. Nowadays, said the Kansas State Collegian, it adds electronics. A fast-paced game updates the practice of dance fitness by making players sweat as they pound their feet to on-screen instructions. Since its release in the 1990s the game has brought about a new dimension to dance. It combines music and technology as well as dance. But it brings the obvious question: is it dancing for the joy of the music and the fun of it or is it exercise that substitutes music for television?

Some social scientists see a connection in the generations of today and yesterday. "Does Generation X have anything in common with those who lived in the Swing Era? . . . If today's Generation X truly does sense some sort of connection with their parallel 'trouble generation' from the turn of the century, it's no surprise that the influence of early hot bands is so prominent in today's definition of popular swing," says a web social scientist. "It stands to reason that today's young people might long for a simpler era and, in retrospect, look at American culture one of the simplest seeming is the Swing Era. Nostalgia for old music is the only way anyone could listen to swing. . . it's grasping for an earlier time, when decisions were black and white, one's life direction was easy to plan, and the music embodied. . . purer than anything today."

Popular NPR DJ David Miller of "Swingin' Down the Lane" says audiences always change but the music from previous eras still remains resonant to the ear.

"In the '80s my audience was composed almost exclusively of people who were at least teenagers during WWII," David continues. "They were listening to 'the music of their lives' and they found it a welcome contrast to what was saturating the airwaves during that time period. In recent years, though, I've noticed a subtle shift. The older people still love my program because it brings back pleasant memories of 'real music.' Young people, too, are coming to appreciate the big band sound. At first I thought it was because of the retro-swing movement, but I'm not so sure anymore. Teenagers who contact me don't make reference to Big Daddy VooDoo or Cherry Poppin' or whoever. . . instead they talk as if they have just discovered music of 60 years ago and like what they hear. Honestly, I think they find it quaint. They often describe it as 'cool' but that's an all-encompassing word for the under-25 set

these days."

Robert J. Robbins who writes about big band and jazz grew up on the 1970s music of Blood, Sweat and Tears and Chicago a decade or so after the big band era but his aunt's gift of a batch of 78 rpm records of Tommy and Jimmy Dorsey, Benny Goodman, Harry James and others got his attention. "I was immediately attracted to the sounds of the big bands which was anything but current at the time. About four years later, I became enamored of the music of Glenn Miller at a time when psychedelia was flowering on pop charts. When I was 19 I attended two concerts which permanently altered my musical outlook and directed me unmistakably toward big band jazz. The first of these featured Maynard Ferguson with his all-star British band which showed me that the music of the big bands was not merely nostalgia but could be decidedly contemporary. Two months later, I heard the Stan Kenton Orchestra for the first time and the Kenton band, with its five trumpets, five trombones, five reeds, piano, bass, drums and Latin percussion roared over me like a tidal wave and I have been a committed Kenton fan ever since."

Michigan big band leader Gary Greenfelder thinks the core of big band music will always be around. "However, it will likely never get big enough for anyone to make a career of playing just that. I, fortunately, decided many years ago to find a different career to 'make money.' I believe that I have found a perfect blend between a career (making money) and playing music (my obsessive hobby). It takes a lot of time and I have chosen to make sacrifices to do so. Being a band leader (as a hobby) has many drawbacks. But I kind of fell in it by accident and have chosen to stay there. The only people that understand the 'behind the scenes' work that a bandleader does. . . are other bandleaders. There is plenty of love for this that bandleaders and players have to have. Not that both don't take lots of time. I do both. In fact, I play both lead trumpet and solo trumpet. I have a big band One Beat Back as well as a small group GI Ensemble. I know it sounds crazy to some. . . but I love playing and will do this as long as I can."

Just read the comments of the territorial bandleaders in chapters 1 and 2 and you know that ideas still flow and efforts continue to conjure the excitement that was the catalyst at the ballroom or dance spot near you. Today you can hear the big band sounds in churches, senior centers, corporate stockholder meetings, non-profit fund-raising events, summer concerts on the green, the traditional college and high school proms, private club holiday dances and neighborhood block parties. Will they go away?

Not as long as audiences keep coming back and new ideas embellish old standards or traditional big band music is recreated by the remaining "ghost bands" and others.

Even zoot suits which evolved from the 1930s and then re-appeared in the play "Zoot Suit" and the movie of the same name in the 1980s returned once more in high schools in the early years of the 21st Century.

Disc jockeys, a term first heard on radio in the 1930s when commentator Walter

Winchill used it to describe the first announcer, Martin Block, to put the disc on the turntable and talk in between recorded numbers have continued although their roles have changed to a more homogenized and packaged form in the 21st century than was envisioned in the trial and error days of radio's beginning. Block, at the time, was using records to fill in between news bulletins regarding developments in the Lindbergh baby kidnapping. He created the illusion as he played recordings that he was broadcasting from a ballroom with top bands performing live, thus, the hit show later called Make Believe Ballroom. Band remotes had special announcers who became familiar faces to bandleaders in different cities. Announcers introduced numbers and offered light conversation to give the music and the players more personal appeal. Today a listener frequently has to wait for a commercial break to find out who played the number or sang it and even then it's not always included.

I talked to many during my research who long for the days of Martin Block, the legendary Symphony Sid and Casey Casem who used their personalities to help project the music and their up-to-date knowledge of the bands and musicians to keep listeners interested. Talk, in other words, made the music even more interesting.

A web site produced by the Department of English in American Studies at the University of Virginia raised the important question though; "Why Swing, Why Today?"

Swing and big band music disappeared before. . . will they again?

Says the Virginia web site: "It's an unanswerable question, but no matter what happens, 'swing' will always mean something to everybody. Swing musicians themselves couldn't define it; Louis Armstrong vaguely referred to 'swing' as 'my idea of how a tune should go.' Swing bands may evolve into new and different entities and swing's centennial celebration in 2035 may feature music nothing like what Goodman and Ellington performed, but one thing is certain: as far as swing is concerned Americans know, and probably always will know that it don't mean a thing without it."

Richard Duffy in a review in Jazz Review a few years ago insists big bands have always been with us. "Actually, big bands never went anywhere; they have, to some extent, succumbed to economics; more importantly, to the many modes of styles of music which constitute simplicity and lie under the umbrella of what is considered today as pop music – this covers a lot of ground."

Succinctly explained and certainly true. One big band leader on the west coast told me that to put together a group of 18 or so seasoned personnel for rehearsal costs thousands. Contrast that to Glenn Miller, Benny Goodman and Harry James when they organized their bands in the 1930s and asked sidemen to rehearse for no pay. In fact, I don't recall a rehearsal band that ever paid me for my time. We had club owners who never paid us for actually performing in front of an audience!

In its special double issue, US News & World Report, July 8-15, 2002, called

"Music & America," the editors chronicled the diversity and expanse of American music but ignored swing and big band and focused on jazz. But the magazine did demonstrate the power of music daily in American lives. "The simplest song can make a sharp point. In the mid '40s, striking tobacco workers in Charleston, SC, fueled their months-long picket with hymns, changing a line of an old black spiritual from 'I will overcome' to 'we will overcome.' The new version caught on, evolving into 'We Shall Overcome,' the rallying cry of the civil rights movement, source of inspiration and courage in frightening times."

Think of the tunes you hum today without thinking of who created them or why and you understand our love affair with music.

Today's big bands attempting to reach beyond a regional image rely on a variety of promotional tools to convey their sound and attract audiences. Individual songs that can resonant with the public are certainly important but they're difficult to achieve in a day when so much radio and television music is canned. Scattered Public Broadcasting stations can be helpful as well as web sites. CDs are a mainstay whether it's a territorial band or a leader of a band with larger aspirations.

Four bands, for example, have gained attention from music critics and audiences in different sections of the country. Some believe they represent the 21st century descendants of the touring big bands of the swing era. They include the United States Air Force's Airmen of Note, a direct descendant of Glenn Miller's Army Air Force Band in World War II; Gordon Goodwin and his Big Phat Band from Los Angeles, Chris Walden and his Big Band, also Los Angeles based, and Maria Schneider and her Big Jazz Band from New York.

Certainly there are others. Big Daddy VooDoo, The Flying Newtrends, Cherry Poppin' Daddies, Squirrel Nut Zippers, Flipped Fedoras, Bill Elliott's Big Band and the list goes on.

THE AIRMEN OF NOTE

The band was created about a year before Glenn Miller organized the original Army Air Corps Training Command band in the fall, 1942. Its purpose, of course, was to carry on the tradition of Glenn's dance band and undoubtedly serve as the best recruiting tool a military branch could have at the time; a band playing popular music, not military marches. Today, the band, which is still headquartered at Bolling Air Force Base, carries out an international mission . . . as a traveling dance band, America's International Musical Ambassadors.

I interviewed the former manager/drummer of the Airmen of Note, Chief Master Sgt Claude Askew Jr, shortly after the band had finished one of its two annual 20 day US tours.

He remembered the "Serenade in Blue" national radio programs that ran for a number of years and the heritage that affects every military musician who auditions

The Airmen of Note band was created about a year before Glenn Miller organized the original Army Air Corps Training Command band in 1942. Its purpose was to carry on the tradition of Glenn's dance band. Today, the band, which is still headquartered at Bolling Air Force Base, carries out an international mission . . . as a traveling dance band, America's International Musical Ambassadors.

or joins the group.

"I was a one striper at Barksdale Air Force Base in 1971 when the Airmen of Note came to a local high school in Shreveport, and they just 'blew my socks off that night.' I was determined to find a way to join the band," he recalls. He said there has always been this argument whether the Miller Band was and is a dance band or a jazz band. "Glenn faced the same argument and I'm sure he'd agree with us. We take the presentation of our music extremely serious when we put on our pinks and green and we go out and represent the Miller Band and the United States Air Force. . . It was probably the best band out there then. . . and we feel that pride today. The argument that it wasn't a jazz band isn't really a debate. . . it wasn't intended to be a jazz band . . . it was and is a world class dance band and I don't think one came close to it."

The band is a part of a rotating group of eight units in the United States Air Force which go on tour abroad and in the states. Stateside tours usually consist of evening programs, high school and college clinics and other such events in conjunction with sponsoring groups such as newspapers, radio and/or television stations or other civic organizations. "While we are certainly a recruiting tool for USAF," Claude says, "we do clinics with high school and college students to 'plant a seed.' We think of ourselves as sharing the opportunity with students for them to see and, in a sense, and hear what we do."

When the Airmen of Note leave a school it makes sure that the music director has copies of the group's CDs and how to contact the band. Any area organization can obtain the Airmen of Note's CDs by contacting high schools, public or private libraries in your area and requesting they write a letter on official stationery to the Office of Public Affairs, 201 McChord St., Bolling Air Force Base, Washington, DC. 20032-0202. The CDs will be sent as reference tools at the library. Airmen of Note CDs aren't for sale generally.

Competition is keen for section positions in the band and college music majors dominate. Claude said that about half of the band is from North Texas State University, one of the oldest jazz education programs in the country.

The band has backed a roster of famed players and singers over the years.

Count Basie singer and soloist Joe Williams called working with Airmen of Note "an absolute gas. They knocked me out. I've never had more fun working with a big band."

The 18-member band is informal about each program although it goes to the gig like any dance band trying to please the crowd. " We sneak a peak between the curtains and try to determine what they'd like . . . although we have a program of music in mind. Our audiences are more and more diverse. Everyone wants to hear Miller stuff and we don't back away from it but we don't try to interfere with the rights of the Miller Estate which granted us use of some of the Miller music. But on a given night you could hear a little bit of a variety of popular groups as well as Miller. I suppose we take about 125 charts with us on any particular tour," Claude continues.

The veteran drummer, who along with alto saxophonist Joe Eckert managed the group in 1998 until his retirement, sees the band meeting a "very worthwhile mission. Our job is to make sure that everyone in those seats gets at least a glimpse of something they came to hear. We want to entertain. . . I don't want to pigeon-hole the band. . . I want the band to be a little bit of everything to everybody."

Glenn Miller would have certainly approved.

CHRIS WALDEN BIG BAND

He started out a teen trumpeter in Germany writing big band arrangements for his high school band and thinking that one day there would be better opportunities. There were. It didn't necessarily happen the way he thought but what in this life ever does?

Chris Walden is one of those gifted musicians who bypassed New York and went straight to where the action was and has been; Hollywood and Los Angeles, CA.

Before the age of 30 he had made a musical name for himself on two continents.

He played with the German National Youth Jazz Orchestra and he wrote more than 400 arrangements for German radio big bands while studying composition and arranging at the University of Cologne. Later he conducted the RIAS Big Band in Berlin and Frankfort's Big Radio Band and served as musical director for the nationally televised German Movie Award Show and he scored some 20 films. Next stop? America.

His talent at 29 caught attention upon his arrival. Within weeks, a network executive offered him a chance to write some music. . . on spec. His Hollywood credits came at light speed for someone his age. He wrote the soundtrack for the Hallmark production "The Last Cowboy," Gene Wilder's A&E movie "The Lady in Question" and the Sci Fi Channel's "Alien Siege" and "Crimson Force" and added a few compositions for CBS and ABC for good measure.

German born Chris Walden is one of the new young stars working in film and big bands on the west coast. His big band plays primarily west coast gigs but his sound has traversed the coasts.
Photo submitted by Chris Walden

Word got around. News traveled like wildfire among entertainers seeking new, fresh material. He has since worked for Sheryl Crow, Christopher Cross, Nancy Wilson and Bill Conti and, not long ago, with Michael Bolton on his Concord release "Bolton Swings Sinatra."

What does he need with a big band?

"My big band fills lots of important roles for me," he says. "I look at my big band work as year to year because, frankly, the band simply doesn't cover its own costs. I don't make money off it. For me running a big band, however, is a luxury I thoroughly enjoy and I'll keep it as long as I can afford it. The money I put into the big band I don't get back directly. . . I get it back indirectly through other writing assignments."

And in the time span it took Glenn Miller to put a successful big band on the road in the east, Chris has launched a 17 plus singer plus leader aggregation on the west coast and scored a major coup early; two 2005 Grammy nominations (Best Large Jazz Ensemble Album and Best Instrumental for his arrangement of "Cherokee") for his first CD, "Home of My Heart" six generations after Glenn. He said he chose the title because musical passion is where his heart is. The CD features long lyrical melody passages which, Chris says, is reflects what he feels.

"I love creating big lush music," he says with a smile.

He's optimistic about big bands, he adds, but he knows the glory days of Glenn, Benny, Harry and others won't be back. "But big bands have come back because of the tremendous number of schools teaching it, young people's excitement about it and the pop music artists who are getting comfortable doing swing and jazz. That really helps all of us."

And he loves it because it gives him the opportunity to express himself musically.

"It's a great feeling of satisfaction to know that I can create my own compositions, arrangements, decide what gigs we play, decide what players I want and, at the other end, get feedback from a live audience," he told me. "A band certainly isn't a democratic organization but you can gain respect from those who play with you and for you. But you don't do that by creating fear as a leader. I try not to be an 'asshole', excuse my language, but I've seen leaders who make playing one of fear of punishment."

Yet, there are the risks as well as the adrenalin of reaching for another rung up the ladder. While in New York City for the Grammy Award event, Chris scheduled a gig but poor advance ticket sales cancelled it. "It simply wasn't going to work, " he said recognizing that he still is a west coast band that rarely gets out of the region because of the cost of carrying top professionals.

Chris uses two musical books; the dance book, which contains over 200 charts, gives him diversity although he says the band doesn't do that many dance dates. The concert charts include "probably 40 to 45 compositions and allow us to showcase our diversity including my movie and television numbers.

"For example, I did a special arrangement of David Foster's "Winter Games" which I made sure was available just as the 2006 Winter Olympics was underway. The good thing about all of this, of course, is that I wouldn't want to do just one thing. . . compose or just arrange. It's nice to go back and forth and go out to a club date or someplace and play for people. "Winter Games" is up front number in a summer 2006 CD called "No Bounds" from Origin Records which adds creative work on light and airy old standards "When You Wish Upon a Star," "Smile" and "People Will Say We're In Love."

With all kinds of contemporary music available, why return to hits of a very different yesterday? "The three Disney songs – "When You Wish Upon a Star," "Someday My Prince" and "Small World" – actually came from my past. I was commissioned by the Frankfort Radio Big Band in Germany to write them for a concert we did under the motto "Disney Goes Jazz. "So I didn't really choose the songs myself but I chose out of the concert these three numbers in my album," Chris says. And he sees this CD as very similar to "Home of My Heart." "It's a good collection of arrangements I've done in the last two years that are quite special to me. However, this time I tried to explore a bit wider range of instrumentation, adding strings and French horns and I experimented with an electric cello and other things."

I think most aficionados would agree with jazz luminary Dave Grusin. After hearing the "Home of My Heart" CD, Dave told publicists: "The performances are superb and the soloists are first rate, but the writing is the star here. . . Chris has truly made his mark, and he owns it."

MARIA SCHNEIDER BIG BAND

She could easily teach entrepreneurial bandleading as well as music creativity 100 to 500. She has that restlessness and free spirit that sets her music apart yet she's well grounded in a world that demands resourcefulness and an appreciation of roots.

Maria Schneider made some quantum leaps from Windom, MN, a village of 3,666 that had far more farmers than musicians among its population, to Manhattan with some impressive stops along the way. She received not one but five Grammy nominations from 1995 to 2005 for her album Concert in the Garden," more than any other jazz artist or album. "Concert in the Garden" won the 2005 jazz album of the year, large ensemble of the year and Downbeat chose her the jazz arranger and jazz composer of the year. In less time than some bandleaders from the early days found success, Maria's work ethic and creativity connected with critics and event planners at home and abroad.

But it started in an unassuming way near her hometown. She studied music theory at the University of Minnesota and then convinced the Eastman School of Music in Rochester, NY to accept her. She earned acceptance to Eastman's summer Arrangers' Holiday and "I worked my butt off. I really didn't sleep that whole time," she said of the experience. On to the Berklee College of Music in Boston and a trip to Miami for a semester. Back to Rochester and the Eastman School where Fred Sturm, Eastman professor of jazz studies, told writer Mark Liu of the University of Rochester Review: "She had such a hunger and genuine interest in learning. There was a tenacity about her – she was going to become something. But it wasn't calculating."

A great description. Months later she was working as an assistant to the legendary pianist and composer Gil Evans and as a protégé of the innovative composer Bob Brookmeyer in New York City. In 36 months, she had decided to front her own group; a jazz big band. Her first gig at Visiones in Greenwich Village on Monday nights was what every player hopes for. . . a long, steady engagement. She was there for five years. She remembers how an argument with the late drummer Mel Lewis over tempo when the band was working on one of her compositions caused Lewis to strongly suggest she should "start your own orchestra." She did just that in 1993. Maria sat down with a rolodex and called musicians she and her friends knew and started rehearsing.

One of her first recruits, pianist Frank Kimbrough, said he was skeptical when he heard that some female was looking for a pianist. His skepticism remained until he listened to a tape of her arrangements. Within 30 seconds of the tape he was convinced the music was special he said.

Yet, she was realistic too. "If I have to be a waitress and have a band on the side, that's fine." It's the price many have paid. . . some still do.

Composer/arranger Monk Rowe says music inspiration "is a very funny thing. . . . sometimes it comes from hearing something, sometimes it comes from meeting people. So I would get these little 'gooses' of inspiration and I'd go to the piano and start messing around and come up with tunes and they would be really be closely identified with persons I was affected by."

Maria's work ethic comes close. But, she admits it starts as a puzzle. "You look at the pieces, try to find some that fit together. Eventually you've got enough connected that you can make out a face in them and then you look for the pieces you need to complete it. . . . The rhythmic, harmonic and melodic flavors in my work are undoubtedly influenced by my love of Spanish, flamenco, and Brazilian music. Jazz is still at my core but the intricacy and development one would find in classical music is more present. Even I become hard pressed to define my music," she told a reviewer.

Yet, she blended others' influence. Maria still remembers when Toshiko Akiyoshi brought her orchestra to Minneapolis and the affect it had on her. "It wasn't that Toshiko was a woman. I loved watching her conduct, so I could see there was someone doing what I wanted to do, and that it could be done; composing, conducting and touring with your orchestra."

Her 17-piece orchestra travels everywhere and brings rave reviews. She has done commissioned work with American and European orchestras and guest conducted in 17 countries. Her first Grammy recording "Evanescence" was nominated for two awards; best large jazz ensemble performance and best instrumental composition.

Now she's working to support herself which is a measure of success in the music business. "The success is nice because it means I can work. But it's important to appreciate the process, not the result. The process is what we live with."

She certainly embellished the process, though. And, while she still soaks up all the musical flavors and constructive advice she can absorb, she told Larry Kelp who wrote the Artist Profile for San Francisco Performances in early 2006, she is now offering advice and inspiration to those seeking to find success in music.

Downbeat columnist Jason Koransky explains: Maria's 2004 Grammy Awards opened a whole new retailing world in the hidebound music business. Instead of relying on retail store sales, Maria used ArtistShare and sold thousands of her CDs through her web site, MariaSchneider.com Others have tried it but it was the first time a Grammy nomination came from web sales exclusively.

But it's her music that reaches across generations and time machines. Said Richard S. Ginell of Variety.com in reviewing Maria's first performance in the Walt Disney Concert hall in early 2006 before a crowd that paid $87 for the best seats: ". . . The Maria Schneider Jazz Orchestra gave us a startling different yet wonderful vision of what a big band can

One of the west coast's hottest new big bands, Gordon Goodwin and the "Big Phat" Band. The band has brought any number of young fans to listen and enjoy big bands. Photo courtesy of Gordon Goodwin

sound like. In fact, there were a couple of passages that rose to the spine-chilling level of sublime – and when was the last time that happened at a big band concert?"

No question, it's a brave new big band world.

GORDON GOODWIN BIG PHAT BAND

You know you're listening to Gordon Goodwin's big band when you hear the number "Hunting Wabbits." But creative arrangements like "A Game of Inches" or "The Jazz Police" could be your sensors too. Every band has a personality and Gordon's group of Los Angeles professionals give the Big Phat Band plenty of pizzazz.

"Big Phat?" It draws curiosity certainly. Gordon's response: "Phat is an acronym for hot, terrific – although my 14-year-old son says it's an adjective that means of very high quality," he told me in an email. I couldn't find it in my dictionary but then new words are being coined as I write this especially by a younger generation that had no idea what "alligator" or "Boogie Woogie" meant.

His first CD album "Swingin' From the Fences" in 2000 was a breakthrough.

"I didn't know whether we could make it work," he said, recalling his attempts to launch a big band in the '80s and '90s.

No question young people are "roots" to his audience in a day when hip hop, rock and other music derivatives brainwash us with the unfounded notion that swing and nostalgia big band are dead. Said Reveries Online Magazine in 2005:

". . . Gordon Goodwin. . . had previously tried and failed – twice – to launch a big band in the '80s and '90s. 'His music is so well known by kids that kids want to hear the band,' comments Jim Warrick, who coordinates jazz studies at a Chicago-area high school In part, Gordon's music is known and loved by kids because he's composed music for movies including 'The Incredibles.'"

Music school directors know Gordon because he keeps them informed. He told the New York Times that he probably appeals to young people because he records with the latest technology, emails continuously, offers an inviting web site, gets recognition with T-shirts and his CDs at performances and he and his talented group stay after to talk and sign autographs.

It was a home gig at California State University at Northridge, his alma mater, that jump-started the Big Phat band. Like Benny Goodman years before, Gordon connected with the kids.

"Swingin' From the Fences" got a Grammy nomination in 2002 when his renditions of "Sing Sang Sung" was named the Best Instrumental Composition and his "Bach 2 Part Invention in D Minor" won the Best Instrumental Arrangement. Add those to his three Emmys and his talent demonstrates its versatility.

A 2003 CD called "Big Phat Band XXL" added the legendary vocalist Johnny Mathis to a super star list of studio musicians.

Said one reviewer: "The heyday of big band jazz may have been back in the last century, but contemporary groups like Big Phat Band have found a market among teenagers, particularly those in school and college music programs. Goodwin, a film and television soundtrack composer who formed his group in 1999, has aggressively courted this young audience. Jazz educators say students are a natural market for big bands because these are the most common type of ensemble in most schools."

"I think what's so terrific is that the kids really get excited. . . they yell and scream," Gordon told me. "That's what really got me started. One of the best learning experiences of my life was attending the Stan Kenton Clinic at Redlands University when I was a kid. It did much to form my musical aesthetic." Animated audiences will always bring people back . . . and they alert concert and dance bookers, too.

He's doing what turned him on in his high school he said in an album liner.

"I always thought big bands were the coolest thing in the world. From the very first time

I heard one back in Jr. High School, the sound of 17 guys roaring away really resonated with me. It became a life-long love, and even though I would study and appreciate other forms of music, from rock'n'roll to classical and would come to make a nice living as a commercial composer, my passion for big bands would never wane."

If it's not the water he drinks in LA . . . it must be in the genes.

The reality, said noted jazz and swing columnist and critic, Ralph Gleason, in Downbeat Magazine in 1960 as a decade ushered in rock music "People are not interested in coming to a ballroom and dancing anymore. . . I know that we play a lot of ballrooms, but I'm certain that most of the people who come through the doors are into jazz. They're not there to dance."

Looking around as dance halls closed doors. . . he was correctly assessing the mood of the country at the time. Just a year earlier, Stan Kenton, addressing a National Dance Band camp in cooperation with Downbeat, warned young musicians they would have to make their own opportunities. But, he added, "remember before Glenn Miller, Ellington . . . there were no bands. . . they made it themselves."

Whether you're a contemporary jazz unit or a band that plays mellow music for dancers, the need is there and the demand continues, says Henry Mason of the Sentimental Journey Orchestra of Atlanta.

"Every bandleader I've talked to is really enthusiastic about the business. One told me he was excited going to every gig these days because 'we're finding appreciative audiences.' We're actually rehearsing lots more than I ever did when I started in this business 20 years ago. We wouldn't do this if we didn't really enjoy it. We try our best to deliver an authentic and high quality product because we feel the music deserves it. Les Brown Sr, for example, upon examining our card and picture said: 'Sentimental Journey'. . .hmmm. . . what a great name for a band.' While most of the great ones are gone now. . . I did manage to meet a few personally like Les, Woody Herman, Buddy Rich, Stan Kenton, Harry James, Count Basie and Buddy Morrow. Everyone of them obviously loved their work and all were encouraging when I told them what I do. The music played well is the best monument they can have . . . and we can have," Henry added.

But, says John Matter, director of the National Ballroom & Entertainers Association, we're still talking about the big band and ballroom "business."

"Ballrooms, like other businesses, have needed to evolve in order to survive. What kept the doors open 20 years ago is not going to pay the bills today. Those ballrooms that have survived deserve a pat on the back. But the future is not bright. Competition for the entertainment dollar is fierce and often times unfair to the ballroom operation. Legislative, licensing and insurance issues have all but closed many ballrooms. The bands will outlive the ballrooms, the venues will be different and the bands will be fewer and probably smaller as we go forward," he explains.

And musicians from sidemen to leaders feel the pinch; it drains their enthusiasm and optimism. Bob DeRosa, a bassist and big band camp organizer from Rochester, NY, sees a declining audience of older people, not a growing audience of younger ones. "As a player, I regularly bemoan the graying of the audience for big band music. Those old folks love to come and dance but their kids, the ones with the money that they could be spending at the bar, are generally home watching TV. Which doesn't bode well for the future of the genre. And club owners – the lowest of all people – are helping to kill it as well. Tried getting any gigs lately? Even free ones? There are real pros – some with PhDs no less – in New York City playing for $75 to $100 a gig. It's a real sin.

But sometimes it depends upon your location, too. Frank Wood, a 30-some year veteran tenor saxophonist from Nevada played with Vido Musso, Johnny Mathis, Rickey and the Four Keys in Long Beach and worked a daytime job at MGM in California. "I've been fortunate to work steady while I was playing. In approximately the 15 to 16 years I was playing steadily . . . I was never out of work. I worked in Vegas show bands for three of those years, incidentally. I really got out of the business finally because my second wife got me a job in the movie studios and I couldn't pass it up. Plus the fact my kids were getting old enough to go to school and I had to settle down. I continue to play . . . lots of casuals," he told me in a letter.

Yet, everyone has an opinion about where big band music is going including those who spent years developing it. Jazz star and longtime sideman, the late baritone saxophone great Gerry Mulligan talked to critics years before his death about his take on where the big band music came from and where it might be headed. "I grew up on the big bands of the '30s and '40s and radio. Every night you heard good bands playing from so many places. I'm not interested in the future of jazz as an entity – it's really a bunch of individuals playing. I'm glad there are young musicians coming along interested in the traditions of music not the technology."

Certainly big band nostalgia, which is quite popular today on eBay, at charity dances and virtually any and all kind of fundraisers, is kept alive because of the memories and even current shows, too. Broadway conductor Keith Levenson created the show "Broadway: The Big Band Years" as a tribute to Broadway composers and lyricists of the big band era. The show kicked off a 10-week tour of mostly one nighters, said Sue Merrell in the Grand Rapids Press in 2005. The touring band, called the Curtains Up Orchestra, played numbers like "Singin' In the Rain," "Some Enchanted Evening," "I Get A Kick Out of You," "Just One of Those Things" and other hits of yesterday.

The encouraging signs though are on campuses. The Ohio State Lantern reported in 2005 that, while the songs and bands are different, the jukebox has returned to hangouts around the university. Glenn Miller's "Elmer's Tune" and "Chattanooga Choo Choo" have been replaced by Bon Jovi's "Bad Medicine" and Billy Joel and Marshall Tucker music . . . even Ohio State Marching Band songs. Said the Lantern: "The jukebox looks as old as it sounds, harboring all of its handwritten selections of classy jazz and blues such as John Lee Hooker, BB King, Etta James and Duke Ellington on one sub page."

The music is also found in strange places played by those who you don't associate with musical instruments or musicians. Imagine going to traditional Symphony Hall in Boston to hear a quintet play a benefit for the Longy School of Music and find yourself watching and listening to New England Patriot's burly linebacker Tedy Bruschi play the saxophone. It provides balance in his life. It provides refreshing creativity that he wants, he says. And he tells sportswriters he picks up an alto saxophone at least three times a week when time permits.

Of course, you could also happen to be in a nightclub on a weekend and be listening to comedian Woody Allen playing his axe, too.

Perhaps things haven't changed as much as we think.

Will There Be Big Bands Forever? Bibliography

UC Roundtable
WIBX (Don Cantwell, Dick Robinson)

Kansas State Collegian
March 9, 2005   http://xroads.edu/~Class /am483_
971projects/graham/conclusion.html

David Miller
Swingin' Down the Lane, email no date

Gary Greenfelder

One Beat Back
email Aug. 23, 2005; June 7, 2006

Ralph Gleason
Downbeat Magazine, April 28, 1960

www.jaybeckenstein.com

Dorsey Tippett
emails, 2005, March 20, 2006

Buddy Rich
June, 1986 USA Today undated

The Grand Rapids Press
March 13, 2005 www.mlive.com

John Matter
email Aug. 16, 2005

Bob DeRosa
Rochester, NY email undated

Frank Wood
email Dec. 27, 2001

Auburn Knights
web site www.auburnknights.com

Chuz Alfred
personal correspondence, Oct. 30, 2000

Campus Jukeboxes Spice Up the Night

Ohio State Lantern, March 14, 2005

Monk Rowe
Utica College Roundtable, WIBX Radio, Dec. 14, Dec. 21, 2001

Bruce Raeburn
email May 15, 2002

Chris Walden
telephone interviews, Feb, 15, Feb. 24, 2006

Costa Release
'No Bounds,' emails May 11, May 15, 2006

The Artist As Businessman
Jason Koransky, Downbeat, February, 2005

www.MariaSchneider.com

Leading Jazz to a Big Band Future
Mark Liu, Rochester Review, Summer/Fall, 2001.

www.allaboutjazz.com.php/news.php?id=4785
December, 2004

www.allaboutjazz.com/php/news_print.php?id=4863
September, 2005

Richard S. Ginell
Maria Schneider Jazz Orchestra, Variety.com

San Francisco Performances
Maria Schneider Orchestra, Feb. 4, 2006

Gordon Goodwin
emails, Sept. 7, 8, 2003

The Definition of 'Phat': Big Band with Big Young Fans
Rutland Herald, April 12, 2005

Reveries Magazine
web March 10, 2005

Silverline Records release
undated promotion

Hard Contact Is Music to Bruschi's Ears
New York Times, Jan. 29, 2004

Dr. Lou Fischer
Capital University, emails, April 8, 18, 2006

Louis "Lou King" DiSario, letter, Feb. 9, 2002

Bob January
"What They Don't Teach You at Bandleader School,"
www.bobjanuary.com/bandlead.html March 28, 2006

"The Definition of 'Phat': Big Band with Young Fans,"
New York Times, March 9, 2005

"Big Band Era Jazz,"
Spokane Public Radio, www.kpbx.org/programs/bigbands.htm

Robert J. Robbins
email, September 20, 2001

TODAY'S MAJOR GHOST BANDS

While Stan Kenton refused to even consider a ghost band playing his charts after his death, other leaders either decided it was in the interest of their spouses and families to be able to sell, lease or barter their image and charts.

Since the 1950s, a number of former major touring bands have continued. The most popular, of course, is the Glenn Miller Band led by Larry O'Brien. To many observers, the band is as busy today as it was when Glenn led it in the 1940s. Here's an incomplete list of bands that have continued over the years:

Dick Johnson and the Artie Shaw Orchestra
www.dickjohnsonjazz.com

Guy Lombardo's Royal Canadians with Al Pierson
2469 Spring Hill Road, Aubrey, TX 76227, Telephone 940-365-9491
email: ApGLO@aol.com

The Russ Morgan Orchestra with Jack Morgan
PO Box 218, Rapids City, IL 61278, Telephone 309-496-2102,
email: RMOband@webtv.net

Jan Garber Orchestra with Howard H. Schneider
1026 Hillside Dr., Kewaskum, WI 53040

Accordionist Lawrence Welk advertising his orchestra in the days before TV launched him to national fame.

Photo courtesy of James Ronan Collection, Iowa

The Count Basie Orchestra with Bill Hughes

Telephone 631-473-4944 Count Basie Enterprises, 407 East Main St, Suite 7, Port Jefferson, NY 11777-1868

The Cab Calloway Orchestra with C. Calloway Brooks

email: info@cabcalloway.cc web: www.cabcalloway.com

Jimmy Dorsey Orchestra with Bill Tole

email: BillTole1@aol.com web: www.jimmydorseyorchestra.com

Eddy Howard Orchestra

Gerald Accola, 245 Beecher, East Dubuque, IL 61025-1103, Telephone: 815-255-3196

Sammy Kaye Orchestra with Roger Thorpe

115 Guilford School Road, New Paltz, NY 12561, Telephone: 845-255-1944
web: www.sammykayeorchestra.com

Hal McIntyre Orchestra with Don Pentleton
email: donpentleton@yahoo.com

Glenn Miller Orchestra with Larry O'Brien
Glenn Miller Productions, 801 International Parkway, 5th Floor, Lake Mary, FL 32746

Woody Herman's Thundering Herd
directed by Frank Tiberi

Lester Lanin Orchestra
Ted Schmidt & Associates, Telephone 800-972-1108, email: TedSchmidt@aol.com

Les Brown Jr. and the Band of Renown
contact American Entertainment Treasures, Telephone 818-209-0669
web: www.lesbrownsbandofrenown.com

The Billy May Orchestra
Visa Management, email: VSAlik@aol.com Ann Vracin

The Gene Krupa Orchestra with Michael Berkowitz
Telephone 800-397-6293, Email: berkowitz66@msn.com

Tommy Dorsey Orchestra with Buddy Morrow
Buddy Morrow Productions, 5415 Lake Howell Rd #224, Winter Park, FL 32792
Telephone: 407-831-1675, FAX 407-339-4071, web: www.buddymorrowproductions.com
email: info@buddymorrowproductions.com

Woody Herman Band with Frank Tiberi
web: www.franktiberi.com

Among other bands of the past that may be available for corporate events, according to Corporate Artists, web: www.corporateartists.com/bigbands.html, are: Artie Shaw Orchestra, Buddy Rich Band, The Dorsey Brothers Orchestra, The Duke Ellington Orchestra, Harry James Orchestra, Nelson Riddle Orchestra directed by Christopher Riddle, Peter Duchin Orchestra, Ray Anthony Orchestra and Larry Elgart's Hooked on Swing Orchestra.

BIG BAND, JAZZ, SWING REPOSITORIES

People like to visit interesting places, do interesting things and what better way to spend a day, weekend or a vacation if you're a big band or swing fan than examining a colorful and exciting part of Americana; the people, places and the sound of the swing era.

I found a number of locations in the United States, mostly at university or college libraries, that could be ideal sites to put on your list of places to visit some day. Obviously, there are more and there's no doubt as big band donors and benefactors see the need to celebrate lives of outstanding and probably forgotten names, bands and dance spots from the early days new exhibits, museums and collections will appear.

Locating your favorite isn't easy, however. Few cities, counties, even universities have actively promoted such sites. And some are buried in congested areas that make getting there once you're in town as difficult as no map at all. Been there. . . done that. That's why I took the time to find as much information and as many ways as I could to help you locate the following repositories that offer a number of surprises to the aficionado. Included below are the organizations, addresses, telephone numbers, web sites and generic information to hopefully make it easier.

ALABAMA JAZZ HALL OF FAME 1631 4th Avenue North, Birmingham, AL 35203. Telephone 205-254-2731; FAX 205-254-2785; email:info@jazzhall. com; web. www.digitrends.com/jazz; Executive Director Ms. Leah Tucker email: LTucker@jazzhall.com. Housed in the historic Carver Theatre for Performing Arts, this museum is closed on Sundays and Mondays. Museum admission is $ (2005) and guided tours are $3 per person (2005). Movies, educational programming, concerts, calendar of jazz events, jazz musicians roster.

AMERICAN JAZZ MUSEUM 1616 E. 18th St., Kansas City, MO 64108; Telephone 816-474-8463 web: www.americanjazzmuseum.com; Email: ajm@kcjazz.org. The museum offers one of the best facilities in the US. A modern 500-seat performing arts center, a theater, and a working jazz club. Located on historic 18th and Vine in Kansas City, this is the place where Charlie Parker, Count Basie, Big Joe Turner and hundreds of others cut their teeth on the jazz of the '20s, '30s and '40s.

BIG BAND AND JAZZ HALL OF FAME FOUNDATION 3817 Via Del Rancho, Oceanside, CA 92056; Telephone 760-945-9833 FAX 760-945-9833; Email: equus100@netzero.net The Hall of Fame is a non-profit organization based in Carlsbad, CA whose purpose is to promote a greater awareness, knowledge and appreciation of big bands and jazz music. It began in 1977 and it has inducted over 200 artists and others who have had a great influence in the popular music world.

BIG BAND RESEARCH AID MUSIC LIBRARY 3rd Floor, Jerome Library, Bowling Green State University, Bowling Green, OH 43403; Telephone 866-LIB-BGSU (toll free) Music Library telephone 419-372-2307; web: www.bgsu.edu/colleges/library/library/music/bigband1.html. General historical surveys of big band music including pictorial histories.

BLACK ARCHIVES, RESEARCH CENTER AND MUSEUM Florida A&M University, Tallahassee, FL 323307; Telephone 850-599-3020; Web: http://168.223.36.3 /acad/archives. The museum is an electronic gallery. For information contact Prof. James N. Eaton

CHICAGO BLUES ARCHIVES Harold Washington Library Center, 400 S. State Street, Chicago, IL 60605; Telephone 312-747-4850. This special archive holds a significant collection of recordings of 78s to CDs and includes a number of noted blues artist's audio and video recordings of oral history.

CENTER FOR BLACK MUSIC RESEARCH Columbia College Chicago, 600 South Michigan Ave, Chicago, IL 60605; Telephone 312-344-7586; FAX 312-344-8029. Research requests should be made to Suzanne Flandreau, librarian and archivist. Web: www.cbmr.org/lib. This is a comprehensive research center which has an electronic index of music collections and vertical file materials. It includes printed music, photos and videotapes and manuscripts.

DELTA BLUES MUSEUM #1 Blues Alley, PO Box 459, Clarksdale, MS 38614; Telephone 662-627-6820; FAX 662-627-7263; Web: www.deltabluesmuseum.org; Email: dbmuseum@clarksdale.com.

EUBIE BLAKE PAPERS ca 1905-1983 Maryland Historical Society Library, 201 West Monument Street, Baltimore, MD 21201-4674; Telephone 410-685-3750; FAX 410-385-2105 web: www.mdhs.org; Email: library@mdhs.org This is a huge archive of 94 boxes of papers, correspondence, manuscripts, photos, etc. WARNING: To the layperson who attempts to download and print. . . this file is 177 pages without any preliminary page to describe it or its size. If you plan to download and print this file. . . make sure you have 200 sheets of paper in your printer bin.

FELIX E. GRANT JAZZ ARCHIVES University of the District of Columbia, 4200 Connecticut Ave NW, Washington DC 20008, Building #41, Van Ness Campus. Web: www.Irducc.wric.org/index.html The archives contains the Grant digital collection, radio interviews and is a resource center to study, preserve and continue the development of jazz.

INSTITUTE OF JAZZ STUDIES John Cotton Dana Library, Rutgers, the State University of New Jersey, 185 University Avenue, Newark, NJ 07102; Telephone 973-353-5595; FAX 973-353-5944; web: www.libraries.rutgers.edu/rul/libs/jazz/shtml.

JAZZ AND MONTEREY JAZZ FESTIVAL Stanford University Archive of Recorded Sound, 541 Lasuen Mall-Braun Music Center, Stanford, CA 94305-3076; Telephone 650-723-9312; FAX 650-725-11445; web: www.sul.Stanford.edu/depts./ars/using.html email: soundarchive@stanford.edu Richard Koprowski, asst. achiver; Aurora Perez, operations manager. No archive holdings are allowed to circulate. Only a small part of the archive is catalogued. First festival included Louis Armstrong, Harry James, Dave Brubeck, Billie Holiday and Paul Desmond.

JAZZ FOUNDATION OF AMERICA 322 West 48th St, 3rd Floor, New York City, NY 10036; Telephone 212-245-3999; web: www.jazzfoundation.org; email: pledge@jazzfoundation.org; Wendy Atlas Oxenhorn, executive director. JFA promotes cultural and educational activities that build awareness of the music and the musicians that make it. JFA operates the Jazz Musicians' Emergency Fund which assists struggling jazz artists many of whom are older and need medical and financial assistance. The foundation was founded in 1989.

KINGWOOD COLLEGE LIBRARY AMERICAN POPULAR MUSIC 1900-1950; web: http://kclibrary.nhmccd.edu/music-2.html American popular music subject guide arranged chronologically.

LAWRENCE WELK COLLECTION North Dakota State University, The Libraries PO Box 5599, 1201 Albrecht Blvd., Fargo, ND 58105-5599; Telephone 701-231-8416; FAX 701-231-7138; web: www.lib.ndsu.nodak.edu/grhc/history-culture/lawrencewelk.

LEN LYONS COLLECTION OF JAZZ RECORDINGS; The Loeb Music Library, Music Building, North Yard, Harvard University, Cambridge, MA; Telephone 617-495-2794; FAX 617-496-4636; Email: Robert J. Dennis, recordings curator rdennis@fas.harvard.edu. The library holds music, jazz, blues, and American popular music collections including 2,500 LP recordings from jazz critic Len Lyons. It also includes the Joseph Jeffers Dodge Duke Ellington Collection of more than 2,000 recordings and other visuals devoted to Ellington's career.

LIONEL HAMPTON INTERNATIONAL JAZZ COLLECTION Lionel Hampton School of Music, Music Building, Room 306 University of Idaho, Moscow, ID 83844-4015; Telephone voice: 208-885-6231; FAX 208-885-7254; web: www.classuidaho.edu/music/lion.html; email: music@uidaho.edu. The Lionel Hampton Center is a collection of musical scores, scrapbooks, records, documents, photos musical instruments (approximately 150,000 items) from Hampton, Ella Fitzgerald, Dizzy Gillespie, Al Grey and Stan Kenton.

LOS ANGELES JAZZ INSTITUTE PO Box 8038, Long Beach, CA 90808-0038; Ken Posten. Archives of jazz and big band and it offers music celebrations of great musicians and bands of the past and present.

NEW HAMPSHIRE LIBRARY OF TRADITIONAL JAZZ University of New Hampshire Library, 18 Library Way, Durham, NH 03824; Telephone 603-862-1535; web: www.library.unh/edu. Created by Dorothy "Dot" Prescott, a longtime supporter of New England jazz. It contains hundreds of jazz-related books and periodicals, photos, videotapes and other archival materials. The library also sponsors annual jazz series.

PAPERS OF BANDLEADER ARTIE SHAW Music Building & Fine Arts Library, Special Collections, Main Library, The University of Arizona Libraries, PO Box 871006, Tempe, AR 85287; Telephone 480-965-6164; Email: askalib@asu.edu. Archives contains songs, music, swing music, students' songs, jazz vocals, manuscripts, photos, financial records; 51 feet of materials. Preliminary inventory available in the library, folder level control.

Harry Onan (in white suit) and his orchestra ready to tour in their customized "RV."

Photo courtesy of James Ronan Collection, Iowa

PAUL WHITEMAN COLLECTION Williams College Libraries, 55 Sawyer Library Drive, Williamstown, MA 01267; Telephone 413-597-2501. This collection comprises nearly 4,000 manuscript arrangements of the 1920s to the 1940s along with contemporary recordings, clippings, and a small collection of photos and artifacts.

REGISTER TO THE BENNY GOODMAN PAPERS Irving S. Gilmore Music Library, Yale University, PO Box 208240 120 High Street, New Haven, CT 06520-8240. Contains Goodman's band and combo arrangements, orchestral arrangements, miscellaneous items. Compiled by David A Gier and Adrienne Scholtz, assisted by James John

REGISTER OF THE COLLECTION OF BIG BAND PHOTOGRAPHS ca 1930-ca. 1945 Music Library/Special Collections, University of California, Box 951490 Los Angeles, CA 90095-1490; Telephone 310-825-1665; FAX 310-206-7322. Timothy Edwards, Music Library Special Collections or Gordon Theil, acting music librarian for special collections. Collections contain 1 box (142 big band photos 1930-1945).

RICHARD F. WRIGHT JAZZ ARCHIVE Department of Music and Dance, University of Kansas, 460 Murphy Hall, Lawrence, KS 66045; Telephone 785-864-3210; Contact Roberta Schwartz at email rfschwar@ku.edu. Considered one of the

Bandleader Joe Enroughty leading his Royal Virginians at the Lewis Ginter Botanical Gardens Christmas Concert/ Dance, 2005.
Photo courtesy of J oe Enoughty

most complete jazz archives in the midwest. Its holdings include major jazz periods from 1920s and 1930s on 78 rpm, the swing and bob eras. The archive is a collection of more than 15,000 33 rpm recordings and 5,000 78 rpm recordings.

SAN FRANCISCO TRADITIONAL JAZZ FOUNDATION 41 Sutter Street PMB 1870, San Francisco, CA 94104; Telephone 415-522-7417; email: info@sftradjazz. org. Created in 1981 as an archive of several thousand items. It preserves live events and broadcasts. Contains some private collections also.

SPECIAL COLLECTIONS OF JAZZ University of North Texas, PO Box 305190 University of North Texas, Denton, TX 76203-5190; Telephone 940-565-2860; FAX 940-565-2599; www.library.unt.edu/music/speccol.htm. The collection contains Duke Ellington, Leon Breedon, Willis Conover, jazz lecture series in this group.

SONNY ROLLINS INTERNATIONAL JAZZ ARCHIVES Carnegie Library of Pittsburgh, 4400 Forbes Avenue, Pittsburgh, PA 15213; Telephone 412-622-3114; web: www.pitt.edu/~pittjazz/sonny.html; email: ndavis@pitt.edu

TED LEWIS MUSEUM 133 W. Main Street, Box 492, Circleville, OH 43113; Telephone 740-477-3630; Coordinator Patty Miller; Web: www.pickaway.com / visitors/html. The museum has a small theater which offers early TV and movie clips that show Ted's work as a jazz entertainer. Ted led one of the first jazz bands and worked with Benny Goodman, Fats Waller, the Dorseys and others. Memorabilia include his famous clarinet, old top hat and sheet music from his famous number "When My Baby Smiles At Me."

THAD JONES JAZZ ARCHIVE William Paterson College Library, William Paterson University, Wayne, NJ 07470; Telephone 973-720-2371. The Jazz Room features artists during the academic year.

THE BOSWELL MUSEUM OF MUSIC PO Box 159, Springfield Center, NY 13468; Telephone 607-264-3321; web: www.boswellmuseum.org; email: boswell@boswellmuseum.org. In the 1930s, the Boswell Sisters – Vet, Connie and Martha – created the "Boswell Sound" – a music that offered the optimism many thought necessary to combat the depression blues of the era. The sisters worked with top musicians and singers like Bing Crosby, the Dorsey Brothers, Goodman and Shaw and others. The museum has educational programs, special events and a collection that includes magazines, newspaper clippings, records, film sheet music, photos, records, film, sheet music, radio programs and oral histories.

THE CIPJ ARCHIVE at California State at Long Beach California State University at Long Beach Library, 1288 N. Bellflower Blvd, Long Beach, CA 90814; Telephone 562-985-7072. Archive Coordinators Keith Bishop and David Zapotocky. The Archives was in process of cataloguing recordings and contents in 2005.

THE GRAYSTONE INTERNATIONAL JAZZ MUSEUM BOOK BUILDING 1249 Washington Blvd Detroit, MI 482126; Telephone 313-963-3813; web: www.ipl.org.ar/exhibit/detjazz/About.html; email: exhibits@ipl.org. The Graystone was one of America's best known ballrooms. It was demolished in 1980. It was bus driver James Jenkins who spent 20 years building the collection of materials currently displayed in the Graystone.

THE CHARLES H. TEMPLETON RAGTIME SHEET MUSIC COLLECTION Mississippi State University Libraries, Mississippi State, MS 39762; Telephone 662-325-2323; web: www.mssstate.edu/web/contacts.php; Contact Michael Ballard, mballard@library.Msstate.edu. Charles Templeton collected more than 22,000 pieces of sheet music from the late 19th century to the early 20th. The music covers the spectrum; Irving Berlin, Scott Joplin, W.C Handy, George Cohan, John Phillip Sousa and others.

THE HAMILTON COLLEGE JAZZ ARCHIVE 198 College Hill Road, Hamilton College, Clinton, NY 13323; Telephone 315-859-4071; Web: http://academics. hamilton.edu/music/home/jazzarchive; Director Monk Rowe email: monkrowe@ hamilton.edu. Begun in 1995, this archive holds a collection of videotape interviews with about 230 musicians, arrangers, writers and critics. It contains supporting materials such as LPs, CDs, photos, books and other assorted items.

THE HOAGY CARMICHAEL COLLECTION Lilly Library, Indiana University, 303 E. Kirkwood Ave, Bloomington, IN 47408. The Hoagy Carmichael Room is located in Morrison Hall. Telephone 812-855-4679; web: www.dlib.indiana.edu/collections/hoagy/ intro/room/index.html. The official Hoagy Carmichael site is Hoagy Bix, 226 West 47th St, New York City, NY 10036; Telephone 212-764-1850; FAX 212-768-9538; email: staff@ hoagy.com. The Hoagy Carmichael site at IU includes manuscripts from 1921 to 1955. The collection at IU is housed at 3 sites on campus and includes more than 3,500 items.

THE JOHNNY MERCER PAPERS 1885-1981 William Russell Pullen Library Special Collections Department, Popular Music Collection, Georgia State University, 100 Decatur St SE, Atlanta, GA 30303; Telephone 404-651-2172; web: www.library. gsu.edu/spcoll/collections/music/81%2D1.htm. One of America's foremost song writers was Johnny Mercer. This archive holds 18 feet of manuscript papers and 10 feet of non-manuscript materials. It's divided into five series: Series l, biographical and personal 1927-1979; series ll correspondence, 1930-1981; Series lll business records ca 1937-1977; Series lV lyrics, music, scripts and shows ca 1930-1976 Series V news clippings and printed material 1928-1981.

THE LOUISIANA STATE MUSEUM JAZZ COLLECTION The Louisiana State Museum, PO Box 2448, New Orleans, LA 70176-2448; Telephone 504-568-6968; FAX 504-568-4995; web: www.http://1sm.crt.state.la.us/collections/jazz.htm; Telephone for jazz collector at 504-568-8215. The collection, once owned by the New Orleans Jazz Club, holds about 10,000 photos, hundreds of Louis Armstrong photos, 10,000 recordings in virtually every format used from piano rolls to digital tape, film, sheet and miscellaneous items

THE MARR SOUND ARCHIVES Miller Nichols Library, University of Missouri, Kansas City, 5100 Rockhill Road, Kansas City, MO 64110; Telephone 816-235-1534; FAX 816-333-5584; web: www.umkc.edu/lib/spec-col/marr.html; Staff contact is Chuck Haddix, telephone 816-235-2798. This is a special collection which holds nearly 250,000 sound recordings in LPs, 78s, 45s transcriptions. There are voices of WWII, Musicians Local No 627 materials, a collection of Nat "King" Cole early years 1936-42 and electronic music or Raymond Scott.

Drummer Von Sterling and Frank Galime (third trumpet from left standing) in a big band TV appearence in 1958.
Photo courtesy of James Ronan Collection, Iowa

THE NATHANIEL C. STANDIFER VIDEO ARCHIVE OF ORAL HISTORY

Black American Musicians School of Music, African American Music Collection, University of Michigan, 106 West Hall, Ann Arbor, MI 48109-1092; Telephone 734-764-8338; FAX 734-763-4452; web: www.umich.edu/~afroammu/contact.html. Archivist Dr. William Shea. Started in 1968, this collection contains 150 videotaped interviews with black musicians who have made significant contributions to music. Interview range from one to five hours and are on VHS. They include: Eubie Blake, Cab Calloway, Ella Fitzgerald, Keter Betts, John Hammond, J.C. Heard and others.

THE WILLIAM RANSOM HOGAN ARCHIVES OF NEW ORLEANS JAZZ

Jones Hall, Tulane University Libraries, New Orleans, LA 70118; Telephone 504-865-5688; FAX 504-865-5761; web: www.tulane.edu/~1miller/jazzHome.html; Curator Bruce Boyd Raeburn. The Hogan Jazz Archive is a department within the Special Collections Division. The archives holds extensive New Orleans jazz research which includes oral histories, recorded music, photos and film and sheet music as well as orchestrations.

"That Swingin' Band" from Rochester, MN, the Bennett-Greten Swing promotion in the late 1930s

Photo courtesy of James Ronan Collection, Iowa

THE UNIVERSITY OF ARIZONA LIBRARY ARTIE SHAW COLLECTION
University of Arizona Library, 1510 E. University Blvd Tucson, AZ 85721-0055; Telephone 520-621-2101; FAX 520-621-9733; email: webadmin@u.library. arizona.edu. The papers of Artie Shaw (1910-1953) mostly musical scores by various arrangers that were played by his bands. Photos of family members, friends, musicians. Publicity articles and programs from theaters and concerts.

VOCAL GROUP HALL OF FAME & MUSEUM 98 East State St., Sharon, PA 16146; Telephone 724-983-2025; FAX 724-983-0446; Email: mail@vghf.org; web: www.vghf.org. Tracy Rogers, museum director. The Hall of Fame has added new home for club activities and museum. Bob Crosby, CEO.

WILLIAM RUSSELL JAZZ COLLECTION Williams Research Center, 410 Charles St., New Orleans, LA 70130; Telephone 504-598-7171; FAX 504-598-7168; web: http://hnoc.org/russell.htm; email: wrc@hnoc.org. This study was begun when the Historic New Orleans Collection acquired the jazz recordings and materials of the late William Russell in 1992. It contains more than 300,000 photos, prints, drawings and paintings as well as 35,000 library items.

WEB SITES ABOUT
BIG BANDS, DANCING, BALLROOMS

www.NYJazzMuseum.com
between 1972 and 1977 one of the most significant
jazz repositories in the world. Highlights book
about the museum by Howard E. Fischer.

www.gapmangione.com
The Gap Mangione band and schedule, bio

www.maynardferguson.com
trumpeter Maynard Ferguson and his band, bio
and schedule

www.bigbandjump.com
Big Band Jump, a 2 hour weekly radio show of
big bands, vocalists

www.jaybeckenstein.com
Spyro Gyra leader from Buffalo, NY; top
contemporary jazz band

www. henrymancini.org
Composer, arranger and movie musical director
Henry Mancini Institute, CA

www.bolewis.org
Bo Lewis Big Band Dance Party

www.montereyjazzfestival.org
Annual Monterey Jazz Festival, CA

www.glennmiller.org
Glenn Miller Birthplace Society, Clarinda, IA,
Society, programs, plans

www.bigbandsinternational.org
Big Bands International Society, newsletter,
membership

www.dukeellington.com
biography of Duke Ellington

www.musicians.com
all about music, players, produced by Virtual
Countries, a Seattle, WA web site

www.JimmyScalia.com
Jimmy Scalia, official archivist for Bobby Darin

www.nfo.net
The American Big Bands database (outstanding archive for any and all information about big bands in US and abroad). Prepared by Murray L. Pfeffer

www.woodyherman.com
The Woody Herman Society supports Woody Herman's music and musicians. Al Julian is director

www.bigband-era.com
David Miller hosts Swingin' Down the Lane for NPR

www.chuckmangione.com
Trumpeter Chuck Mangione's web site, schedule and bio

www.americanjazzmuseum.com
The American Jazz Museum, Kansas City, MO

www.louisprima.com
A tribute to Louis Prima, swing era band leader; photos and story

www.monkrowe.com
Monk Rowe, resume, bio, director, Hamilton College (NY) Jazz Archive

www.jazz-clubs-worldwide.com
type of jazz clubs and location

www.redhotjazz.com
A history of jazz before 1930

www.allaboutjazz.com
Jazz talk site, free monthly newsletter

www.concordrecords.com
A major jazz recording company

www.mannheimsteamroller.com
one of the country's most popular new age touring bands and shows with Chip Davis and Mannheim Steamroller

www.zildjian.com
Cymbal manufacturer for major drummers of past, present

www.dorisday.com
big band singer with Barney Rapp, Les Brown, actress

www.tuxjunction.net
George Spink's jazz and big band collection

www.sierramusic.com
Bob Curnow's music publishing Site, Sierra Music

www.bigbandworld.com
A Canadian big band magazine

www.geocities.com.gkiiorchestra Gene Krupa, Krupa fan club

www.gkrp.net
Gene Krupa story

www.drummerman.net
Gene Krupa bio

www.jazzlegends.com
Home page About Jazz features

www.grovemusic.com
Comprehensive music dictionary

www.sonymusic.com/artists
Descriptions of recording company's performers, records

www.selmer.com
Instrument site to locate top high school, college jazz bands

www.swingfever.com
San Francisco Bay area's swing band with musicians from top groups like Brubeck, Basie, Goodman and others

www.clevelandjazz.org
Jazz history by Joe Mosbrook of one of the
country's outstanding concert jazz orchestras

www.downbeat.com
Professional monthly magazine for all
musicians

www.ludwig-drums.com
Drum manufacturer site

www.jazztimes.com
monthly jazz magazine

www.jazzimprov.com
JazzImprov, source for everything related to jazz

www.cmjo.com
Chicago Metropolitan Jazz Orchestra, with band
alumni from big bands of Kenton, Rich, Herman,
Ferguson and others. Plays original Kenton
arrangements

www.museum.media.org/duke/duke.html
The Duke Ellington Society, Duke Ellington
Appreciation Page

www.library.ucla.edu/libraries/music
Collection of big band photos, ca 1930 to 1945

www.iaje.org
International Association for Jazz Education

www.pyramidband.com
The Pyramid Dance Bands, a professional
ensemble from Northeastern US and southern
Canada.

www.jazzreview.com
A monthly jazz newsletter

www.glennmillertribute.com
Tribute web site presented by Tom
Daugherty band

www.littlebigband.com
A creative big band page for those interested
in helping children find out more about big
bands, big band sounds

www.jazzeast.com
Nova Scotia's online source for jazz

www.teorecords.com
Teo Macero, one of the major producers of big
band albums for Maynard Ferguson, Woody
Herman and others

www.tritonejazzfantasycamp.com
One of those lifetime experiences designed for
adult players (21 and over) to spend a week
immersed in listening and playing great music
with outstanding players of today.

www.oscarpeterson.com
Canadian jazz pianist

www.bigbands.com
Big bands/Horace Heidt Productions

www.jangarber.com
site for the Jan Garber band with Howie Schneider

www.tomdaughertyorchestra.com
Leading big band, featured at the Glenn Miller
Society annual celebrations, led by Tom
Daugherty, trombonist

www.tommydorseytribute.com
Tribute site presented by Tom Daugherty band

www.nbea.com
The National Ballroom and Entertainers Assn.
Site for ballrooms of past, present and listing
of big bands

www.chriswalden.com
composer, arranger Chris Walden and his
Big Band

www.airmenofnote.com
USAF jazz ensemble, big band, Bolling Air
Force Base, Washington DC

www.seniormusicians.homestead.com
Columbus, OH jazz site

www.crystalballroom.net
Crystal Ballroom, Staunton, IL

www.casalomaballroom.com
Casa Loma Ballroom, St. Louis, MO

www.stpete.org/coliseum.htm
Coliseum Ballroom, St. Petersburg, FL

www.dbqfair.com
Grand Ballroom, Dubuque, IA

www.hollywoodballroom.com
Hollywood Ballroom, Silver Spring, MD

www.medinaentertainment.com
Medina Entertainment Center, Hamel, MN

www.mosleyonthecharles.com
Mosley's On The Charles, Dedham, MA

www.riversideballroom.com
Riverside Ballroom, Green Bay, WI

www.southernrhapsodysociety.com
Southern Rhapsody Dance Society, Pleasant
View, TN

www.willowbrookballroom.com
Willowbrook Ballroom, Willow Springs, IL

www.cadencebuilding.com
Cadence Jazz Book Publisher

www.gordongoodwin.com
Gordon Goodwin, leader of the Big Phat Band, one
of the West Coast's exciting new big band sounds

www.lajazzinstitute.org
Housed at California State University at Long
Beach to preserve and document jazz and big
band in southern California

www.swingmusic.net/getset.html Offers
excellent discussion of big band era and web
icons about big bands, photos, combos, vocalists
jazz radio archives, etc.

www.wikipedia.org
Flapper Era, Jazz, Swing definitions, explanations.

www.jocelynmedina.com
Young jazz singer formerly of Clinton, NY
who works east coast clubs and lives in Spain.

www.anitaoday.com
The big band singer Anita O'Day's official web site

**www.bigbandsandbignames.com/
GuyLombardo.html**
A 1957 Craig's Big Bands & bignames.com about
Lombardo leaving the Roosevelt Grill in NYC

www.NelsonRiddle.com
was a trombonist and arranger who played
a significant role in such bands as Charlie
Spivak, Tommy Dorsey, Eddie Sauter, the
Elgart Brothers, Bob Crosby and others.

www.marvinstamm.com
The biography of one of America's top
contemporary trumpet players

www.countbasie.com
The official Count Basie web site

www.artieshaw.com
The official site of bandleader Artie Shaw

www.peggylee.com
The former big band singer Peggy Lee's site
with many photos

www.duke.edu/web/danceclub
A ballroom and club dancing group listed as the Graduate Student Dance, Chapel Hill, NC

www.unc.edu/student/orgs/ballroom/home.html
The University of North Carolina Ballroom Dance Club and Team

www.austinballroomdancers.org
The Austin Ballroom Dancers is devoted to promoting ballroom dancing, Austin, TX

www.triangleswingdance.org/About.asp
TheTriangle Swing Dance Society covers the Raleigh, Durham and Chapel Hill areas in North Carolina.

www.piedmontswingdance.org/index. html?ckset=ok&refer=
The Piedmont Swing Dance Society in the Piedmont Triad of North Carolina.

www.sif.net/swing.htm
The Syracuse (NY) Swing Dance Society which promotes dances such as jitterbug, lindy and hustle.

www.jazzfoundation.org
The Jazz Foundation of America (JFA) was established in 1989 to promote the cultural and educational values of jazz. The organization assists struggling jazz artists with a Jazz Musicians' Emergency Fund to help those who are getting older, who are sick and in need of medical and financial assistance.

www.onlinepot.org/reefermadness/ swingbands.htm
A Jack Hanley story from Radio Stars, 1938 explaining the facts of habitual use of "reefers" among musicians.

www.btinternet.com/~j.r.killoch/porcino.htm
A review of trumpeter Al Porcino's big band live show in Munich, Germany, December, 1999

www.streetswing.com/vsdc.htm
San Fernando (CA) Valley Swing Dance Club

www.lib.neu.edu/archives/collect /findaids/ m31find.htm
Northeastern (MA) University Libraries Glen Gray and the Casa Loma Orchestra recording collection, 1915-1979

www.bigband.com/mainpage.htm
The Great American Dance Band and sounds of America's big band era. Band is located near Stanford University

www.philcollins.com
English rock, pop singer/drummer who between 1984 to 1990 had a streak of 13 straight US top 10 hits.

www.earshotjazz.org
A Seattle, WA based non-profit music, arts and service organization begun in 1984 to support jazz.

www.johnnymercer.com
Song writer who wrote such pieces as Laura, Moon River, That Old Black Magic and many others, Johnny Mercer was also a singer and co-founder of Capitol Record Co.

www.kaykyser.net
The so-called "ol professor of swing and "College of Musical Knowledge," Kay Kyser was a part of the big band era but was also a showman and entertainer. Had a top rated radio show for 11 years on NBC.

www.alumniband.homestead.com/index.html
A great web site about a marvelous band of some of America's great sidemen who played in the big bands during the 1930s,'40s and '50s. The band is based in the Los Angeles, CA area.

www.lib.uchicago.edu/e/su/cja/oralhist.html
Chicago Jazz Archive, Jazz Oral Histories, Joseph Regenstein Library, Unv. Of Chicago

www.davepell.com One of the popular brush cut saxophone players from the 1950s and the Les Brown Band of Renown, Dave Pell offers arrangements, price lists and his work on CD from the Dave Pell Octet and Dave Pell Big Band.

www.davehanlonscookbook.com A popular Central New York band, winner of regional awards, which has been a solid territorial band since 1983.

www.ku.edu/~sfa/mad/jazzarchive Richard F. Wright Jazz Archive, Department of Music & Dance, University of Kansas

www.lib.uchicago.edu/e/su/cja/jazzarch.html Chicago Jazz Archive, Joseph Regenstein, University of Chicago Index of Listings by Location of jazz, blues, big band and singer collections and museums.

www.wnur.org/jazz/internet.html A general jazz information resource from WNUR-FM Northwestern University

www.satchmo.net The official site of Louis Armstrong house and archives

http://brubeckinstitute.org
This is the Dave Brubeck Institute at the University of the Pacific which involves his papers, research and clinics

www.jazzonline.com
a discussion site on jazz

www.culturekiosque.com
Commentary about jazz, CD reviews and interviews with international jazz critic Mike Zwerin

www.dickjohnsonjazz.com
The Artie Shaw Band led by clarinetist Dick Johnson

www.mp3.com/ray-anthony/artists/5181/biography.html
A brief biography of bandleader Ray Anthony, his musical roots and those he worked with.

www.gigmasters.com
Here is a worldwide talent agency for musicians and bandleaders seeking work.

www.savoyballroom.com
The beginning of the Lindy Hop as a dance at Harlem's Savoy Ballroom, NYC

www.buddymorrow.com
Official web site of Tommy Dorsey Orchestra, conducted by Buddy Morrow.

www.dickhyman.com
Piano player and organist Dick Hyman is a major jazz and big band instrumentalist

www.alhirt.com
Trumpet player, New Orleans-born Al Hirt was a legendary person in jazz and swing.

www.bennygoodman.com
The king of swing, Benny Goodman, was world renown for his music and given credit by jazz historians for launching the swing years. The site offers all facets of Benny's life. It is handled by the Benny Goodman Estate

www.maynardferguson.com
The Maynard Ferguson Tribute Page offers articles, tour dates, pictures, merchandise and fan club information.

www.billyeckstine.com
A great singer and bandleader, Billy Eckstine's albums are displayed on this site.

www.bennycarter.com
Bandleader, alto saxophonist Benny Carter provides a look at his life and work in this web site.

www.jimmydorseyorchestra.com
A very popular bandleader of the 1930s, 40s, Jimmy Dorsey Orchestra continues directed by Bill Tole. This is the official web site.

www.ww2aaf.org/band/band.html
Brooks Tegler's recreation band of the World War ll Army Air Force band from Washington, DC

http://annapolisjunctionbigband.com
A Maryland big band

www.musicunlimited.com/bb.htm
The James Bazen Big Band

www.bigbandtheory.com
The Jet Propulsion Big Band from Pasendena, CA

www.auburnknights.com
One of the country's oldest college affiliated dance bands from Auburn University

www.tomdaughertyorchestra.com
Tom Daugherty's big band

www.WRRSwing.com
Pete Jacobs and his Wartime Radio Revue Band from California

www.thesjo.com
The Sentimental Journey Orchestra with Henry Mason from Atlanta

www.xaviercugat.com
This is a web site yet to be developed for the popular Latin/Cuban sound of bandleader Xavier Cugat.

www.russcarlyle.com
A big band singer who started by winning an amateur radio contest at Danceland in Cleveland, OH in 1935, Russ Carlyle went on to sing with bands such as Blue Barron. He was named one of the top four singers in the country by Billboard.

www.bigbandonline.com
Andrew Thielen Big Band

www.cabcalloway.com
This is the official homepage of the Hi De Ho bandleader and singer, Cab Calloway. The band today is directed by his grandson, The Price of hi De Ho, C. Calloway Brooks.

www.bunnyberigan.com
Bunny Berigan, one of the great trumpet players of the 1930s, is remembered by fans. This site offers direction to the Bunny Berigan Foundation and archives. The Bunny Berigan Collection is now at the University of Wisconsin Mills Music Library

www.texbeneke.com
Don't be misled, this web site is actually The Big Bands web site of Chris Valenti who presents Big BandRadio.com and the Big Band Broadcast. It offers Valenti's sampling from the big band era.

www.countbasie.com
Here's a web site devoted to the current Count Basie Band directed by Bill Hughes. It offers highlights and tour plans for the Basie Band.

www.fredwaring.com
Fred Waring and his Pennsylvanians, a combined orchestra and choral group, traveled the world with a particular musical style. This site, which is under construction, describes his life and times.

www.joevenuti.com
Jazz violinist Joe Venuti is featured on this site. It's under construction by Robert E. Mohr, a longtime jazz officinado.

www.rudyvallee.com
A vocalist/bandleader, Rudy Vallee was a popular musician/singer who started at the Unv. Of Maine. He was a popular radio, Broadway and movie actor.

www.buddyrich.com
Considered the world's most celebrated drummer, Buddy Rich was a vibrant part of the development of the major big bands. This is his official web site.

www.louisprima.com
This is the official web site of singer/ trumpeter/bandleader Louie Prima.

www.russmorganorchestra.com
In the 1930s, 40s Music in the Morgan Manner on radio was a part of the development of the big bands. Russ Morgan, a trombonist, offered a popular sound. His son, Jack, another trombonist, joined the band and has continued music in the Morgan way today.

www.halmcintyre.com
A founding member of the Glenn Miller Band, Hal McIntyre, a saxophonist, started his own band in the 1940s. Today, Don Pentleton has taken the baton to head the McIntyre sound and band.

www.lesterlanin.com
One of the most successful society bands in the country, Lester's bands played 15,000 weddings, 6,000 debutante parties and continues after his death.

www.sammykayeorchestra.com
He thought he wanted to be an engineer when he went to Ohio University but his music success while on campus produced a successful sweet band from Ohio. His "So You Want to lead a Band" program popularized his band and music. The band is now being led by Roger Thorpe.

www.louisjordan.com
He was a first class cutup but his music became popular through the 1940s and 50s. Louie Jordan had what was called his "Tympany Five" to handle good swing and comedy numbers.

www.gordonjenkins.com
A composer, arranger and leader of a soft and sweet sounding big band, Gordon Jenkins was a favorite among Hollywood producers.

www.bullmoosejackson.com
Here was a guy who knew how to work a crowd and work up a sweat. A singer and saxophone player, his crooning started when he was with the Lucky Millinder band and the singer didn't show up. He was pulled out of the section to sing the appropriately named song, "Hurry, Hurry."

www.macfilms.com/jazz.htm
A 35 page examination of movies with big bands and musical groups. A musical performance catalogue of jazz and big bands.

www.answers.com/topic/fletcher-henderson
This is a Wikipedia dictionary biography of one of America's pioneers in swing big bands, Fletcher Henderson. His arrangements were considered the critical to the development of the Benny Goodman band.

www.aragon.com
The Aragon Ballroom was built in Chicago at the exorbitant cost of $2 million. It was named after a providence in Spain and it replicated a Spanish palace. It opened July 14, 1926.

www.hypermusic.ca/jazz/bigbande.html
Hyper Music History of Jazz: Big Band Music: The Early Years.

www.afana.org/jazzorgan.htm
"The Jazz Organ: A Brief History" by Geog Alexander copyrighted in 1988. A 26 page, carefully documented article on the jazz organ.

www.bigbandnostalgia.com
This is a band that features the music of legendary bandleaders like Harry James. It's located in Camp Hill, PA.

www.nfo.net/usa/females.html
This article is a special feature of the Big Bands Database Plus – Females and All That Jazz. It's a 10-page description of women starting with African-American female vocalists in the 1920s and 30s singing what is called the "classic blues."

www.porthalcyon.com/features/200503/ canteen01.shtml
The Halycon Weekly Press examination of the USO Canteen of the 1940s called "See You At The Canteen" (part 1 in a series).

www.bigbadvoodoodaddy.com
This is one of the national retro big bands of the 21st century based in California. The band was launched as a three-piece jazz, blues and swing combo in 1989.

www.home.earthlink.net/ %7Eswingband2000
The Alan Glasscock Orchestra from Dallas/Fort Worth, TX offers the southwest a band that recreates the sound of big bands of the past like Miller, Dorseys, Goodman, James, Shaw and others.

www.swingshiftworld.com
The Alan Gresik Swing Shift Orchestra which opens its evenings with the announcement "Its 1939 and we are on the air! " The Swing Shift band has been the house band at the Green Mill Lounge, Chicago's hottest jazz club.

www.thebigbandsound.com
A 20-piece jazz orchestra from Poughkeepsie, NY which has played throughout the east since 1975.

www.hometown.aol.com/tunes1342/tunelov7.htm
Here's a celebration of music, sponsored by The Tune Lovers Society, to recall tunes from the past with a site called Carry A Tune Week

www.clairdee.com
A jazz singer with a great repertoire and her band.

www.bates.edu/x13981.xml
The story of the Little Big Band in 1941 at Bates and going to college and enjoying great music of the big bands. Written by Bruce Park, Bates '44.

www.allaboutjazz.com/php/news.php?id=4785
A December, 2004, posting about composer Maria Schneider and her CD "Concert in the Garden" which was nominated for four Grammys but not available in a retail store. Story on All About Jazz web site.

http://oceancounty.lib.nj.us/Link2Topic/ music.htm
The Ocean County, NY Library Online music resources which includes a big band/swing section.

www.spaceagepop.com/marterie.htm
A biography of bandleader Ralph Marterie, a musician and later leader during the 1940s, 50s and 60s.

www.spaceagepop.com/zentner.htm
A biography of bandleader Si Zentner, a big band musician who took a big band on the road in 1959 when big bands were leaving national tours.

www.thedailystar.com/opinion/columns/ simonson/2004/08/simonson0816.html
"The Closing of a Dancing Landmark," Oneonta Daily Star story by Mark Simonson about the closing of George F. Johnson Pavilion in Johnson City which was built in 1926 and was used during the 1920s, 30s and 40s when big bands came to Johnson City, NY

http://newarkwww.rutgers.edu/ijs/fw/ fatsmain.htm
Rutgers' Institute of Jazz Studies online exhibit about legendary pianist Fats Waller

www.pbs.org/jazz
Here is a web site about the biography section of Jazz: A Film by Ken Burns. It also includes audio clips.

www.smithsonianjazz.org
The Smithsonian Jazz is a program to preserve and promote America's foremost music and offer information about exhibitions, performances, recordings, radio, publications and educational programs.

www.savoystyle.com
The story of the famous Lindy Hop dance is presented via dancers' biographies

www.writerjackweb.com
Here is my web site which monthly devotes a column to spotlight big bands, sidemen, leaders and ballrooms.

www.lavaysmith.com/links/linksmain.html
Here is a web site devoted to jazz and blues artists chosen by invitation only.

www.melmartin.com
Mel Martin, a jazz saxophonist who heads the group Bebop and Beyond.

www.charlesmcneal.com
Charles McNeal is an alto and tenor man and his web site offers jazz transcriptions which can be downloaded for free.

www.marcusshelby.com
Bass player and composer and leader of the Marcus Shelby Jazz Orchestra.

www.blueroomboys.com
A San Francisco area swing band led by Michael Mcintosh on the piano.

www.swingorchestra.com
The Bill Elliot Orchestra is one of the leading big bands playing 1930s, 40s and 50s charts. The band has appeared in movies like The Dorothy Dandridge Story. Bill teaches at the Berklee School of Music, Boston.

www.georgegee.com
a New York City-based big band that plays in the tradition of Count Basie. Led by George Gee, this 10-piece band is considered the Make Believe Ballroom Orchestra.

www.mightyrhythmkings.com
Melissa Martin and the Mighty Rhythm Kings are a jump blues band from Philadelphia.

www.sultansofswing.com Arranger David Berger's big band with thre e CDs out to promote their music.

www.cityrhythm.com
Here's a Philadelphia based band that performs nationally as well in their native state of Pennsylvania. It has recorded five well received CDs.

www.winikermusic.com
A band that calls itself a Boston wedding band also plays for Boston Red Sox parties, New England Patriot events and museum and cultural activities in Massachusetts. It's a 21-piece group that played at President Bill Clinton's Inaugural Ball.

www.vaughnmonroesociety.org
One of the very popular crooners and big band leaders, Vaughn Monroe, was a trumpet player and trombonist. He went on the road with Camel Caravan promoting cigarettes and easy to listen to music for dancers.

www.legendsofswing.com
A Claremont, CA swing band that offers salutes to Goodman, the Dorsey brothers, Glenn Miller, Harry James and others led by trombonist Gary Tole.

www.stanbann.com
A Twin Cities, MN big band that offers a range of musical interests for dancers and listeners.

www.stompyjones.com
is a swing and jump blues band that features original material and classics in the San Francisco area.

www.moonlightswing.org
This is a not-for-profit living history big band that emulates the Glenn Miller sound and offers the harmony of the Crew Chiefs, the Modernaires and even the Four Freshmen. It reproduces the big band sounds of WW II. Led by Don Treco and located in Sacramento, CA.

www.docscantlin.com
Here's a 15piece group that uses Cab Calloway's hi-dee-hi-dee-ho music to take you back to a Harlem nightclub and those tunes of the 1920s and 1930s.

www.johnhoward.com/sfso.htm
The San Francisco Starlight Orchestra offers the authenticity of the 1920s and 30s dance style with arrangements from the Jazz Age. Music from orchestras like Duke Ellington, Paul Whiteman, Bennie Moten, Ben Pollack and others.

www.dickcampobigband.com
A New England big band, led by drummer Dick Campo, that plays for charity balls, concerts, swing dances, weddings and other events.

www.moodswings.com
A swinging big band of young musicians, who work as computer professionals and doctors during the day. Based in Baltimore, it plays the Mid-Atlantic region and sports elegant tuxs or rocket red zoot suits as the occasion demands.

www.johnnyknorr.com
A very traditional band which plays "The Music you Like" is located in Oregon, OH but travels from Chicago to Washington, DC to offer a program of the old favorites and custom arrangements adding Rhumba, Samba. Disco and Rock to swing and foxtrot.

http://hometown.aol.com /groovinhigher jo/ myhomepage/tunes.html
The Groovin Higher Jazz Orchestra features some outstanding section leaders and solo the Tacoma, WA region. It's a 21 piece jazz aggregation that loves to wail and plays pieces from the libraries of Kenton, Rich, Bellson, Count Basie, Woody Herman and others.

http:jazzexpressbigband.com
The Jazz Express of Waukesha, WI is another big band – 20 players – comprised of teachers, engineers, artists, small business owners and others who feature Ellington, Basie, Rich, Herman and Kenton among others to offer a traditional sound. Band began in 1979.

www.starliteorchestra.com
A 17 piece band based in Washington, DC which is a cooperative of local professionals with a common interest in playing classic arrangements as well as popular. It plays many community charities.

www.cyberjaz.com/steelpier
The Steel Pier Remembered Big Band offers those on the East Coast great memories of the big band sounds of the 1940s at the world famous Marine Ballroom at the Steel Pier, Atlantic City.

www.billporterorchestra.com
A former USAF band trombonist, Bill Porter toured with a number of big bands like Harry James and Woody Herman and returned home to Chicago to create his own big band playing in the area and record.

http://members.aol.com/famemgt/fame/ crosby.htm
The Bob Crosby Orchestra is back working engagements thanks to the permission of the Crosby Family. The 14-player band includes the eight member Bob Cat ensemble. Bobby Levine, who was with Bob Crosby for 35 years, leads the group.

www.tomsmithbigband.com
Tom Smith and his big band play swing and jazz in the Long Island region and elsewhere. A vocalist with a Sinatra tone and sound, he offers a range of smaller groups to the bigger group.

www.rosevillebigband.org
Here's a novel and, at the same time, unique big band that plays Dorsey, Miller and other classics in Minnesota as a band sponsored by the Roseville Parks and Recreation Department. It evolved from a stage band and a municipal band to become a municipal band in 1988.

www.thesjo.com
The Sentimental Journey Orchestra plays the southeast from its base in Atlanta. It began in Decatur, GA with strong emphasis on the Les Brown Band of Renown sound.

www.scottharris.com/bigband
A northern California big band with 15 pieces Scott Harris combines the traditional 1930s sound to capture the era playing a wide range of other music.

www.tuxedojunction-bigband.com
 Steve Lallier's Tuxedo Junction Big Band from Dallas, TX offers swing and society music with recordings to keep the sound alive.

www.jumpstreetswingband.com
An 18-piece big band that began in 2002 is led by trumpeter Matt Reed and bassist Eric Simons. Jump Street is located in metro Detroit but takes its extensive library throughout Michigan and border states.

www.bedfordbigband.com
Here's a band that entertains parties, dances and events in southern New Hampshire for the fun of it. The Bedford Big Band non-profit musical group of 23 musicians and singers who thoroughly enjoy the classics from the big band era.

www.devilsworkshopbigband.com
Richmond, VA was home for New Yorker Stephen Norfleet's 17 piece band but the improvisational group includes a mix of Big Apple musicians and others and plays regularly in Manhattan and Brooklyn. The band has made its mark, though. Downbeat gave its album CD "Idlehands" a four star review not long ago.

www.jeremyshradermusic.com/hepcats/NMHm.htm
A 16-piece group that plays for weddings, parties and special nights is based in Tennessee and it's called New Memphis Hepcats. The repertoire includes the classics from Ellington and Goodman and swing easily to Sinatra and Kenton.

www.tcjs.org
The Twin Cities Jazz Society, a very progressive and aggressive group in middle America offers a diversified array of programs, bands and interests. It's a non-profit, all-volunteer organization but it has demonstrated its value to the mission of promoting swing, jazz music. There are approximately 50 jazz clubs represented in the Twin Cities area and 46 big bands plus 20 collegiate jazz ensembles.

www.open.org/~petwir/salembb
The Salem, OR Big Band has been performing since 1989 at public, private and special jazz events. It's an 18 piece band which features vocalist Christie Tanguy.

www.berkmusic.com
Michael Berkowitz's big band which plays throughout the country and abroad offers tributes to Gene Krupa, Harry James, Buddy Rich, Nelson Riddle, Artie Shaw and others. He worked with Riddle and Johnny Green and later he worked on Broadway on various shows. A talented drummer, his band was sold out for three nights at Birdland.

www.singers.com/jazz/vintage/modernaires.html
A brief biography of the early days of the Glenn Miller singing group that rocketed to fame in the 1940s. Excellent information about the group's CDs.

www.mikehenebryorchestra.com
A Cypress, CA swing era big band with an amazing library of more than 1,900 charts from the 1935-1948 period. The arrangements, Mike says, are genuine. . . a number of Artie Shaw's own and over 300 from Benny Goodman's own library. It's a band that re-creates the best of the popular sounds of past and present.

www.bigband-ri.com
The Moonlighters Orchestra serves the New England area and plays the music from the 1940s to the 1990s. It began in 1977 in Rhode Island.

www.stormloader.com/brje
The Baton Rouge Jazz Ensemble is a 19-piece big band that began in 1993. It's a non-profit organization of part-time musicians who seek to expose Baton Rouge, LA residents to the sound of the big band era.

http://onebeatback.com
This is metropolitan Detroit big band that plays for the love of playing the big band and swing era music.

http://rhythmsociety.net
Another Detroit-based band that plays the music of the swing era. A 16-piece group, it is influenced by the Count Basie and Harry James sounds and it adds a flavor of its own with singer Paul King who gives listeners and dancers a Mel Torme-Joe Williams-Frank Sinatra-Cab Calloway flashback.

www.stagedoorcanteen.net
The Stage Door Canteen big band recreates the music of the 1940s that was made popular entertaining troops at the USO. It's a 12-piece band led by Berklee grad Roger Gamache.

www.capitolint.com/bigbandcavbio.htm
An all-star group that plays the big band sound with a show called "Big Band Cavalcade." Led by Rick Schalk of Chicago, former associate conductor of the Guy Lombardo Orchestra, this band features people from the Dorsey brothers, Les Elgart, Lionel Hampton, Russ Morgan, Buddy Morrow bands and others.

www.atlantabluenotes.com
The Atlanta Blue Notes, is a band of local Atlanta area musicians who provide big band swing and the most danceable big band sound south of "New York, New York," the web site proclaims.

www.bigbandonline.com
Drummer Andrew Thielen leads this big band that plays places like Hilton Head, Planet Hollywood, North Carolina, South Carolina, Georgia, Virginia events and a PBS special too. The band is based in North Myrtle Beach, SC.

www.bigbandtheory.com
Here's a futuristic big band that may play earth stations in space some day. It's a band comprised of staff, contractors or retirees from the Jet Propulsion Lab in Pasadena, CA. It probably has the largest percentage of non-musical PhDs for any big band in the country. It plays Goodman, Dorsey, Ellington, Basie and others from the pre-Sputnik era.

http://members.aol.com/bigband200
The Don Burns Orchestra, which began in 1967, started with 11 players and today boasts 17 musicians and two vocalists. The band is based in Warren, OH but books gigs throughout Ohio and western Pennsylvania offering the sounds of Goodman, Dorsey, James, Miller and others.

www.bigband.com
The MJP Big Band is another Ohio group that performs at community events. It's is based in Madison, OH

www.vanguardjazzorchestra.com
The internationally known band of the late Mel Lewis and Thad Jones based in New York City. It began in 1966 and has performed continuously ever since and continues to play every Monday night at the celebrated Village Vanguard.

www.sandiegoswings.com/bigbandexpress
Marty Conley's Big Band Express plays music from its extensive library of original Dorsey, James, Miller and Good-man books and adds contemporary sounds, too. It's led by former chief instructor at the Navy Music School in DC, Marty Conley. The band is based in San Diego.

www.bobjanuary.com
This is a band for all occasions but Bob has a New York Dance Band Orchestra that replicates the sounds of Glenn Miller with strings as well a plays Franz Lehar and Xavier Cugat. At the same time, he offers a tailor-made Original Swing Era Big Band which features Count Basie, Ellington and his own compositions and what he calls a Satin Swing Orchestra, a smaller group that plays for ballroom dancing.

www.jazzreview.com
 A web magazine about jazz complete with calendar, jazz features, reviews and resources.

www.roselandballroom.com
You'll find an occasional dance among the many events that take place at 239 West 52nd Street, New York City today but it's one of America's legendary ballrooms and the site that launched the Woody Herman Band

www.news.com.au/common/story_page/ 0,4057,528431%5El3780,00.html
The death of big bandleader Ray Conniff

www.lkwdpl.org/lore/lore37.htm
Story of bandleader Sammy Kaye as it appeared the Lakewood, OH SunPost, Dec. 21, 1989.

www.swingshiftdanceband.com
A Washington DC 18-piece band which creates the big band sound of Miller, Basie, Tommy Dorsey and others and features trumpeter and director Gary Henson who offers the Maynard Ferguson style.

www.lasalledanceorchestra.com
This 12 –piece band takes you back to the era of lawn parties, flappers and dress white events. It recreates the rhythms and dancing of the Jazz Age with vocals and dancers. Its played for members of Congress, World Bank executives and others.

www.tomcunningham.com
A big band with a big Basie, Goodman, Ellington and Miller sound that plays for presidential and gubernatorial inaugurals and has made TV appearances. Features Robin Cunningham as vocalist.

http://www.snow.prohosting.com/lombardo/ joeband1.html
Joe Enroughty and his Royal Virginians is that special sweet band that takes you back to the music of Guy Lombardo, Sammy Kaye, Jan Garber and others.

www.lesbrownsbandofrenown.com
A review of Les Brown Jr and the Band of Renown along with bios of both of Les Sr. and Les Jr. along with great band photos.

www.nymdbb.com
Claims to be New York's "most dangerous" big band led by Edward deCorsia. A 17-piece big band that has been in business for 8 years and offers dancers and listeners in the Big Apple area rock, Latin, standards, pop, swing and more.

www.bgsu.edu/colleges/library/music/ bigband1.html
This is a big band research aid available at the 3rd floor of Jerome Library, Bowling Green State University, Bowling Green, OH

**www.bigbandlibrary.com/
listingofghostbands.html**
Here's a list of the "ghost" bands that have
played and continue to tour

www.iowaballroom.com/p/people.html
A chronology of Iowa ballrooms, their owners,
performers

www.terrygibbs.net
Legendary vibraphonist Terry Gibbs who
played with big bands during the early and
later periods of swing

www.franktiberi.com
Frank Tiberi, longtime Woody Herman
saxophonist, leads the Woody Herman
Thundering Herd Band

ACKNOWLEDGEMENTS

There are so many who have helped me create this book. And what's so difficult as you get to the end of researching, interviewing, re-interviewing, re-scheduling to meet busy schedules, organizing and writing it is not forgetting the people who made it possible. First though an apology to whomever I may miss in retracing my steps of research of nearly three years. While it may sound lame, I estimate I contacted more than 800 sources and made probably 1,500 contacts. I believe about 40 percent responded either negative or positive. They took the time from their busy lives to write, email or call. Some went a step further offering illustrations and other materials. I'm very grateful as I'm sure readers are, too.

I want all to know that you're very much a part of these pages either in spirit or name and I appreciate your efforts.

Two long time musical friends, Chuz Alfred and Jim Booker, shared their family musical experiences with me after my first book, "The Big Band Days" was published. Their recollections touched pertinent parts of this work.

Throughout my life, I've always admired my musical friends and their heritage. I came from a non-musical family and I didn't receive support because, while my parents loved to listen to music, they sensed my interest and they made it clear to me it was nonsense. "Foolishness!" my dad said emphatically. I'm sure they felt I didn't have the talent and it was better to be negative than positive. But my mother loved to dance and, later in life, she began playing the piano and told me that she had learned to play early in her teens but stopped because there was no money to continue. She said that dad told her there was no money for a piano. She was most surprised when he purchased the instrument when they were in their late 60s.   Musicians to them, unfortunately, were people of little consequence to society, they said over and over. If you weren't in business or committed to business there was nothing to discuss.

I waged a personal war within myself for years because I felt the guilt of doing something that was, in their eyes, immoral, frivolous and senseless. Yet, I told myself, it was something I felt good about doing and being a part of at the same time.

Fortunately, I was later able to write about popular music and the people who shaped and played it which filled my creative need. I still cherish the stories of USO Tours while I worked for the Pacific Stars & Stripes, Tokyo.

I not only wrote about music . . . I talked about it on two radio stations in central New York where I was able to broadcast more than 1,000 public affairs shows years later that focused on big band music.

And that's where I met a versatile jazz musician/composer/arranger, Monk Rowe, who had the same commitment I had to swing and big band. His work as director of the Hamilton College Jazz Archive was featured in my first book, "Big Band Days," and it certainly continued to be an important research tool in this book, too. Our shows on great bandleaders, players, arrangers and other parts of the swing era offered good musical selections and great big band conversations which gave me commentary for various sections of this book.

I'm indebted to John Matter, who operated a family ballroom in Iowa for years and the National Ballroom Owners & Entertainers Association who have supported my efforts. It's the only organization I know that speaks for the nation's ballrooms. It was John and the NBEA who showed me the major role ballrooms played in the big band business. They helped create my approach to this book.

Finding usable illustrations for such a book is always a task but thanks to James Ronan, also of Iowa, I was able to tap into his personal postcard collection of big bands and ballrooms of the 1930s to 1950s. James is a big band and ballroom enthusiast who vividly remembers the days when dancing was the weekend entertainment.

Phil Holdman of Chicago and his nostalgic "Browsers" newsletter provided fascinating memories of not only the Windy City's involvement but of the touring bands who traversed the midwest.

Dick Jurgens Jr., son of popular big band leader Dick Sr, supplied various parts of his interesting web site about his father's band, its members and friends.

And the memories also poured in from friends and distant acquaintances about their ballroom and band experiences. A delightful group of Buckeye Lake women – Donna Braig, Paula Kirk, Betty Perkins and Marty Frankenbury – who grew up with Central Ohio's two ballrooms, the Crystal and Pier, gave me their recollections of how the dance pavilions impacted their lives.

I couldn't have navigated the west coast without the help of a former student, Bruce Manning of Los Angeles, who put me in touch with a number of ex Palladium announcers and dancers.

Master Sergeant David Nokes of the USAF Airmen of Note helped me gather information about America's oldest touring dance band, the Airmen of Note.

Other friends have passed away since I started this project but their contributions were invaluable to me and to their fans. Trumpeter Frank Galime of Utica, NY, gave me anecdotal memories as did emcee/entertainer Lou DiSario of Philadelphia, PA. Both gave of themselves in performance after performance . . . and both loved being a part of the big band life.

Certainly dancers have been the catalyst for the success of bands, music and ballrooms. And some steered me across their dance floors of the past. Thanks to Carolyn Ziebell of California, Barbara Rhodes of New York and George Dale McFarland of Ohio among others for their memories.

Finally, to a "band of brothers" in uniform – bandleaders, musicians and singers – who gave me their descriptions of what compels them to get on the bandstand each week, heart felt thanks and best wishes for whatever success they seek in a field where rags and riches have always been side by side. Helping me with this task were: Gary Greenfelder of the One Beat Back Band of Detroit, Chris Walden of the Chris Walden Big Band in Los Angeles, Joe Enroughty of the Royal Virginians in Richmond, VA; Gordon Goodwin of the Big Phat Band in Los Angeles, Pete Jacobs of the Wartime Radio Revue in California, Andrew Thielen of North Myrtle Beach, SC and his big band; Richard Machuzak and the musical technicians at the NASA Jet Propulsion Lab Big Band Theory at Pasadena, CA; Doc Scantlin and his Imperial Palms Orchestra; Brooks Pegler, a big bandleader and re-creationist who fronts the World War II Army Air Corps Review Big Band of Leesburg, VA; Vocalist Dorsey Tippett who sings with possibly the nation's oldest collegiate band, the Auburn Knights; Henry Mason of the Sentimental Journey Band of Atlanta, GA; Tom Daugherty Pfrogner and his band from southwestern Ohio; James Bazen who offers three different versions of big band in Washington, DC and another re-creator, Pete Jacobs, and his Wartime Radio Revue of California.

Each provided a slice of their musical experiences. At the same time, each gave us a Kodak picture of the importance of big band music in their lives, too.

I hope you enjoyed this continuing story as much as I did writing it.

AUTHOR
John "Jack" Behrens

"My big band days were spread over parts of two decades (1940s, '50s) but they were certainly a special six years. I met bandleaders, musicians, singers and played ballrooms, clubs and dancing and drinking spots I never forgot. I met people I never forgot either. And who could forget as a guy who weighed 140 pounds hauling 100 plus pounds of a Slingerland drum set throughout the midwest? Probably why I had three hernias later in life," Jack told radio listeners in 2002.

While his first book, "The Big Band Days" (1stBooks/2003), was a memoir, this book is devoted to letting many others from the early swing years to today's "second swing era" tell their experiences and describe their feelings about the music they play, listen and dance to . . . and why it is important to them.

A nationally known award-winning columnist, editor, writer and professor of magazine, Jack founded the journalism program at Utica College of Syracuse University (1972) and continues to teach from time to time today. The Reader's Digest Foundation named him a Reader's Digest Fellow in the 1980s. President Ronald Reagan invited him to the White House and the island nation of Antigua used his advice to launch its telecommunications program. Columbia Scholastic Press Association awarded him the coveted Gold Key Award for his efforts to found and continue the Student Press Archives which continues today.

He has written more than 14,000 magazine articles, columns, essays in national and international periodicals and with the publication of "Big Bands and Great Ballrooms" he has authored 20 books including an E&P best seller, "The Typewriter Guerrillas " (Nelson-Hall/1976).

His memories of big band, quartet and trio work in the 1940s and 1950s are vivid, though. "Like thousands of others we were the weekend's entertainment where we lived. We loved every minute we played, came to hate the travel and setup sometimes at places that had no bandstand and no microphones and the fact that we weren't paid more times than not. But the excitement of playing for an audience was addictive."

Printed in Great Britain
by Amazon

57497658R00118